6—

SOLUTIONS

Other FuturePace Books by Leslie Cameron-Bandler:

Know How
Guided Programs for Inventing Your Own Best Future
(with David Gordon and Michael Lebeau)

The EMPRINT Method
A Guide to Reproducing Competence
(with David Gordon and Michael Lebeau)

Personal Business
Freedom and Power Through Emotional Choice
(with Michael Lebeau)

SOLUTIONS

Practical and Effective Antidotes for Sexual and Relationship Problems

by Leslie Cameron-Bandler

Published by FuturePace, Inc., P.O. Box 1173, San Rafael, California, 94915.

ISBN 0-932573-01-0

Library of Congress Catalog Card Number 85-070138

Design by James Stockton & Associates, San Francisco.

Excerpt from the *Silent Language* by Edward T. Hall. Copyright © 1959 by Edward T. Hall. Reprinted by permission of Doubleday and Co., Inc.

Diagram and excerpt from the *Dance of Life* by Edward T. Hall. Copyright © 1983 by Edward T. Hall. Reprinted by permission of Doubleday and Co., Inc.

Printed by Malloy Lithographing, Inc., Ann Arbor, Michigan

Dedication

*I dedicate this book with great affection
to my brother Wade—
may you live happily ever after, and*

*To my parents Harry and Joyce—
for teaching me to stand on my own feet
instead of someone else's toes.*

Acknowledgment

I want to express my appreciation to Michael Lebeau. Without him this book would not be in your hands. In addition to making it possible, his editing has made it easier to understand and more enjoyable to read.

LCB

Preface

This is a book about fulfillment and choice. The practical and effective solutions presented in the following pages will enable you, if you choose, to convert the promise of personal satisfaction and fulfillment into reality.

Although the material in this book is used by clinicians in the field of psychology, all of the concepts and methods are discussed in everyday terms. Each important point is amplified with anecdotes and actual examples from my rich background in helping people achieve happier and more fulfilling lives. Even though the presentation of this material is oriented around couple relationships and sexual functioning, it is important to know that these techniques are just as effective in producing desired change in all of the other significant areas of life. *The following set of resources is a therapist's guidebook that anyone can use to resolve problems and make their life more of what they want it to be.*

This revised and expanded edition of this work (formerly titled *They Lived Happily Ever After*) contains all of the methods and techniques formulated by my colleagues and me during our development of the field of Neuro-Linguistic Programming (NLP). That remains unchanged; none of the original book has been deleted since each item has proven its value in creating positive change. But while this book has received a generous and enthusiastic response over the years, time has not stood still and even an excellent product of the past needs updating and improvement.

In addition to stylistic revisions, I have added several important new techniques that I developed during the past few years. These techniques work to remedy problems that were generally considered unsolvable when I first wrote this book. The new sections on the threshold pattern in relationships (Chapters 9 and 17) are especially relevant to anyone who wants to understand the process of falling in and out of love, and to everyone who wants to know what to do to maintain a loving and supportive relationship.

I have written this book for anyone who wants the experience of sexual fulfillment and nurturing relationships to reside within the realm of choice and control. The information contained in the following pages is for *seekers* and *doers,* people who will not settle for less when they know that more is within reach.

Be comfortable and curious as you read this book. Recognize yourself and others in the descriptions and stories. Practice the techniques—they work. Use what you are about to learn, and enjoy.

September 10, 1984
San Rafael, California

Table of Contents

I Preliminaries

Chapter 1: The Puzzle of Marital Difficulties

Once upon a time, in the not-so-mythical land of Nom, two very nice people fell in love. They decided to live together for the rest of their lives to capture the good feelings between them. They thought love could conquer all and fantasized a future of continued joy and growing happiness.

As time passed, however, some mysterious evil lurked furtively at the edge of their joy. Slowly, unseen and unheralded, it began to work its way into the core of their relationship. In the beginning both assumed it was only a passing mood of the other. But as time passed each became more suspicious that the other was in some way bewitched. Every day it became more of a struggle to keep any semblance of the happiness that once had flourished. Things worsened until it was obvious to each of them that even pretending they were still happy was a dreary chore. Finally they fell to accusing each other of being the basis of the evil, each professing their own innocence. They sought allies in their friends and relatives; sides were chosen, and open hostilities broke out.

The hostilities continued to escalate until expert consultants were brought in. Three consultants insisted the problem was definitely the man's fault. Another three insisted the problem was surely the woman's fault. Each side compiled elaborate data and theories to support its claim, and the result was further escalation. The man and the woman could no longer look at one another without feeling angry or empty. Sometimes they also felt guilty, because in occasional moments of solitude they would each ask themselves, "Could it be my fault?" or "Can't they see I'm also to blame?" More time passed until finally the matter was brought before a court of law.

Charges and counter-charges were made. A wise and shrewd judge presided. After a time he leaned over the bench and said, "Before we proceed any further with this case, there is something I must tell you. Whoever is found guilty will be sentenced to a life of complete and utter unhappiness, and will be tortured constantly by excruciating guilt. The other will be free to try to find a life of joy again. Though the odds will be against you, it is not impossible. Therefore, I will offer you a choice. If either of you is sure beyond a doubt that you are right, I will proceed to hear this case and make my decision. However, I am not perfect and my decision may be in error. So each of you will risk your future on my fallibility and the strength of your claim. Or, you may elect to seek the help of a court-appointed experience technologist, who will provide you with alternatives to knowing who is right."

This second alternative was both frightening and intriguing to the man and the woman. Neither was really sure who was indeed right, and everyone had heard of the powers and mysteries of the experience technologists. After great discussion, and against the advice of their attorneys, consultants, friends and relatives, they decided to face the unknown of the experience techologist rather than risk their future to the whims of a court proceeding.

The next morning, they both arrived at the laboratory and waited anxiously in the office of the technocrat supervisor. An attendant entered and silently signaled them to follow. They walked down long corridors lined with rooms full of huge machines and scientific paraphernalia. Finally they entered a small room, completely darkened except for a soft red luminous glow. Two chairs stood in what appeared to be an otherwise empty room. The attendant left as the two sat down and glanced nervously about. A door of the little room opened and a figure passed in. The red glow reflected off the white lab jacket, producing an eerie image. The man and woman noticed that the glow seemed to radiate from everywhere and nowhere at the same time. The figure introduced itself as Technician Four, and as he waved his hand a small computer terminal emerged from the floor. Deft fingers played across the keyboard and words emerged on the monitor.

Technician Four turned to them and said, "Do you know why you are here?" The man and the woman hesitated, glancing sidelong at each other. "Then let me explain as briefly as I can. You are people who, through whatever mechanism, have chosen not to find out what went wrong and who was at fault. You have chosen instead to create a future which is satisfying in itself. With a satisfying future you will have no need to know what went wrong in the past. My file states the problem as a common one: Once there was great love between you, but now it is gone. Let me ask you a simple but complex question, 'Where does love go when it goes away?' If there is an answer to this question, therein lies a way to create a satisfying future." The man and the woman were quite confused by all this and could only shrug. Technician Four nodded, "We at the Institute of Generative Experience offer a variety of futures to people who have your problem. I would like to outline each one briefly so that you may come to an agreement on which one you will choose."

Nimble hands wove another intricate pattern on the computer keyboard. The red luminescence seemed to shiver for a moment. Then it began to coalesce into an image of a translucent red pyramid suspended in the center of the room. The rest of the room lay in absolute darkness.

Technician Four spoke, "I want each of you to think of one of the pleasant memories from your past—one which is representative of the joy you wish to have now." The man and woman gazed at the hologram. Suddenly each could see a memory appear in the pyramid. Each saw their own memory, and each felt sadness that the joy they once shared was no more. The technician continued, "To each of you has appeared an event. If you enter the pyramid, you will not only see the event from start to finish, but you will also hear, feel, smell and taste all that occurred in that time and place. You may try it if you like." They both stepped into the pyramid. For a moment they only glowed in the shimmering light. Then they were lifted up and plunged into the memory—first the woman's, then the man's. Each memory was joyous and satisfying to both. The technician tapped out the sequence, "b-r-e-a-k" and "return."

The pyramid disappeared and the room glowed red again. The man and the woman stood together, staring at each other as they had when they first were in love. They sighed deeply and returned to their chairs.

"Our first alternative," Technician Four intoned, "consists of equipping your home with as many of these pyramids as you like. Each pyramid holds three events of approximately six hours in length. They are quite expensive, so you may choose to order some now, and some later." The man and the woman looked at each other with intense interest. "However, I must warn you that most of our past clients have had one or two problems. Some became bored with reliving the same memories over and over. They continued purchasing pyramids until they ran out of money or pleasant memories. A more serious problem has been that some couples have stayed in a memory pyramid so long we were unable to get them out." The technician paused, "Yet, with judicious use, the memory pyramid offers an alternative to unpleasantness."

Technician Four turned to the computer console. The luminescence shivered again, this time coalescing into a pulsating gray image of a brain, suspended where the pyramid had been. "The second program is simpler and somewhat cheaper, but it is much more permanent in nature. The brain you see before you is a blank hologram which can be filled with any thought or belief we choose to put in it. It is nothing more than an elaborate memory bank that stores both data and the programs to run that data. More simply put, we can fill it with facts and the belief systems to process those facts." The technician punched out a sequence, then looked intently at the man and woman. "This program offers the following possibility: Each of you will believe beyond a doubt that the other is at fault, and you will have the illusion that the other has accepted this to be the complete truth. You need only to step into the hologram to try it." Technician Four paused and gestured towards the brain. The woman rose and walked into the image. She suddenly recalled events which had never really transpired. She knew for certain that she had been wronged, and maliciously so. She felt complete righteousness, but it did not fill the emptiness inside her. The man followed and had the same experience. "Of course, with this alternative it is imperative that you never meet again. I can see that the other drawbacks are self-evident to you. Still, this is a choice most people consider."

The brain disappeared, leaving only the red luminescence in the room. "The third choice we offer is a very popular one. You may have a future of new experience together, without any risk of unpleasant feelings." A new configuration of keys was rhythmically tapped out. The red luminescence trembled once more, but this time no hologram appeared. Instead, a green aura appeared around the man and the woman, glowing brightly from head to toe. Technician Four requested that each review the kind of pleasant memories they had hoped would have permeated their entire relationship.

Separately they began to review memories from the time they first fell in love and decided to live together. Pleasant memories and feelings filled their thoughts and bodies. The technician then instructed them to interact in any way they wished. They turned to each other and began to speak, and the strangest things happened. No matter what they said or did, they only had feelings similar to the ones they had when they were in love. Both experimented. They tried being insulting and mean, but the result was always the same pleasant response.

Finally Technician Four pressed the appropriate keys and the red luminescence washed away the remnants of the green glow. "This option offers a future of varied behavior with a limited range of feelings. The advantage is, of course, that this removes all the unpleasant low spots in a relationship. However, it also eliminates the possibility of any new highs." The man and the woman once again looked at each other with interest.

At this point the technician rose from the chair and signaled them to follow. Again they passed down long corridors lined with rooms until the technician turned sharply into one of them. The walls were lined with tubes about three feet in diameter and eight feet high. These were stacked one on top of the other, side by side. There must have been tens of thousands in the room. Each one appeared to be made of some sort of glass and was filled with the red luminescence.

Technician Four looked at the awed faces of the couple and spoke without emotion, "What you see here is the fourth and last option. If you are placed inside this tube, you can live the life you believed you would have when you first fell in love. We need only scan your expectations on that day, program a module for you, and your life's dreams will come true. You will only experience this. It will not really happen, but you will not be able to tell the difference. You will spend the rest of your life in what resembles a coma, while internally you will experience a full life. We will monitor your life support and draw off any excess energy you produce to pay your way." The technician waved a hand and the two tubes opened, still glowing red. "These two have been programmed for a short demonstration." The technician gestured to the couple.

The man cautiously entered, the door closed softly behind him. A strange, light-headed feeling came over him. At once he found himself holding the woman's hand in the technocrat supervisor's office. He heard himself say with conviction, feeling the belief and truth of his words, "We have decided we do not need your services. We are going to make our own pleasurable future." Then, as they left, he looked into the woman's eyes and knew, no matter what, they would find and keep the love they both had shared. Three days of continued joy, rich with good times, good loving, and caring communication were experienced by the man, furthering his conviction. He had totally forgotten he was in the tube, when suddenly the environment around him dissolved and he stood staring at the technician. As he stepped out, the woman was just stepping out of the tube next to his. They looked at each other, but said nothing. Technician Four led them back to the technocrat supervisor's office and told them they must now decide their fate. They were then left alone.

In an hour the technocrat supervisor came into the office and asked, "What is your decision?" The man and the woman looked at each other. At last the woman said, "We have decided not to use your services, however tempting they may be. We are going to try to build our own future out of the joys of our past and do a better job this time. We know it will not be as easy as you can make it, but we hope it will be better. Although things may not be perfect, we will continue to learn from our problems and work together for our happiness. If we fail we will return, but do not expect us." With that, they turned and left.

The technocrat supervisor raised an eyebrow and turned to the wall. With a wave of the hand the wall disappeared, revealing Technician Four standing there. The technocrat supervisor said, "Once again you have succeeded. You are to be commended on this effort. Return now to your duties." The technician smiled, the technocrat supervisor smiled, and the man and the woman lived happily ever after.

And they lived happily ever after. Is this just a therapist's fairytale? It certainly describes a desirable ending. Rather than deciding who is right or wrong, retreating into the past, or living an illusory future, these two people came to the best of all solutions. Each of them would behave toward the other in ways that would elicit the most desirable responses, as well as respond to difficulties as if they were opportunities for enrichment. Moreover, they decided to do this on their own, without hanging onto a therapist's apron strings. Of course, this is just a story, only fiction. Besides, just how did these two people come to this happy ending? Was it chance, or the technician's trickery, or was there a deliberate plan? If there was a deliberate plan, can you find it?

The technician had elaborate tools which produced elaborate effects. These elaborate and useful experiential effects can actually be produced now by non-mechanical means. I can produce them, and so can you, with the knowledge and skills presented in this book.

The discovery and development of the knowledge and techniques presented in the following sections began in the early 1970's when Richard Bandler and John Grinder combined their remarkable skills of detecting and using patterns of human behavior to produce change, and applied those skills to the development of a useful therapeutic model of the English language. They called it the meta-model.[1] With the meta-model they succeeded in creating a set of linguistic strategies which could be used in responding to the verbal patterns spoken by any individual. (See Appendix I for a useful summary of the meta-model.) The meta-model provides the foundation for the material in this book.

The beginning of my association with Bandler and Grinder precedes the meta-model days. That association began with extensive training experience and developed into professional collaboration. The discoveries we made as a result of modeling various people's experience led us to the development of the field of Neuro-Linguistic Programming (NLP).

NLP has reoriented much of clinical psychology toward, in my opinion, a different and much more productive direction. NLP provides many new perspectives on old understandings. More important, NLP provides tools which can lead to specific desired results quickly and effectively.

As a co-developer of NLP I have specialized for many years in working with troubled couples, as well as couples and individuals suffering sexual dysfunction. As a result of my experience and background I developed therapeutic models and techniques for correcting relationship problems and sexual dysfunction. These models have come about as a result of studying such therapeutic wizards as Fritz Perls, Virginia Satir and Milton Erickson; doing therapy with countless couples, individuals, and families; and through seminars with a variety of professional communicators.

My purpose in modeling human experience is to overcome limitations and transform them into possibilities rich with choices. The purpose of this book is to make available to you the information and skills which make it possible to be successful in helping people establish enriching and fulfilling couple relationships, including mutually satisfying sexual expression. The skills presented in this book include perceptual and behavioral options you need to transform a person's experience from a set of limitations to a set of choices. Each model and change technique includes a behavioral outcome that is easily testable and verifiable in *your* sensory experience, leaving no doubt about its validity.

A model is a representation of experience, in the same way that a map is a representation of an area of territory, or a model airplane is a representation of a full-sized functioning airplane. The models presented here are blueprints for moving from unwanted to wanted experience. These models of change satisfy four conditions: (1) they work to produce the results they were designed for, (2) they are described in a step-by-step manner, so they are learnable and reproducible, (3) they are elegant, i.e., they use the least number of steps necessary to achieve the outcome, and (4) they are independent of content and deal with the form of the process, and therefore have universal applicability.

The models of change presented here use explicit, operational procedures to move a person from one specific experience to another. It is possible to give people directions that, when followed, will result in their arrival at the desired location. What is needed is knowledge of the present location, knowledge of the desired location, and knowledge of the possible routes between the two. If you have an overview of a maze, it is quite simple to chart a path from the center of the maze to freedom. Without such an overview you would waste precious time and energy on circular wanderings and dead ends. This book shows you how to determine the present or existing experiential location and how to specify the desired experiential location; it also provides choices (with instructions) for going from one to another. The instructions that are provided with each choice include ways to insure that the experiential traveler will be able to get to the desired experiential location again, unaided.

Helping clients reach their chosen destination is a little like putting together an enormous jigsaw puzzle. It helps to look at the picture on the box to know how it will be when completed. It is much more difficult if you have no idea what the puzzle is meant to look like. Imagine putting together a 3,000-piece jigsaw puzzle with no concept of the total picture. You have no opportunity to pattern, but are forced to act with excruciating care in a trial and error process, with a minimum of assurance that you are proceeding correctly. It is much more efficient to know the outcome you are moving toward.

The puzzle pieces for the human problem solver are the structural elements of experience: attitudes (beliefs), emotions (internal states), thoughts (internal processing), actions (external behavior), and physiological responses. The human puzzle is not static but alive; it moves through space and time like a living tinkertoy set. There is a finite number of connecting pieces and lengths of stick, but an infinite variety of objects can be made with them. There are laws though. Certain principles and combinations make it possible for wheels to roll, and if these requirements are not met, there will be no movement.

Understanding Sexual Dysfunction

Before knowing how it is possible some people have dysfunctional sexual experiences, we need to understand how it is possible others have wonderful sexual experiences. Knowing the variables of subjective experience makes that possible to understand. Simply put, there is an alignment of attitude, emotions, thought, actions, and physiological responses that automatically culminates in orgasmically great sexual experience. When a person has dysfunctional sexual experiences, some portion of their experience is out of alignment. The task is to determine which portion needs changing—beliefs, internal state, internal process, external behavior, or physiological response—and adjust it.

For instance, if a person's internal dialogue is distracting—"It just won't happen this time either" or "He doesn't really care about me"—it will be difficult for her to reach a fulfilling sexual experience. The same is true if there is an attitude of "this is being done to me" or if there is no personal sensual enjoyment in the simple but profound experience of being a man or a woman.

A woman who came to me for assistance in attaining sexual pleasure demonstrated how a belief that is out of alignment can be detrimental. I learned that she knew most of what there is to know about sex: what to do, and how to think—that is, what kind of words to say to herself and what sort of pictures to make. Her husband was a good lover, and she was in love with him.

What was out of alignment? Not her attitude toward sex, but her attitude about being a woman. An attitude is a perceptual filter based on a belief. Adopting a belief results in a person primarily noticing and responding to examples that verify and conform to the belief. If counterexamples are detected, they are justified as aberrations. She believed that being a woman meant being weak and submissive, traits which were disgusting to her. This became evident when I directed her to feel the ongoing body sensations that let her know she is a woman. As she did, her teeth clenched, she frowned, stiffened her neck and shoulders, and shook her head no very slightly. These nonverbal responses alerted me to the need to learn more about how she experienced being a woman. She pictured women as weak and submissive, traits she deplored. Each time she felt the body sensations that were unavoidably those of a woman, she pictured herself as weak and submissive and felt disgusted. She never actually felt weak and submissive, but she so strongly attached "being a woman" to those traits, that feeling womanly brought the response of disgust—as if she had actually been weak and submissive. She saw herself as being strong and competent, traits she associated with being masculine, and dressed accordingly. However, her entire movement repertoire was certainly womanly.

By first changing her pictures of women to include decidedly feminine qualities of strength (the kinds of strength it takes to be gentle, giving, caring, loving, as well as competent and tenacious), and then putting these qualities into her pictures of herself, she experienced being a woman as a cherished attribute. It was then a relatively small step to attach these new pictures to the sensations she associated with being a woman. This intervention led to many other benefits in her life besides the sexual pleasure she requested.

Understanding Marital Disagreements

How is it possible that two people who genuinely love one another can bring each other so much pain? A couple volunteering for a demonstration in a training seminar said they wanted "to be happy with each other and improve communications." He described the present state as "She attacks me and tries to make me feel bad." Her description of the present state was "He keeps information from me; he won't tell me what I need to know." When I asked them to role-play a typical situation—a way in which their natural communication styles could emerge—their differences were quickly apparent.

The phone rang and he answered. It was their teenage daughter asking to spend the evening shopping:

He: Fine (*hangs up*).

She: Who was it?

He: Ann.

She: What did she want?

He: She's going shopping.

She: What did you say?

He: Fine. (*So far everything is OK; but now the problems begin.*)

She: Who is she shopping with?

He: I don't know.

She: Where are they shopping?

He: I don't know.

She: Does she have any money?

He: I don't know.

She: Did she have her jacket?

He: How the hell should I know?!

His experience was "She is attacking and belittling me, and trying to make me feel stupid." Her experience was "I'm worried about our daughter, and if he was concerned about me and the family he would have gotten more information from her."

By attending to the nonverbal cues (discussed later in this book), the structure of their difficulty became evident. She needed a very complete internal picture of what was going on in order to feel secure about anything concerning a loved one. Her questions were all directed toward achieving that full picture. An incomplete picture led to feelings of insecurity and fear.

He, however, paid more attention to a person's words and voice tone. Since their daughter had *sounded* fine, he felt confident that there was nothing to worry about. But since he also believed that he should always know the answers to his wife's questions, not knowing the answers in this situation was equivalent to being stupid—a terrifying possibility for him.

My interventions removed the negative connotations of their behavior and reestablished the experience of each being loved and valued by the other. We jointly designed a questionnaire form, including the required who, where, what, and when, to complete the woman's pictures. The last line read, "Because I love you, Mom." These were placed by the phone and message board for all family members to fill out. Everyone came to use them consistently and with good cheer to keep Mom happy.

At the end of the therapy session I had them engage (as a behavioral test) in a similar interaction. This time both behaved in more useful and loving ways. He did his best to provide sufficient information to complete her picture and at the same time he watched and listened to be sure she was reassured and comfortable. She, in turn, concentrated more on his efforts to reassure her than on her internal picture. She felt more comfortable as a result of his obvious concern, even when her picture was not as complete as she would have liked. They each felt they were on the same team for the first time in a long while.

In another situation, a colleague and I treated a woman who suffered from torticollis (a condition involving the turning of the head to a fixed, rigid position, resulting in almost no neck mobility). We discovered that the cause of this psychosomatic symptom was an incident of forced fellatio at age eight. The turning away of the head was the manifestation of the woman's unconscious desire to avoid another similar incident. Learning the cause of the symptom was important to the treatment of the torticollis, and it also helped explain the woman's present state of severe sexual dysfunction. Although it was not the reason the woman sought therapy, treating the present sexual dysfunction was essential to treating the symptomatic manifestation of torticollis. This case exemplifies the need for tools to do sex therapy that can be integrated into an ongoing general treatment program.

As I travel around the country conducting seminars in change and communication, I meet many practicing sex therapists. Some are highly regarded for their professional skill, and they do help their clients achieve richer sexual experiences. Not infrequently, however, even these therapists have approached me confidentially to ask for help. One woman sex therapist could not reach orgasm without the use of a vibrator; another couldn't reach orgasm during intercourse. A male teacher for both a medical school and a family therapy training center sought consultation because of periods of impotency.

My experience indicates that a significant number of sex therapists and educators suffer from the same kinds of sexual dysfunction they treat. This is due in part to their operating assumption that sexual response is something separate and distinct from the rest of their behavior. In fact, many people still treat human sexual behavior as though it is separate from all other human behavior. It is, however, a gross distortion to view sexuality apart from the totality of the human system.

The Needs to Be Fulfilled for Couples

If the human community is to continue to form and live in the family groupings that have existed in the past, we need to find ways to improve the quality of primary couple relationships. For significant economic and social reasons it has become a matter of choice to be in, or remain in, a couple relationship. It is critical, therefore, that being committed to another be an enriching experience in actuality, not just in ideals. Since people often seek some form of counseling when they are making important decisions concerning their relationships, it is the opportunity and responsibility of the therapeutic community to assist them in attaining the kind of experiences they desire.

Satisfying sexual contact contributes significantly to making a relationship successful. Pleasure is inherent in sexual experiences, and moments of shared physical intimacy, in which two people pleasure one another to fulfillment, can provide a foundation for a relationship that can withstand potentially destructive external pressures. Sexual behavior can convey passion, intimacy, love, and tenderness. Though words may enhance, the vitality and depth of feeling of the communication is expressed through immediate sensory experience. The touches, smells, sounds, and sights of lovemaking are profound communications. Lovemaking is a natural and poignant human experience that no one should be needlessly denied.

It is crucial for therapists to have available and adopt effective methods for dealing with sexual dysfunction. According to Masters and Johnson in *Human Sexual Inadequacy*, "a conservative estimate would indicate half the marriages . . . either as presently sexually dysfunctional or imminently so in the future."[2] Sexual functioning holds a unique position within the realm of psychotherapy. Unlike other psychological problems for which the therapist has the burden of interpreting behavior as progress or relapse, success or failure in sexual functioning is definite. The client's manifest physiological response is a direct demonstration of whether or not the desired changes have been made. Therapists can look forward to the satisfaction that can result from definitive feedback.

In presenting the patterns, methods, and techniques contained in this book, I have omitted lengthy definitions of what clinically constitutes sexual dysfunction. There is much of that already published. I have also avoided focusing on explicit sexual techniques. There are also many sources for that information, if it is needed.

What I *am* offering you in the following pages are solutions. Psychology offers an immense body of knowledge concerning diagnosis, but almost nothing about what to do about the diagnosed problems. The solutions presented in this book are a partial remedy. The presentation of each change technique includes step-by-step instructions together with the responses each technique will elicit from your client. Examples are given of client behaviors that indicate when each of the various techniques is the optimal choice as an intervention. Specific client behaviors worth detecting—the ones that reveal the significant underlying structure—are discussed in detail. This will assist you in being able to recognize what holds your client in their present state, making it impossible for them to reach the desired state without your assistance.

Models for Solving the Puzzles

Many therapists avoid working with couples. They find dealing with more than one person at a time overwhelming, and tend to consider sexual dysfunction an area best left to specialists. These therapists could begin to enjoy and find fulfillment in doing couple therapy if they first accepted a simple fact: The information needed when working with couples is different from what is needed when working with an individual. Too often therapists accrue two separate sets of data when working with two people. Instead, attention should be focused on the nature of the interactions between the two people.

The complexity of working with more than one person needs to be reduced to manageable proportions. This can be done by learning which aspects of your clients' experience are important and which are irrelevant for the purpose of facilitating change. Once you know what is important, you can organize your perceptions to search for and detect that information. You also need an adequate repertoire of change techniques to deal with the variety of situations that your clients will present. The following sections are structured to provide the learnings, help you reorganize your perceptions, and give you the additions to the repertoire of techniques you need to be an effective agent of change.

The application of these models for behavioral change to seemingly impossible problems is, to me, a fascinating process. My personal bias about what constitutes a fulfilling solution leads me to present the application of this material in the context of couple relationships and sex therapy. This personal bias, as well as my professional experience, has convinced me that all professionals in the varied therapeutic professions have need of additional skills in dealing with couple relationships and sexual expression.

My purpose is to make the relevant patterns and techniques comprehensible and rich with experience by providing detailed descriptions and meaningful clinical examples. Each technique is presented in a step-by-step format and many of them are suitable for self-help.

Be warned, however, that the integration of these skills carries certain freedoms and responsibilities: the freedom to change yourself and others, and the responsibility to choose what changes would be best for all concerned. To facilitate understanding and integration of the material, this book is best read, studied, and re-read a section at a time. It is meant to become assimilated into your experience, your beliefs, and your approach to life. It is up to you, through study and practice, to carry this knowledge into your experience.

This book offers a theoretical framework as well as specific therapeutic skills. These techniques are universal in their application to human behavior, and are only implicitly sexual as discussed in this book. They are useful, therefore, with any type of problem. I sincerely urge you to generalize their use to other contexts. They can provide concepts of organization and methods of intervention that can be used by any person, in any context, regardless of previous training.

In summary, although there is a body of knowledge concerning sexual behavior, and there are procedures for dealing with sexual dysfunction and couple relationships, there is still much room for improvement. The existing procedures cannot be used with a severely disturbed individual, or someone not involved in a couple relationship. Existing procedures are especially inadequate when internally generated experience interferes with the natural sequence of physiological responses during a sexual experience.

This is not a criticism of existing treatment procedures. The existing body of knowledge has successfully diminished the need to develop new skills in this area, but has not abolished it. I doubt that anyone would say we know enough to stop now. Instead, I hope they would be eager to add new choices to their existing procedures. One way of accomplishing this is to first recognize that sexual behavior and expression are not separate from the rest of human experience, and then to integrate sex and couple therapy into general treatment programs. Another is to move the practice of therapy away from theories and toward experiential models that provide specific methods of knowing what to do with the problems our clients bring to us.

You have the opportunity to add the following NLP techniques to the useful choices that are already a part of your behavior. Do keep in mind that yesterday's science fiction is today's science and not all technology is built of machines. You can open the doorway to becoming an "experience technician" with the pages that follow.

Chapter 2: The Factors that Make a Difference

Some years ago in the town of Grand Lake, Colorado, on the snowy western slope of the Rockies, there was a tradition that everyone had to use skis to get around in the winter time. New schoolteachers transferred into the area had to learn to ski, and even the school principal and the school band were on skis. Small children learned how to ski soon after they could walk. When one watched these people move about it was as though the skis were an actual extension of the foot, a highly adapted organ for locomotion. Each person had developed his own highly individualistic style, just as everyone has his own way of walking. When skiing competitions took place some of the villagers were better than others, while many did not compete at all.

. . . At the same time, there were a few hardy souls in Denver and other nearby towns who used to take to skis for pleasure, as a part-time activity . . . Some of them had very real talent, others weren't so skilled . . . They were not highly conscious of how they skied, what technique they used, or how the skill could be taught. They would say, "Watch me," or "Do it like this," and that was about as far as they could go. I never will forget the time when one of my friends who had been watching this weekly trek to the mountains finally decided to come along. He was an excellent athlete who had once been a Golden Gloves champion, so he had no lack of natural co-ordination and control. However, when he first put on skis the result was comic and disastrous at once. As soon as he tried to take a step, down he went. Encumbered by his skis, he could barely get up. The newcomer was beset by all sorts of problems which demanded skilled and technical analysis if they were to be solved quickly. Unfortunately the best that these Sunday skiers could manage was something like this: "You bend your knees and take off. Eventually you'll get the hang of it."

. . . At the same time . . . thousands of feet of film were being taken in the Alps of wonderfully skilled skiers rushing down slopes, turning, climb-

ing, and coming to a stop. These films were analyzed, and the whole pro-
cess was broken down into its components or isolates, as they can be
called. In addition to the components, broader patterns were also ana-
lyzed. After a while it was decided that skiing was not an art which had to
be restricted to the gifted. Anyone with patience and a modicum of control
could be taught to ski, since the components had been so well identified
that they could be talked about and described technically. Moreover, the
uniformity of skill that could be achieved by these new technically trained
skiers was so amazing that it made possible the later tremendous popularity
of the sport. [3]

Edward T. Hall
The Silent Language

As Edward Hall noted, by breaking down the activity of skiing
into its component pieces and identifying significant patterns,
methods of instruction were created which could bring high levels of competency to virtually anyone. Similarly, my colleagues
and I have identified the significant components and patterns
from the countless successful therapeutic interactions we have
studied. This has made it possible for us to create methods to
skillfully acquire the talent necessary to bring such interactions to
success on a consistent basis. These experiential components and
behavioral patterns have been organized into procedures which
can be followed to achieve specific outcomes—as presented here,
proficiency in couple and sex therapy.

The components of these procedures are based on the five
sensory systems: vision, kinesthetics, audition, and olfaction/
gustation. Seeing, feeling, hearing, and smelling/tasting are primary experiences. We experience any one, or any combination
of them, directly with the senses. There is a difference between
these components of primary experience, and representations of
experience such as language and numbers. Words and numbers
are *abstractions* of primary experience. They are symbols, and are
meaningful only to the degree and extent to which they are
connected to primary experience. Hence, the meaninglessness of
reading a book in an unknown language. This is not a statement
concerning the lack of importance of words, but a discrimination
that recognizes the function words serve in generating experience. There are several properties of language (words) which are
not properties of the basic sensory components and vice versa.

Each basic component functions three ways in forming experience: (1) as an input system through which we perceive our
environment, (2) as an internal representational/processing system we use to apply meaning to incoming data, as well as carry

out such activities as thinking, making choices, learning, fantasizing, etc., and (3) as an output system used to externally manifest our behavioral responses to the environment.

Human experience is generated as a result of the interactions among the external world and what our senses detect of it; the internally generated imagery, internal dialogue, smells and tastes, sounds, and feelings that our minds produce; and the various external behaviors we generate to act directly in the world. The understanding that human behavior (including, of course, sexual behavior) is only one aspect of a functioning system involves more than merely appreciating the importance of a systemic approach to therapy. We think in pictures, sounds, feelings, and words. When these internally generated processes are not aligned with the sensory experience available to us from the world, a certain incongruity arises. This incongruity can be useful in many contexts. For example, we can daydream through long, boring meetings, or place our consciousness on a pleasant memory or fantasy while enduring a visit to the dentist. These internal processes allow us to plan, remember the past, and project into the future, but they can also limit our ability to achieve desired experiences.

I'm sure you are familiar with persons who stop themselves from doing anything new because they think they will look silly. Specifically, they picture themselves doing the new behavior badly, and feel embarrassed—as if the internally generated picture had actually occurred. By responding to their pictures rather than to what is actually occuring around them, they inhibit their behavior rather than risk experiencing the imagined possible embarrassment.

Another example of internal process distracting from and limiting desired experience is one most therapists are familiar with: having their work supervised at various levels of training. Often in such circumstances, the therapist being supervised is so distracted by internal projections of the supervisor's assessments that the quality of the therapist's work diminishes radically. This is not surprising considering the fact that a therapist's success depends on being completely available to sensory experience.

Internal processes play a significant role in the context of sexual experience. If either person is reciting multiplication tables or carrying on an internal dialogue about tomorrow's shopping list, the intensity of the sexual experience will be drastically diminished, regardless of the quality of foreplay and sexual expression. The same would be true if, while making love, you pictured a conflicting scene (say, an argument with your mother) or heard internal voices (your father saying "Nice girls don't do such things" or your own voice asking "I wonder if he is getting tired?"). Similarly, if you were to remember inappropriate feelings from an unrelated experience—like taking an exam or driving through traffic—the totality of the experience would be lost. In such instances, your experience would become an incongruent mixture of the present lovemaking and other unrelated pictures, sounds, words, or feelings.

Even when these internally generated processes are congruent with the ongoing sexual experience, they can still detract from the intensity of it. For example, if while making love you pictured each area of your lover's body that you touched with your right hand, it is quite likely you would be more aware of the images than the feelings. Or, if you constructed an image of how you and your partner appeared to an unseen spectator, you might lose all conscious awareness of the body sensations caused by direct stimuli. Bill Masters discusses this loss of perception in *The Pleasure Bond*:

There probably isn't anyone who, while having intercourse, doesn't become a spectator for a time. On occasion we watch what we ourselves may be doing or what our partner is doing. It's perfectly natural to consciously observe the procedure; in fact, it's quite stimulating to do this now and then.

What is important is the degree to which we assume this spectator's role. In some cases, being the spectator on occasion may reflect a detachment from any emotional involvement. This too is natural and no cause for concern. But it does cut down on the input of the stimulus. For instance, if you are the spectator during sexual activity, some degree of your wife's pleasure and excitement doesn't really get through to you, which means you lose that stimulation. And to a degree your own pleasure is dulled because you're not lost in the experience—you're observing. I am not saying that you experience no pleasure at all. I'm just saying that some of it is blocked. A level of perception is blocked. [4]

These internal processes can also be used at times to enhance our sexual experiences:

All of us use fantasy, to a greater or lesser degree. It is a form of self-stimulation. It helps us move from where we are to where we want to be, when the occasion warrants. In that sense it is a bridge and can be very useful. [5]

Perhaps Bill Masters' analogy of a bridge is especially appropriate here. In cases of sexual dysfunction, internally generated experi ence often lies on one side of a wide and deep chasm while external sensory experience lies on the other side. If internal experience can be directed so that desirable fantasies are produced—fantasies somehow congruent with the ongoing external sensory experience—the chasm can be bridged and the two sides can reach alignment.

The techniques of change presented in this book offer infinite possibilities for constructing these kinds of bridges both *between* individuals and *within* an individual. When building such bridges, it is important to remember that because our consciousness is a limited phenomenon, our subjective experience is largely contingent upon what that consciousness is focused on. It is possible to be conscious of internally generated experience or external sensory experience, or a diluted mixture of the two. There are times when each of these three foci of attention is useful. For the person who has been occupied primarily with incongruent internally generated experiences, a diluted mixture of congruent internal fantasy and external sensory experience is a move towards focusing full consciousness upon the intense, externally generated experiences provided during a sexual encounter.

Fundamental to my approach while working with couples is the premise that people respond to one another constantly and intensely. This premise naturally leads me to detect, in each couple I work with, behaviors that each person manifests that elicit particular responses from the other. Although you will be directed in the following chapters to attend to the components of experience previously described, the focus will be on how those components influence the experiences that are generated by the interaction between two people. Whereas the concept of an alignment of internal and external experience is useful regarding sex therapy with the individual, the concept of a reciprocal system is useful with couples. Intervening successfully with a couple is a matter of influencing each person's behavior and the responses their behavior elicits.

The following interaction demonstrates how these components can interact to produce an unfortunate communication:

Paul: I feel unloved, she never responds to me sexually. (*His voice is whining and plaintive, his hands are resting limply in his lap, and he is looking at the floor.*)

Hazel: (*She says to herself, All he thinks of and wants is sex. I'm not even a person in his eyes. Feeling mistreated and unloved, she turns away from him and says out loud:*) And I never will.

Paul: (*He sees her turn away and hears her words; he feels hurt, rejected, then angry in quick succession. Face flushed, he speaks loudly.*) Then leave me now, bitch!

Paul's external behavior affects Hazel's internal experience, she manifests some external behavior which, in turn, affects his internal experience, and so on.

Of course, undesirable interactions are not always initiated by direct verbal communication. Here is an example—from another couple that came to me for help—of how problems can begin independent of words. One afternoon he arrived home from work before she did. He wanted a snack and was curious about yesterday's sports results, so he spread out the newspaper and helped himself to leftovers (a benign activity in and of itself). She walked through the door a few minutes later and saw him reading the newspaper and eating. All day long she had been making pictures of (and anticipating with excitement) the two of them going out to dinner that evening; when she saw him eating at home by himself she was disappointed. She automatically and erroneously assumed that his behavior meant he didn't stop to consider what she might have wanted to do that evening. She used this false assumption as evidence that he didn't care about her. Feeling worse, she said to herself, "I never get what I want." He looked up in time to see her frowning and, with a sinking sensation in his stomach, asked, "How are you?" She glared at him and replied, "As if you care!"

Besides demonstrating how internal experience contributes to the overall interaction, these examples help demonstrate that our responses to one another are not purely "wired in" cause and effect relationships. Rather, the effect (response) that is elicited by a cause (stimulus) depends to a great extent upon the meaning attached to the cause. If you lay your hand lightly on someone's arm, they will feel the temperature and the pressure of its weight, first in contrast to, then added to, their own. This is a simple cause-effect (stimulus/response) relationship.

If, however, the person understands the touch of your hand as a communication of affection, it will have the distinct meaning of affection to them, *whether or not* that was what you intended. The meaning attached to a behavior is called a *complex equivalence.* In this example, lightly laying your hand on their arm (a complex of behaviors) equals (means, is the equivalent of) your being affectionate toward them. Complex equivalences are pervasive in our experience and typically lie far outside conscious awareness. Not only do you know very little about what your behavior means to others, but others usually are not aware of the basis for their judgments concerning what they believe your behavior means.

When uncovering the structure of the present state and desired state with couples, a relevant question to answer is "What are the cause-effect and complex equivalence patterns that bind the present state in place?" In bringing a couple to their desired state, these patterns must be changed so that they become bonding instead of binding. Part III contains methods of changing distinct behavior as well as changing the responses to the behavior. Usually there is a need to do some of both, but changing the meaning of the offending behavior can often effectively change each person's experience of the other in a lasting way.

To facilitate creating a relationship that is mutually enriching and fulfilling, it is useful and appropriate to accept the presupposition that the meaning of a communication is the response it elicits from the other person, regardless of your intent. Accepting this premise will lead you to attend very closely to the response any communication (verbal or nonverbal) elicits, since the response determines its meaning. In practice, this means being sure of the intention behind your own communication and endeavoring to align the expression, as closely as possible, with the intention. Attending closely to our receiver's responses, we always need to remain willing to adjust our expression, if necessary, to elicit the response we intend.

If we go back to the example of Paul, the man whose lover was sexually unresponsive, and uncover his intent, the resulting interaction would be quite different:

Paul: (*to himself*) I want her to know I love her and want her. (*takes her hands in his, looks at her and speaks gently*) You are so important to me. I love you and yes, I also want you.

Hazel: (*softens the tension around her eyes and mouth and relaxes her hands in his*) Do you mean that?

Hazel's response indicates that Paul is beginning to communicate effectively with her. The expression of his communication is aligned with his intention by virtue of the response he is able to elicit from her.

By responding to the intentions behind behavior and believing that the meaning of a communication is the response it elicits, each person can connect with the other in ways that enrich personal and mutual experience. Each of them can be assisted in knowing and expressing what they want from one another, as well as what they want to give to one another, by incorporating cause-effect and complex equivalence relationships into their interactions. By installing these patterns, which are bonding and self-sustaining, you will genuinely surpass the wonders of any storybook "experience technician."

A Roadmap to Follow

The material in this book is meant to act as a guide. You can use it to guide your behavior as you assist people in developing strategies at the unconscious level that will help them to generate more satisfying and enriching sexual experiences. The sequence of the material provides a structure for organizing your behavior in a way that will assist you to act effectively when dealing with sexual dysfunction and other relationship problems.

For this presentation to be useful, it must reduce the complexity of successful interventions to a degree that is easy to handle. I have kept that requirement in mind throughout this presentation. While offering numerous techniques for successful therapeutic intervention, the patterns are presented in simple, easy-to-follow steps with several examples to further elucidate each technique. These patterns of communication and change have been used by my colleagues and me, and have been taught to psychotherapists in workshops all over the country, always with great success. If you are careful to make the necessary distinctions, and organize your experience in the sequence and in the categories prescribed here, then you can expect to be consistently effective in assisting your clients in reaching desired goals.

The form of this book is itself a strategy. I have found this strategy to be a useful way to organize my behavior in accomplishing any desired goal. It has three basic steps:

☐ Establishing rapport and gathering information concerning the client's present state and desired state.

☐ Evolving the client from their present to their desired state.

☐ Future-pacing; integrating the desired state experience into their ongoing behavior.[6]

These three steps facilitate effective therapeutic change when two vital ingredients are added: sensory experience and flexibility of behavior. External sensory experience is needed to detect the observable behavior that constitutes the present (or problem) state and the observable behavior that would constitute the desired (or cured) state for any individual or couple. Once this is known, it takes flexibility of behavior to move clients from where they are to where they want to be. If you are flexible in your behavior, you can shift from one method of intervention to another until you achieve the desired results. Again, the steps are:

☐ Find out where clients want to go and where they are now.

☐ Pick a method of getting to that desired state and use it.

☐ Notice whether the desired destination has, indeed, been reached. If it has, take measures to insure that it can be reached in the future without you. If the desired destination has not been reached, then pick another method and use it. Continue to use different methods until success is achieved.

This may sound like an incredible oversimplification of the very complex activity of doing therapy, yet it is for me the most elegant possible organization of behavior for doing therapy. Again, this strategy constitutes the form of this book. The content of this book concerns itself with five topics:

☐ What information concerning the client's present state and desired state is vital to gather with your senses.

☐ How to gather the vital information.

☐ Methods of establishing rapport consistently and meaningfully with any client.

☐ Techniques for evolving the client from present state to desired state.

☐ Methods to effectively future-pace the learnings and experiences accomplished within the therapy session into the client's ongoing behavior.

As with any book, the form and content of this text is a representation of the author. This is how my perceptions and behaviors are organized. It is with this strategy and these methods of intervention that I change myself and those who come to me seeking change.

This strategy for therapy can be likened to building a new house for someone. I learn about the existing structure and what is desired in the new one. Do they want doors with locks, or open arches for coming and going? Are large communal spaces appropriate, or cozy cubbyholes for privacy? What do they want to see, hear, and feel in their new dwelling that is not available to them now? What aspects of their present home would they like to integrate into the new one?

Once I know all of this I can choose the materials and tools suitable for constructing that new house; and I have a variety of materials and tools so that I can adjust from what doesn't work to what does. While construction is under way, I'm careful to build in endurance to insure the lasting quality of their new home. I also take care to install possibilities for future expansion.

Each of these "dwellings" is built upon the foundation of my own philosophies, including the belief that each human being has, somewhere within, all the resources needed to accomplish any change. My primary function is to access and organize those resources in a way that produces lasting, desired change. I'm a believer in the possibilities, rather than the limitations, of human experience.

The information and techniques of intervention in this book have made it possible for me to actualize my good intentions and personal philosophies. It is toward the actualization of your own good intentions I would now like to move you.

II How to Establish Rapport and Gather Information

Chapter 3: The Importance of Rapport

No communication is totally independent of context, and all meaning has an important contextual component. This may seem obvious, but defining the context is always important and frequently difficult. For example, language is by its very nature a highly contexted system . . . rooted in abstractions from reality. Yet, few people realize how dependent the meaning of even the simplest statement is on the context in which it is made. For example: A man and a woman on good terms, who have lived together for fifteen or more years, do not always have to spell things out. When he comes through the door after a day in the office, she may not have to utter a word. He knows from the way she moves what kind of day she had; he knows from her tone of voice how she feels about the company they are entertaining that night.

In contrast, when one moves from personal relationships to courts of law or to computers or mathematics, nothing can be taken for granted, because these activities are low context and must be spelled out. One space inserted between letters or words on a computer where it does not belong can stop everything in its tracks. Information, context, and meaning are bound together in a balanced, functional relationship. The more information that is shared, as with the couple referred to above, the higher the context. One can think of it as continuum ranging from high to low.

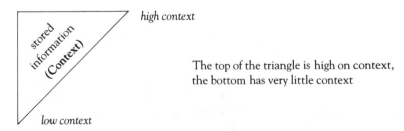

high context

The top of the triangle is high on context, the bottom has very little context

low context

Pair this triangle with another in a balanced relationship. In this second triangle there is very little information at top and more at the bottom.

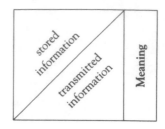

Combine the two and it can be seen, as context is lost, information must be added if meaning is to remain constant. The complete relationship can be expressed in a single diagram; there can be no meaning without both information and context. [1]

Edward T. Hall
The Dance of Life

Edward Hall's excellent description is useful to us on at least two counts. First, couples almost always treat their communications as high context ones. That is, they presume to know the meaning of each other's behavior and they respond to the assumed meaning, treating their perceptions as reality. Because of the assumption of shared meaning, little or no specific information is offered. This leaves them with the disadvantage of not realizing when even a simple miscommunication has taken place. For example, a couple came to me seeking help in improving the general tone of their relationship. They took turns telling me about their most recent argument; each wanted me to understand how the other was obstinate. He began to describe what had taken place, and where. "When we got to Ghiradelli Square I became depressed and . . ." She interrupted him immediately and corrected, "You were depressed *before* you ever got to Ghiradelli Square." With this they were off and running into a great argument over when he had actually become depressed. Since I had no assumption of it being a high context communication, it was easy to pursue the specific information about which they were arguing. To him, Ghiradelli Square started as soon as it was in sight. To her, it did not start until they stepped foot in it.

The second use of Edward Hall's description—of how the balance of "stored information" and "offered information" leads to more or less meaning—concerns the problem of bringing the therapeutic interaction to a high context communication as efficiently as possible. The solution involves knowing and being able to discern, out of all the possibilities, what is relevant information to remember and utilize for the purpose of effective therapeutic intervention. In the example given above, there were two pieces of information worth storing. One, that beginnings were determined more visually by him and more kinesthetically by her (which could indicate a more general pattern difference as to how each organized their experience), and two, that they were willing to fight and bring obvious discomfort to one another in order to demonstrate their "rightness."

We need to reach high context communications with our clients as quickly as possible. We have hours, not years, to spend with the people who come to us for help. The way to accomplish this is to accept that the first interaction begins at the lowest possible context, and then proceed to gather the information which is most relevant to comprehending the underlying structure of the client's experience. Essential to gathering the necessary information is the ability to achieve and maintain rapport with your clients. This presents a bit of a dilemma. If you review an interaction in which rapport was achieved and maintained, it will contain the characteristics of very high context communications. The parties experience little effort in being understood and believing that their concerns are highly regarded by the other person.

Specific methods exist for achieving the experience of rapport with others quickly and easily. With these methods, your client will experience the interaction as a high context communication while allowing you to gather the needed information graciously in order to make your map of their experience an accurate one. But I warn you to be cautious: There is a difference between giving your clients the experience of being understood and regarded, and actually understanding what their communications mean. If you make the mistake of automatically believing you know what they mean, you are doing them a great disservice. Remember: Until you have acquired and stored the relevant behavioral information, you are giving them the comfortable and secure experience of participating in a high context communication, while actually participating in a very low context one.

Though rapport skills are useful to any communicator, they are essential for the therapist. A good many other professionals, such as scientists, engineers, and architects have the opportunity to succeed without consistently high quality interpersonal interactions. Effective therapy doesn't happen without them.

Mirroring

When my colleagues and I analyzed the seemingly magical therapeutic interactions achieved by such wizards as Virginia Satir and Milton Erickson, we discovered certain common behavioral patterns. One of these patterns is *mirroring*. Mirroring is the process of offering back to the client portions of their own nonverbal behavior—just as a mirror does. Mirroring is a way to imitate the high context messages the client is giving without attaching meaning to them; knowing that they do carry significant unconscious meaning for the client.

You are already familiar with macro types of mirroring in your ongoing experience. An example of mirroring on this scale is behaving suitably—like not swearing in church or in front of Aunt Milly, whereas you might swear when with a peer group, knowing it will make some of your friends more comfortable with you. Another example of mirroring on this scale is dressing appropriately for a particular occasion. As a more refined example, we tend to match our table manners and body postures to the level of formality we perceive to be congruent with the place and people with whom we are dining. Mirroring on its various levels is the behavioral equivalent of agreeing with someone verbally.

To mirror effectively you must be able to make refined visual and auditory distinctions regarding your own, as well as your client's, behavior. The portions of your client's behavior that are worthwhile mirroring include body postures, specific gestures, breathing rhythms, facial expressions, and voice tone, tempo, and intonation patterns. Matching some or all of these will assist you in achieving a harmonious interaction. In fact, by mirroring it is possible to disagree with the content portion of a person's communication (what they are saying) and remain in complete rapport.

Mirroring is also a means to achieve *entrainment*, or synchronicity, which is recognized by many in the field of cultural anthropology (as well as others) as being relevant to human functioning. To quote Edward Hall again from *The Dance of Life*:

Entrainment is the term coined by William Condon for the process that occurs when two or more people become engaged in each other's rhythms, when they synchronize. Both Condon and I believe that it will ultimately be demonstrated that synchrony begins with the myelination of the auditory nerve about six months after conception. It is at this point that the infant can begin to hear in the womb. Immediately following birth, the newborn infant will move rhythmically with its mother's voice and will also synchronize with the voice of other people, speaking any language! The

*tendency to synchronize with surrounding voices can therefore be charac-
terized as innate. Which rhythm one uses, however, is a function of the
culture of the people who are around when these patterns are being
learned. It can be said with some assurance that normal human beings are
capable of learning to synchronize with any human rhythm, provided they
start early enough.*

*Clearly, something so thoroughly learned early in life, rooted in the or-
ganism's innate behavior program and shared by all mankind, must be not
only important, but also a key contributor to the survival of our species.
In the future, it is entirely possible that synchrony and entrainment will be
discovered to be even more basic to human survival than sex on the individual level and as basic to survival as sex on the group level. Without the
ability to entrain with others—which is what happens with certain types of
aphasia—life becomes almost unmanageable. Boston pediatrician Dr.
Barry Brazelton, who has spent years studying the interaction between
parents and children from the moment of birth, describes the subtle, multi-
level synchrony in normal relations and then states that parents who batter
their children have never learned to sync with their babies. Rhythm is so
much a part of everyone's life that it occurs virtually without notice.* [2]

To begin learning how to mirror, take the time to watch other
people interact. Watch children playing; observe in restaurants,
meetings, and cocktail parties. Anytime you are near people who
are interacting, notice how much mirroring is going on. Also
notice the quality of interaction that occurs when mirroring is
absent.

After a short period of time in an observer's position, you will
know that people instinctively mirror each other. You can now
begin to do so deliberately to achieve specific outcomes. Start by
mirroring just one aspect of another person's behavior while
talking to them. When this is easy, add another discreet piece—
like their voice tempo—and another, and then another, until
you are mirroring without thinking about it, but can consistently
observe it in your behavior in retrospect.

The more you practice, the more aware you will become of the
rhythms that you and others generate with gestures and breathing
patterns, and in voice tones, tempo, and intonation patterns. Be
sure to notice the degree to which couples are out of sync when
they are miscommunicating, in contrast to how they are in sync
when doing well with one another. The difference in degree to
which a couple is mirroring before and after you work with them
is an important indicator of change. To illustrate across contexts:

*These studies covered a wide range of groups from the Indians of the
Southwest to Eskimos in Alaska . . . Again, the Colliers found rhythms.*

*A quite remarkable but not unexpected discovery was that the teacher de-
termined the rhythm of the classroom. Classes taught by Native Americans who had not been trained by white educators had a rhythm close to
that of natural, relaxed breathing and ocean breakers (i.e., about 5 to 8
seconds per cycle). That is much slower than the frantic quality of a white
or black classroom in the urban settings which most American school-
children encounter today. Native Americans who had been through U.S.
educational mills produced rhythms that were in between. The Colliers'
material made me realize that it was only when the Indian children were
immersed in their own familiar rhythm that they felt comfortable enough to
settle down and learn.* [3]

When mirroring to establish rapport with couples, be sure to
be subtle. Choosing to mirror tempo patterns and smaller hand
gestures is better than shifting from one overt whole body posture
to another. As you turn your primary attention from one person
to another, be sure to attend to the responses that are being
elicited in each person as a result of your behavior and their
partner's behavior. If either person starts to drift into their own
internal experience while the other is talking to you, bring them
back into the interaction. This will provide them with the opportunity to gather significant information concerning their own
responses to their partner's communications. Following are a few
verbalizations that are useful in accomplishing this graciously:

> "I need to find out what each of you wants from the other.
> Sometimes people ask for something their spouse never had
> any idea they wanted, and I'd like to know if you've heard this
> before. If so, what, if any part of it, is different?"

> "You wouldn't be here if you didn't want to reach greater
> understandings, and I know Sally's about to say something
> that's important for you to hear. Are you ready?"

> "I need to hear what Jim has to say now, and I'll want to know
> your understanding of his reply."

> "Even though you may think you've heard and seen it all
> before, I promise you there is something that you still don't
> know that is very important to you both."

> "I know you'll be curious about what sense I make of what she
> is about to say."

> "While I'm listening to you, Sally, I'll also be watching Jim to
> see if he can really hear what you are saying."

In addition to engaging the listener, these questions and statements influence the speakers to consider the impact of their communication.

Many therapists think that mirroring is the same as mimicking, and they are reluctant to mirror because they are afraid they will offend their clients. We have very strong cultural restraints with regard to mimicking others. These cultural restraints are so strong that this tremendous means of learning is often denied us from a young age. "Don't be a copycat!" we are chided. If we detect someone mimicking us we feel that they are likely to be making fun of us and we often are offended. However, mirroring is not mimicry. Mimicry is usually characterized by some exaggeration of a behavioral feature. Mirroring is the subtle, behavioral reflection of those meaningful, unconscious communications each of us offers to the attentive receiver.

Though mirroring might feel awkward to the novice, its value in achieving and maintaining rapport makes it worth doing whatever is necessary to become skilled. It requires effort to learn how to mirror effectively: You need to tune your perceptions to portions of your own and other's behavior of which you were previously unaware. This is true for all of the behavioral information you will be directed to recognize and respond to in the following chapters.

Chapter 4: Assessing Cognitive Behaviors

There are clinicians who say that sexual dysfunction is not a problem; when there is a difficulty, they treat the relationship as the problem. But what does it mean for a relationship to have problems? The word "relationship" is a distortion of the process word "relate." There is no tangible object called a "relationship." It is, instead, a process of animate beings relating to each other. Some clinicians believe that caring and trust make a relationship work. But what is "caring" and what, specifically, is "trust"? They are merely words implying events that are not defined with regard to any particular person's experience. If we simplify "relationship" by construing it to be the verb "relate," we can ask meaningful questions: Who is relating to whom? How does their relating to each other bring about unhappiness and dissatisfaction? How can they relate to one another in ways that generate more desirable experiences? The answers to these questions will reveal useful information about the structure of a client's present and desired states.

Often it is easy to detect when people are not relating well—they tell you. They tell you verbally as well as nonverbally. Their verbalizations are representations of their experiences, just as maps are representations of territories. People use words to describe what they *believe* happened. They can never tell you what actually happened, just as a map can never be a complete representation of a territory. Consequently, an important concept to understand is that what people *tell* us is not what *actually* happened, but only what they consciously experienced. There is a tremendous difference between the two. Thus if two individuals tell me differing stories about the same incident, I know they are both right. Typically, it is not that one is telling the truth and the other is lying. Rather, out of *all* the possible things there are to pay attention to in the situation, each tells only what they were *aware* of in their experience.

The content of people's verbalizations tell you what they believe. The process portion of people's verbalizations tells you how they reached those beliefs. Almost every couple I have worked with disagrees about what takes place between them: He says *a* and *b* happened, and she says it is more like *x* and *y*. Noticing how their descriptions differ is important to understanding how they miscommunicate. It is here, at the process level of their communications, that you begin to find how best to direct the process of change. The words each of us use to express ourselves are indicators of the elements of our conscious experience and can point the way out of dissatisfaction and towards fulfillment.

Representational Systems

During any moment of time, we can only be conscious of a small portion of our experience. For instance, even as you read this sentence you could be aware of the sounds around you, the quality of the air you are breathing, the type of print you are reading, the size of the margins, the taste in your mouth, or the weight and position of your left hand. As you read of each possibility, you likely shifted your conscious awareness to what was being suggested. It is unlikely you were consciously aware of any, or all, of those portions of experience prior to my directing you to them. It has been postulated that human consciousness can hold constant seven, plus or minus two, chunks of information at a time.[4] This means consciousness is a limited phenomena. The specific portions of your experience you bring into consciousness is determined by the interaction of your present sensory capabilities, present motivations, and childhood learnings.

If you attend a lecture given by an erudite and fascinating speaker, it is unlikely that you will be conscious of the color of shoes and dress of a stranger sitting two seats away. Your attention will be on the speaker. If, however, the speaker is a bore, you may become aware of feelings of boredom or loneliness that motivate you to look about for someone with whom to make personal contact. In that case you may become very aware of the color of shoes and dress worn by that stranger. Thus your present motivation would determine the aspects of your experience you brought into conscious awareness.

As a child, you learned to value some aspects of family communication over others. If your mother told you, "Everything is O.K.," but had clenched teeth, made a fist, and had tears in her eyes, which message did you trust?—the one you heard or the one you saw? If your father scolded you verbally about some misdemeanor, but smiled jovially and slapped you on the back, which message did you believe? Predictably, a child from such a family would learn to value, and thereby attend to, the visual portion of experience over the others. He would trust and be more aware of what he saw than the words he heard. If told, "I love you," he might reply, "But you don't look like you love me. How can I believe you?"

As a listener, you can discern the portion of experience a person is representing internally in conscious awareness by attending to the process words used: adjectives, verbs, and adverbs. These *predicates* specify a process of seeing, hearing, feeling, and tasting/smelling. The following are examples of predicates (process words):

Visual	Auditory	Kinesthetic	Olfactory/Gustatory
see	hear	feel	taste
picture	tone	touch	smells
bright	loud	warm	fresh
clear	tune	smooth	fragrant
vague	amplify	soft	stale
focus	harmonize	handle	sweet
flash	screech	grasp	pungent
perspective	shout	tight	sour
dark	scream	rough	bitter
colorful	ringing	hard	salty

Suppose you are gathering information from a married couple and the husband says:

> Well, the way things look to me is that . . . I really can't see any future in our marriage. I am willing to try because the way I see myself is as a person who is very concerned, but I really can't imagine that things will get better. It is just too dark and gloomy.

And his wife says:

> Well, I really feel that things can be better. We have a lot to build upon and if we work on our relationship and try very hard we can smooth out our difficulties.

If, while listening to this communication, you pay attention to what they say and you take the content as being important—that he doesn't believe it will work out and she does—then you have to start guessing about which one of them is right and which one is wrong. If you deal with the content, you don't find out anything about the process by which they disagree. You don't learn how they came to represent the experience of their marriage as, on one hand, being hopeless and, on the other, promising. Instead, you are limited to responding to their verbalizations by forming judgments, opinions, and interpretations of them, as if their descriptions were real world experiences—which they are not. If you believe either her or him, you are responding to the content they are talking about, and this places you in the same dilemma they are in with each other. The degree to which you will be able to actually *understand* their situation is the degree to which you respond to the form of their verbalizations. They do not understand each other; they disagree about *reality*. Your job as a professional communicator is to concern yourself with process—not with "reality."

How is it, then, that two people who live together disagree so widely? By observing the process that is indicated by their words, the first thing you will notice about this couple is that they are talking about different portions of the same experience. He is talking in visual terms, about internal pictures and images he sees or does not see, i.e., internally generated images, not just things in the outside world of sensory experience. She, on the other hand, is talking about feelings. You can identify this by noting the process words—the adjectives, verbs and adverbs—in the sentence. If you attend to the nouns in the sentence, you can get caught in content. If you attend to the predicates (the process words) you identify something about the process. All of the predicates in his sentences relate to making pictures—"look," "see," "imagine," "dark,"—and they all presuppose seeing. All of her words relate to constructing internal feelings: "feel," "hard," "smooth out." This immediately reveals that they both are describing internally generated experiences about the condition of their marriage. It also reveals that they are each aware of, and talking about, different portions of their experience; he, the visual portion, and she, the kinesthetic (feeling) portion. This indicates that there is an important difference in how these people organize and express their perceptions. This difference is *significant:* It demonstrates how they don't get along. In fact, this difference in process is responsible for a great deal of miscommunication. It is as though two *different languages* were being spoken *but no one noticed.*

These language patterns are a significant part of the behavioral information that reveals the structure of an individual's present state. Each sensory-specific process word used—visual, kinesthetic, auditory, and olfactory/gustatory—indicates that the speaker's internal experience is being represented in that sensory system. The habitual use of one category of sensory-specific words over another is indicative of a *primary representational system.* A primary representational system is an internal sensory system that is more highly developed and is used more often (and more fully) than the others.[5] As a result, the individual will make sense of the world primarily in that system. If the primary representational system is visual, sense of the world is made in pictures; kinesthetic, in feelings; auditory, in sounds; and infrequently, olfactory/gustatory, in smells and tastes.

So what does it mean to relate to a person in an *effective* way? Partly, it means talking about the same portions of experience at the same time. To illustrate this, here is an example taken from a therapy transcript:

Shirley: I just really don't like how he is always pawing me in public. He makes a scene and doesn't even see how everyone looks at us. It just attracts a lot of attention and I want him to show me more respect in front of other people.

Bob: But I like to be close to her. I want to make contact with her when I'm feeling affectionate and sometimes I feel affectionate outside of closed doors. She pushes me away and I think that's really cold to do to someone you're supposed to love. She used to like my reaching for her. Now, I don't feel appreciated by her at all.

As in the previous example, the words used by Bob and Shirley indicate that they are aware of two very different portions of their experience—this time with regard to his touching her in public. Look at the predicates. They disclose useful distinctions about what portion of experience Shirley and Bob are each conscious of. Her words, "scene," "see," "show," "looks," all presuppose a *visual* primary representational system. His words, "contact," "feel," "pushes," "cold," "reaching," all presuppose a *kinesthetic* primary representational system. Their words indicate that they are each attending to a different portion of experience; she, the visual portion; he, the kinesthetic portion. In order for them to reach an understanding, a bridge must be built between their different experiences.

Listening to any conversation as well as reading transcripts of couple counseling, sex counseling, and so on, can provide you with a wealth of pertinent examples of the use of representational systems. While researching transcripts, I became aware of an interesting phenomenon. Married persons who participate in extramarital affairs typically refer to their marital relationship using kinesthetic predicates, solid, stuck, cemented, etc., and to their extramarital affairs with visual predicates, how they were attracted by what they saw, that these relationships were more colorful, etc. I also discovered that persons who participated in group sex and considered themselves swingers used a high proportion of gustatory process words. They likened sexual intercourse to going out to dinner and stated that, like gourmets, they sought varieties of cuisine and found the thought of monogamy bland and tasteless.

Predicates that do not indicate any of these four portions of experience are *unspecified.* That is, they are unspecified as to how the process is being represented or executed—whether in pictures, smells/tastes, feelings, or sounds. Here are some examples of unspecified predicates:

think	learn	change	consider
know	nice	respectful	remember
understand	intuit	trusting	believe

When presented with such words, you can ask, "How, *specifically,* do you think (know, understand, learn)?" This question will elicit either a verbal response richer in process detail, or a nonverbal behavior (see next section on accessing cues) specifying the internal process. Of course, people do not consciously sort through and choose the words or syntax to describe their experience. Their words are, however, a representation of what, out of all the experiences available, they are consciously aware.

Accessing Cues

Although language indicates what part of a person's internal experience is in conscious awareness, we must look elsewhere for behavioral information about how the specific experience came *into conscious awareness*. Most of the time in the therapeutic context people talk about either their past or their internal experience. A client seldom speaks about current experience: the color of the therapist's chair, the weight of the client's arm resting on their thigh, the sounds of the ventilation equipment, or any sensory experiences which are occurring while the client sits there in your office. Usually the client describes internal responses to the present therapeutic activities or internal representations of past or projected future events.

In order to speak of such internally generated experiences, each of us must, in some way, gain access to those internal experiences. To illustrate this point further, I would like you to do the following:

1. Think of a pleasant childhood experience you shared with a close friend.

2. Recall the clothes you wore at your high school graduation.

3. Remember your first French kiss.

4. Remember a time when your curiosity overcame your fears.

To accomplish any of these tasks, it was necessary for you to gain access to certain distinct classes of past experiences. The process of obtaining the information (the process of getting internal information—the pictures, sound, words, and feelings that make up memories, fantasies, etc.) is referred to as *accessing*. The specific nonverbal behaviors that disclose information about how such experiential information is made available to the conscious mind are called *accessing cues*. Accessing cues are those eye movements that indicate how a person is thinking—in pictures, words, or feelings.

In addition to words and syntax, people offer to the careful observer-listener a plethora of meaningful nonverbal communication that is also generated unconsciously. There has been much irresponsible speculation and interpretation concerning human nonverbal behavior or body language. (Witness the many irresponsible interpretations of what it means if a woman's legs are crossed or not, etc.) I believe that some of the most relevant information concerning nonverbal communication is provided by accessing cues. My colleagues and I found—in the course of our studies of human behavior—that eye scanning patterns were definitely related to the internal processing necessary to bring into consciousness information regarding past remembered or future constructed experiences.

As stated in *Patterns Of The Hypnotic Techniques Of Milton H. Erickson, M.D.*, Volume II:

> . . . each of us has developed particular body movements which indicate to the astute observer which representational system we are using. Especially rich in significance are the eye scanning patterns which we have developed. Thus, for the student of hypnosis, predicates in the verbal system and eye scanning patterns in the nonverbal system offer quick and powerful ways of determining which of the potential meaning making resources—the representational systems—the client is using at a moment in time, and therefore how to respond creatively to the client. Consider, for example, how many times you have asked someone a question and they have paused, said: "Hmmmm, let's see," and, accompanying this verbalization, they move their eyes up and to the left. Movement of the eyes up and to the left stimulates (in right handed people) eidetic images located in the nondominant hemisphere. The neurological pathways that come from the left side of both eyes (left visual fields) are represented in the right cerebral hemisphere (nondominant). The eye scanning movement up and to the left is a common way people use to stimulate that hemisphere as a method for accessing visual memory. Eye movements up and to the right conversely stimulate the left cerebral hemisphere and constructed images—that is, visual representations of things that the person has never seen before.
>
> . . . accessing cues which may be detected visually. Specifically (for the right-handed person):

accessing cue	representational system indicated*	
eyes up and to the left	eidetic imagery	(V)
eyes defocused in position	imagery	(V)
eyes up and to the right	constructed imagery	(V)
eyes down and to the left	auditory internal	(A)
telephone postures	auditory internal	(A)
eyes left or right, same level of gaze	auditory internal	(A)
eyes down and to the right	kinesthetics	(K)[6]

* V = Visual, A = Auditory, K = Kinesthetic

As you face a person and their eyes move in the direction shown in the following drawings, the internal process designated is being accessed.

Specifically (for the right-handed person):

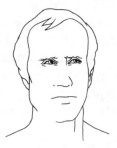

Eidetic Imagery
(images that are recalled from the past just as they were seen originally)

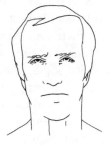

Visual Imagery
(eyes defocused, fixed position, usually some pupil dilation—could be eidetic or constructed)

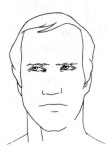

Constructed Imagery

Auditory Internal
(often internal dialogue)

Telephone Postures
(internal dialogue)

Auditory Internal
(often internal dialogue)

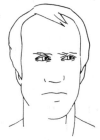

Auditory Internal
(often internal dialogue)

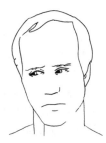

Kinesthetics
(feelings and emotions)

You probably have had the experience of asking a question of someone who then broke eye contact, shifted their eyes up and left, and said, "Hmmm, let's see." And they did. At other times, possibly their eyes went up and right, or defocused while they stared straight ahead, or shifted down and left or down and right. Or perhaps some sequence of these eye scanning movements occurred. You may not have known it, but that person was indicating how they were accessing the information needed to answer your question.

Miscommunication resulting from a lack of understanding of accessing cues is widespread. When accessing, people are not in external sensory experience. Therefore, they miss sensory input. Therapists and people-helpers frequently hear people complain:

> "He just doesn't listen to me. He's right there in the room and I tell him something and then he pretends he never heard me." (This woman failed to notice when her husband was actually available to *consciously* receive information. Though he was in the room with her, and was even maintaining eye contact, his pupils were dilated, indicating visualization.)

> "You did not tell me that. I never heard you say any such thing." (He's right. He didn't hear her say any such thing.)

> "Didn't you see where I put it? You were right there." "No, I wasn't. You did not put it down while I was there." (And they are both right, because his conscious mind was attending to his internal images rather than to what was going on in his external experience.)

When a person's consciousness is attending to and absorbed in internal processes (visual, auditory, and even kinesthetic), input often goes unnoticed. If the input reaches a certain threshold, it will bring the person back out to sensory experience; otherwise, the sensory input will go in, but may not be available to that person consciously. I teach couples, families, and business people how to tell—by watching for accessing cues—when a person is consciously listening, seeing, etc.

The following examples of accessing cues include the relevant eye-scanning patterns:

Sue: I just can't see it (*eyes up, left*). John has never been able to do it before, why should he start now?

John: Did you hear that (*eyes down, left*)? I ask myself, why bother even trying? It seems like (*eyes down, right*) there's just no pleasing her.

In this example, Sue is recalling eidetic images. Naturally, she can't see what hasn't occurred in the past. It would be important for her to build a constructed image of John doing what he has yet to do; seeing that constructed image would assist her in feeling hopeful about future possibilities. John is talking to himself, internally, and then experiencing the feelings he gets from that dialogue.

Will: Do you see how she's dressed? I remember (*eyes up, left*) how she used to look. If she loved me, she wouldn't let herself go to pot like that. I see myself (*eyes up, right*) as an attractive man, and it's embarrassing (*eyes up, right*). Of course, I wouldn't say this in front of her.

Will compares a past image of his wife with her present appearance, then constructs images of how he sees himself and how others see the two of them. Throughout, he is comparing what he sees in sensory experience with his internal images, and the sensory experience rates a poor second.

Or, from a women's rap group:

Sal: (*Eyes up, left*) He's too fast. I put on a negligee and light a candle, turn back the sheets, get all ready and he doesn't even notice (*eyes up, left*). He'd rather just grab for me in the night.

Stella: (*Eyes down, right*) I wish Jim would just reach for me. I feel (*eyes down, right*) so pressured all the time to perform and dress up and look just so (*eyes down, right*). I get tired.

June: (*Down, left*) That's not important. What's important is the (*eyes up, right*) essence of how you approach each other. That you do it in love (*eyes up, right*) as well as lust (*eyes down, right*).

Sal is accessing past images and places importance on visual aspects of the lovemaking experience. Stella expresses kinesthetic priorities which are congruent with her kinesthetic accessing cues. June's accessing cues indicate that she tells herself something internally, makes a constructed image concerning the "essence of how you approach each other," and then accesses kinesthetically in connection with the experience of lust.

While using your ears to detect the words that indicate a person's representational system, you can use your eyes to notice their accessing cues. Accessing cues are those eye movements that indicate how the client is thinking: in pictures, words, or feelings. They give you vital information concerning the client's internal behavior. Although accessing cues alone will not fully inform you of the internal experience that is occurring, by detecting accessing cues you can discern the internal processes that are being used to generate a person's overall experience.

Lead Systems

Just as people typically favor one representational system, which is evident by the process words they use most often, they also typically favor one internal process for *initiating* the accessing of information. You can determine which internal process is favored for initiating the accessing of information by noting which accessing cue is habitually used first. This favored internal process, either the visual, kinesthetic or auditory, is referred to as the *lead system.*

In a recent workshop, I asked two men to join me in front of the audience. I used them to illustrate the concept of different lead systems. (I had discerned previously by their behavior that they processed information very differently from one another.) After asking the audience to watch them closely, I instructed these men merely to think of the answers to the questions I was about to ask them. I then proceeded to ask a series of questions:

1. What color are your mother's eyes?

2. How many doors are there in your house?

3. Which door slams the loudest?

4. Where is reverse in your car's gears?

5. How does it feel to be sunburned?

6. Can you hear your mother calling your name?

One man first looked down and to his right in response to each question. The other first looked up and to his left in response to each question. The first searched kinesthetically for the answers, while the other searched visually. Both found the answers to each question, but they used different systems of accessing to do so. They each used their own most typical lead system.

While some people's accessing cues would have varied with each question, these gentlemen's did not. That is why I chose them to illustrate lead system behavior. Rather than accessing visually for a question that asked for visual information (color), or auditorily for one that asked for sound (loudness, mother's voice), or kinesthetically (the feeling of being sunburned), they habitually used one internal process to access the answer to each of the questions. This was confirmed to the group by the men's descriptions of their internal experience in response to some of the questions:

Question 1

Man I: I got the feeling of my mother, then I saw her face and looked at her eyes.

Man II: I just saw her face and focused on her eyes.

Question 2

Man I: I walked through my house, starting at the front door, and counted the doors on my fingers.

Man II: I saw pictures of the doors in my house like index cards and they just flipped in front of me and each card was numbered.

Question 3

Man I: I felt myself slamming each one and listened.

Man II: I saw each one slam and heard them.

Question 5

Man I: I just felt my skin turn hot and sensitive and it tightened.

Man II: I saw my face in a mirror and it was all red.

Their descriptions tell how they use one system to lead them to information contained in other modalities of experience. These two men would be apt to remember a shared experience differently—by recalling and expressing it through differing sensory modalities. Their descriptions show how internally generated experience is influenced by what lead system is used.

There is one lead system in particular to watch for when treating sexual dysfunction. It is the constructed visual lead system, and the accessing cue for it is up and right. Often—not always, but often—people who habitually access constructed images see themselves in their internal pictures. When asked to remember being kissed for example, they see themselves being kissed rather than seeing the other person's face approaching and feeling their lips making contact. An example of the meaning of such internal processing in the sexual context is provided by Masters and Johnson in *Human Sexual Inadequacy*:

As sex play is introduced and mutual attempts made by marital partners to force an erective response, the impotent husband finds himself a spectator to his own sexual exchange. He is mentally observing his and his partner's response (or lack of it) to sexual stimulation. Will there be an

51

erection? If and when the penis begins to engorge, how full will the erection become? When erection is obtained, how long will it last? The involuntary spectator in the room demands immediate answers for these questions from the anxious man in the bed, so intensely concerned with his fears of sexual performance. Rather than allowing himself to relax, enjoy sensual stimulation, and permit his natural sensual responsivity to create and maintain the erective process, he as a spectator demands instant performance. In the spectator role, a dysfunctional man completely negates any concept of natural sexual function. He cannot conceive of involuntary sexual responsivity sustaining an erection as a natural physiological process on the same natural plane as that of his involuntary respiratory responsivity sustaining his breathing mechanism.

Not only is there at least one spectator in the impotent male's bedroom, frequently there are two. For the wife, who is physically attempting to provide her husband with an erection, simultaneously may be mentally occupying an equal position of watchfulness, critically observing the apprehensive male's level of sexual responsivity. Is there to be an erection? If so, how full an erection? Will it be usable? Will it be maintained? Is she stimulating her husband satisfactorily? If he obviously isn't responding, what could she be doing that is wrong? All these questions arise when, in her spectator role, the wife quietly observes the progress of the particular sexual episode in her marriage. Is it any wonder the wife of the impotent male usually is not fully sexually responsive herself, even when the occasional sexual opportunity presents? Even in the immediacy of sexual opportunity, she frequently is psychologically caught in the corner observing the physical proceedings rather than physiologically tied to the bed totally involved with her own mating.

Neither partner realizes that the other is mentally standing in an opposite corner, observing the marital bedding scene in a spectator role. Both partners involuntarily distract themselves in their spectator roles, essentially uninvolved in the experience in which they are involved, to such an extent that there is no possibility for effective sexual stimuli to penetrate the impervious layers of performance fear and involuntary voyeurism. [7]

Asking questions about past or anticipated future sexual experiences is a good way to elicit lead system information. If you detect a person using a constructed image lead system, ask them directly whether they see themselves in the picture or see the experience as though they were inside it.

If they are watching themselves, you can use the technique of overlapping representational systems (presented on pg. 177) to assist them in stepping into the picture and experiencing it more fully.

Chapter 5: Utilizing Representational Systems

We ask a lot of our clients in therapy: to reveal what is unknown even to them and to follow instructions without information about what the instructions are for, or what they will lead to. We need our client's trust if we are to help them, and the first step in gaining that trust is to establish rapport.

You have established rapport with your client when they are convinced that you are knowledgeable, that you hold their best interest in high esteem, and that you understand their experience. Establishing rapport is prerequisite to your client's belief that you are able to assist him or her in making changes that will improve their quality of life.

This section builds on the foundation already established and describes how representational systems and accessing cues can be powerfully utilized to establish rapport and facilitate the process of change.

Matching

To gather information effectively or begin a process of change, it is always important to establish rapport between you and your client at both the conscious and unconscious levels. *Matching,* the process of generating verbal and nonverbal behavior which paces that of your client, is a technique for creating conscious and unconscious rapport. When you use the technique of matching, your clients will have the subjective experience of being really understood. After all, you are speaking their language— verbally and nonverbally.

The process of matching representational systems and accessing cues requires that you (1) recognize what representational system and accessing cues your client is utilizing and generating, (2) be flexible enough in your own behavior to communicate in the language of any representational system and to direct your own eye movements at will, and (3) in order to accomplish the above, be able to keep your own consciousness attentive to sensory experience rather than accessing internally yourself. Because of the tradeoff between internal and external experience, if your consciousness is on internally accessed experience, you will miss the verbal and nonverbal communications offered by your client. I am shocked every time I notice therapists conducting sessions with their eyes closed. For successful intervention, you must be alert to sensory experience.

The following examples taken from some of my therapy sessions demonstrate and clarify the technique of matching:

June: Well (*eyes up, left*), it's *clear* to me he isn't interested in changing what's going on.

LCB: Oh? The way you *see* it (*eyes up, left*) your husband is satisfied with what is happening now.

June: He must be. I can't (*eyes up, left; head shakes no*) *envision* him being any different, either.

LCB: So you don't have (*eyes up, left*) a *picture* yet of how you'd like him to be? (*Eyes up, right*) Imagine that. (*I lead June with the nonverbal behavior of a constructed image accessing cue, which is congruent with imagining a picture she has never seen before.*)

Meg: He just doesn't *see* how I am.

LCB: Oh, who does he *see* you as?

Meg: I don't know; I just know it isn't me.

LCB: How will you *show* him the real you so he can take a *look*? (*This asks Meg to begin eliciting with her own behavior the response she wants.*)

Joe: Listen (*eyes down, left*), there is nothing but *discord* in our relationship, and everything I've ever tried to do has only *amplified* (*eyes down, left*) our problem.

LCB: Hmmm, if I *hear* you right, then you would like things to *quiet down* and perhaps have some *harmony* develop between the two of you.

Joe: Yeah, now you're *tuned in* to what I want.

Shirley: If I could just *feel* like he was trying. But he just *turns away, pulls* the covers over his head, anything but *face up* to what's going on.

LCB: If I *grasp* what you're saying, then you *feel* like he is *out of touch* with what's going on and you have to *knock him over* to get his attention.

In instances where unspecified predicates are used, the accessing cue can indicate how to effectively structure your communications so as to establish rapport by matching your client.

Betsy: I want you to know that he (*eyes up, left*) really tried. I don't think (*down, left*) there is anything more to do.

LCB: So, you *see* what already has been done and you *tell* yourself there isn't anything left?

Jimmy: (*Eyes down, right*) there isn't anything left here for me. It's a disaster.

LCB: You *feel* like there isn't anything to *hold onto* and perhaps nothing that can or will *hold onto* you?

Sam: We would be (*eyes up, right*) okay if there was more respect around here.

LCB: What do you *see* yourself doing that would *show* your wife how much you respect her? (*This suggests to Sam that he begin to take responsibility for generating the respect he desires.*)

Theresa: Well, just when (*eyes down, left*) we're getting along, something happens and *bang* (*eyes up, left*) we're at it again.

LCB: *Sounds* (*eyes down, left*) to me like just when you tell yourself it's okay, *bang* (*eyes up, left*) and you can *see* trouble happening all over again.

Translating

When you are working with more than one person you need to establish rapport with each by matching predicates and accessing cues. You also must be able to bridge the communication gaps that develop between persons. One of the easiest and most effective ways to bridge such gaps is to translate, in experiential terms, from one representational system to another.

To some highly visual people, the experience of living in a very untidy house is comparable to a highly kinesthetic person sleeping in a bed full of cracker crumbs. For a kinesthetic person, being pushed away would be like being left out of the picture for a visual person. For the auditory person who responds to words primarily (as opposed to tonal and tempo qualities), being illogical could be the equivalent of an unpleasant rockoplane ride for a kinesthetic person, or a psychedelic light show for a visual person. Translating experience from one modality to another creates understanding and appreciation. To be successful at translating you need to be able to represent various experiences in any modality. For instance, the auditory experience of silence could be likened to the kinesthetic experience of numbness, or the visual experience of total darkness. The visual process of imagining could translate as the kinesthetic process of constructing, or the auditory process of orchestrating. These are all brief illustrations of experiential translations.

The following two examples taken from couple therapy transcripts demonstrate the techniques of matching predicates and accessing cues, translating positions in experiential terms, and using unspecified predicates to talk to two different persons at the same time.

Transcript A

Joe: (*Eyes up, left*) Well, I think our difficulty is different from most other people.

LCB: Oh, how do you see it?

Joe: Well, she is the impatient one (*eyes up, left*). I like to plan how it will be. You know, set the stage.

LCB: How do you plan?

Joe: (*Eyes up, right*) Well...

LCB: I understand. So you enjoy picturing what will take place.

Joe: Yes. I really get off on planning and changing the plans until it's just perfect, then I like to live out those fantasies. And they all have Janis in them. I want you to know that.

LCB: So let me see if I understand you (*eyes up and left, mirroring Joe's up and right accessing cue; gestures with hands up in front of eyes*), you create a visual fantasy of you and Janis making love from beginning to end—an elaborate and detailed fantasy. And when it looks right

to you, then you want to make that fantasy into reality by having the two of you act it out. Is that right?

Joe: Yes.

LCB: Okay, now I'm going to ask Janis some questions and I want you to watch closely. Janis (*I reach over and lightly touch her left arm*), and what do you feel you want?

Janis: Well (*Eyes down, right; then down, left*), I just feel like all that is so silly. I don't want to be part of a play. I want to feel wanted without all the buildup. It doesn't have any spontaneity.

Joe: See, she just isn't very romantic!

Janis: And you're not very spontaneous either!

LCB: Whoa! Wait a minute (*holds Janis's arm, puts hand in stop gesture in front of Joe's face*). Now, Janis, suppose you tell me what you *do* want, instead of what you don't want. Can you get in touch with how you'd *like* it to be? And you watch closely, Joe.

Janis: (*Eyes down, right*) I just want it to be more fun. I'd like him to let me surprise him; but no, it's always according to plan. And the lighting has to be just right and the soft music playing. I want to just grab him sometimes, you know. When I feel like having sex, I want it right then.

LCB: Right then and exciting! You feel like you would be happier if, when you felt the urge to have sex with Joe, you could reach for him, or let him know, and he would respond. You would like to feel like there could be more surprises.

Janis: Yes, that's it. Surprises.

LCB: Now, Joe, I want you to pay close attention because I'm going to show Janis what you want in a way I think will make sense to her. Okay?

Joe: Okay, This ought to be good.

LCB: Janis, have you ever prepared a four or five course meal?

Janis: Well, yes, a couple of times.

LCB: And have you had the pleasure of enjoying having a four or five course meal served to you?

Janis: Yes.

LCB: And each course was well planned and designed to

whet your appetite for the next . . . correct?

Janis: Well, yes.

LCB: When you prepared such a meal, would you have felt disappointed if your guests had put all five courses on the table at once and just dived in; or worse yet, if before you started serving they satisfied themselves on a leftover tuna fish sandwich?

Janis: (*Laughing*) Well, yes. Yes, I'd feel disappointed, even mad.

LCB: Well, that's something like what happens to Joe. He makes plans that are intended to delight you and take you exciting places, and he gets disappointed if you sate yourself on the appetizer.

Janis: But . . .

LCB: Before you but, I want to know if you can be in touch with how that would be for him.

Janis: (*Nods head up and down.*)

LCB: Good. Now, I'm going to let Joe in on how it is for you. So, hold on there for a moment. Joe, have you ever taken a tour with a tour guide . . . as a student or something like that?

Joe: Only once, in Hawaii.

LCB: Well, on that tour the guide had a very specific itinerary. And probably you pictured beforehand some of what you would see.

Joe: Yeah.

LCB: While you were on this tour, if you looked this way or that, you may have seen a fascinating side road or curio shop. And you wanted a closer look. But, alas, it was not included on the tour and the opportunity to explore that unexpected object of interest just disappeared as your tour guide directed your attention back to the planned itinerary. Can you see how frustrating that would be? It could even lead to your being disillusioned with going on such tours, don't you think?

Joe: Well . . . you mean, I'm being like a tour director?

Janis: Yes. Yes, you are.

LCB: Of course, sometimes being taken on a tour can be a very delicious experience, like being served an eight course meal. And other times, exploring a new avenue on the spur of the moment can be thrilling. Don't you agree?

Transcript B

LCB: Tell me what you would like to be different in this relationship.

Ron: (*Frowns; eyes down, left; then down, right*) Well, I think it would help if there was more (*Eyes down, right*) cooperation.

LCB: And what could your wife, Sue, do that would help you to feel like there was cooperation?

Ron: Oh, if she'd just understand that I work hard and sometimes the pressure gets to me, you know? It's rough going at work and I come home and she just piles more on.

LCB: So, you feel like she adds to the burden, and what you'd like is for her to lend a hand and lighten the load. Is that right?

Ron: That's about it. Yeah.

LCB: Well, you hold on for a moment, Ron, while I talk to Sue. Sue, I'm sure you want to reply to what Ron has just said, but first, I want you to tell me what you want to be different.

Sue: (*Eyes up, left*) It doesn't matter.

LCB: (*Eyes up, and right, mirroring Sue's accessing cue*) What doesn't matter?

Sue: (*Eyes up, left*) What I want, that's what. Nothing's going to change. Never has, never will.

LCB: You don't like what you see going on now, right? (*My eyes lead Sue's up and left.*)

Sue: That's right.

LCB: Well, if you could take that picture you have of what's going on with you and Ron and change it . . . what would you change in that picture so it would look better to you?

Sue: Well, I'd like to see that he appreciates me. Oh, shit! Look at him. What's the use? Every time I think, Oh, maybe things could be better, but it's just one disillusionment after another. If I think it's gonna get brighter, sure enough—click—it's lights out and I wanna tell you it's dark as hell.

LCB: Let me see if I understand. The picture I have is that you get your hopes up, you imagine how good it could be and—click—something happens that makes those hopes disappear. Right?

Sue: Yeah.

LCB: Sue, I want you to watch closely and see if I can get Ron to see a little of your point of view, okay?

Sue: Okay.

LCB: Ron, what Sue would like you to be in touch with is how disappointed she gets sometimes. Have you ever built a sand castle on the shoreline as the tide came in, and even though you really worked hard to keep that castle standing, the tide would come in and knock it down. Until finally, you quit trying to build or rebuild the sand castle. It just seems like too much for you to handle alone. That's what Sue feels happens to her hopes. They get built up only to be knocked down. So now she pretty much doesn't hope.

Ron: I never meant to knock down her hopes.

LCB: I believe you. While you think a bit about that, I'm going to talk to Sue about what you want.

LCB: Sue, let me see if I can give you a picture of Ron's request. Have you ever been away from home, come home and found the house a mess? As you looked around and saw all the things that needed to be done, it seemed an overwhelming and very gloomy task and, worst of all, there was no help in sight. Well, I think that's how it sometimes looks to Ron.

Now, each of you are here to obtain help from me in order to relate to each other better. And I agree that you need that help. But what neither of you has been aware of is how much the other one needs you; how much Sue needs your help in building hopes and dreams that come true and how much Ron needs your help to clear the path so he can see what there is to hope and dream about. Each of you has perhaps thought that if the other won, you would lose. But not so. If either of you wins, you both win; but if either of you loses, you both lose.

In these two examples, I matched predicates and accessing cues in order to build trust and rapport, translated each client's position to the other in experiential terms, and used unspecified predicates to talk with both of them at the same time. These techniques, though simple, are very useful.

The next transcript is from a therapy session with a twenty-eight year old woman. As the session proceeds, the value of knowing the relevance of accessing cues and predicates becomes more and more evident. Using the meta-model, together with matching and mirroring, I gather pertinent information while moving in useful and appropriate directions with the client, JoAnn. I encourage you to study and use meta-model responses; I use them throughout this session. The meta-model is summarized in Appendix I.

JoAnn is an assistant fashion buyer for a small but prestigious women's clothing store. She is strikingly attractive and picture perfect: tall, slim, immaculately dressed and coifed. Sexual dysfunction was not the primary reason for JoAnn entering therapy, but became important to the change process.

LCB: JoAnn, tell me, what is it that you hope to change for yourself?

JoAnn: (*Eyes up, right*) Well, I just see myself being depressed too much of the time.

LCB: Depressed about what?

JoAnn: (*Eyes up, left; left hand gestures*) Mostly my husband.

LCB: What do you see concerning your husband that you find depressing?

JoAnn: Well, (*Eyes up, left*) I don't know. He's not even around anymore.

LCB: Oh. Does his being out of the picture depress you?

JoAnn: Yeah. (*Eyes up and left*) Hmmm, it's just that he left me and I'm alone now.

LCB: That's how you see it, huh? He left you?

JoAnn: Oh, yeah. There's no two ways about it. *He* left me. I didn't want to split up.

LCB: When did this happen?

JoAnn: (*Eyes up, left*) Two years ago.

LCB: How would you like your experience to be?

JoAnn: (*Eyes up, right: then down, left*) I don't know. Not depressed.

LCB: I'm wondering if you could tell me how you *want* your experience to be.

JoAnn: Well, (*Eyes up, left*) if I could just be happy again.

LCB: What do you see that could make you happy?

JoAnn: (*Frowns*) Hmmm (*Eyes up, left*) If things were like they were.

LCB: (*Smiling*) And just how were they then? (*I lead JoAnn's eyes back to up-left by shifting my eyes up-right.*)

JoAnn: Oh, no. I don't want that (*Eyes up, left; eyes up, right*). I'd be happy if I could see I was making progress.

LCB: What would you need to see happening to know you were making progress?

JoAnn: Mostly relationship stuff (*Eyes up, left*) . . . men.

LCB: What men, specifically?

JoAnn: Any man (*Eyes up, left; then up, right*).

LCB: ANY MAN?

JoAnn: Well, no. But I don't have anyone really special.

LCB: A woman as pretty as you are doesn't have men in her life?

JoAnn: There are men (*Eyes up, left; then down, right*), but none special. Actually, I don't like men much (*makes face*).

LCB: Oh, do you like women? (*analogue gesture, eyebrows lift, etc.: sexual connotation.*)

JoAnn: No! God, no!

LCB: Okay, okay. What do you mean you don't like men?

JoAnn: My husband used to accuse me of being lesbian.

LCB: Oh, I'm sure you have ideas about what prompted such an accusation. I mean, your response was certainly adamant enough. But first I need to know what specifically you would need to see happening to know you are making progress.

JoAnn: I'd need to know I could make it work with a man (*eyes up, right*).

LCB: What does it mean to make it work?

JoAnn: That's not very clear to me (*frown*).

LCB: Well, use your imagination and paint a scene that would depict your making it work with a man.

JoAnn: (*Eyes up, left; eyes up, right; back left, then right, hold.*)

LCB: Can you imagine it?

JoAnn: Um Hmmm.

LCB: (*Reaching out, touching the client to reinforce the experience and to associate this particular touch with the experience.*) Keep looking at that scene so it becomes clear to you just what you're setting your sights for.

JoAnn: It's kind of vague. I can't really see him clearly. Just me, but I know there's a man there. Mostly I know he loves me and he's pleased with me.

LCB: Okay (*removes hand*). JoAnn, come back here. Hello. Now, what stops you from getting what's in that picture? You are certainly attractive enough to have men approach you. True?

JoAnn: Well, yes. But I can't keep them . . . I don't know. I'm just so depressed (*Eyes down, right*).

Detecting and responding to representational systems, predicates, and accessing cues helped me establish rapport and gather pertinent information concerning how JoAnn was creating her experience. Later, as the session proceeded, JoAnn concluded that a central facet of her problem was her sexual dysfunction. She wanted a successful relationship with a man, and she realized that necessary to that success were sexual experiences that would be intimate and satisfying, which they had never been to her. While there was an abundance of opportunities for her to experience sexual encounters, she knew "some things" had to change before she could enjoy them. But at the time, she did not know which things could or should be changed.

A significant part of the structural puzzle that supported JoAnn's problem was her habitual use of a visual lead system and a visual representational system. Sexual functioning is primarily a kinesthetic experience, so to achieve the desired changes it was necessary to increase JoAnn's behavioral flexibility to include conscious internal and external kinesthetic experience.

Because consciousness is a limited phenomenon, problems often arise if it is focused on anything other than the kinesthetic portion of experience during sexual activity. Fortunately, most highly visual people are flexible enough to be able to switch to a kinesthetic representation. They may depend on sexually stimulating visual input to trigger kinesthetic responsivity, or they may use internally generated visual images to accomplish the same thing. It is important to stress that people whose favored lead system is visual feel as much as anyone else. They may not, however, be conscious of those feelings unless they purposely shift attention to that aspect of their experience. Where sex is concerned, most do. When they do not, dysfunction often occurs.

When a person habitually brings only one representational system into consciousness, often all their fear and misery is stored in another system. When that other system is kinesthetic, there are only bad feelings when it is brought into consciousness. Or, for the person who usually accesses kinesthetically and rarely uses the visual system, there are only terrifying pictures. They unconsciously avoid bringing that other system into consciousness as a way of protecting themselves. In such cases, a person's rigidity in using only one system is the very best choice they have.

A young male client of mine typified this set of circumstances. He had a decade-long history of migraine headaches. Like JoAnn, he accessed and represented visually despite the intrinsically kinesthetic nature of the questions I asked him. Except for the horrible headaches, he drew a blank where feelings were concerned. His entire head, neck and facial asymmetry were indicative of his habitual visual accessing (i.e., the right side of his face sloped down; left nostril shorter and higher; left side of mouth higher than the right; head forward and bent, chin up so that the back of his neck was constricted from habitually looking up; narrow chest and shoulders; breathing high in chest; eyebrows lifted, compressing his forehead; lines from squinting to focus internal pictures). I observed similar physical patterns with JoAnn.

At one point I used my hands to move his head down and to the right, and told him where to put his eyes in order to elicit a kinesthetic response. When I asked him, "What is there?" he replied, "Sadness," and tears welled up in his eyes. Merely changing his head position caused the sadness to "disappear" (his word), but upon each readjustment to the kinesthetic accessing position, the sadness and tears returned. He had not been conscious of feelings unless they were overwhelmingly bad or had reached a certain threshold of pain, as the headaches had. My intervention resulted in his comfortably being able to access kinesthetically. He then could receive and respond to subtle messages from his body about situations and activities that if not attended to could have been headache-producing. He learned how to generate responses that were beneficial rather than debilitating, as the headaches had been.

JoAnn also remained fixed in a visual lead and representational system, alternating between eidetic (eyes up and left) and constructed (eyes up and right) images, despite being asked questions such as:

LCB: And as you remember his words, how do you *feel*?

JoAnn: I just *see* myself as a failure.

LCB: When do you *feel* really sexy?

JoAnn: I know I'm sexy. I can *see* that men want me. I just don't enjoy it.

LCB: What do you remember most about sex with your husband?

JoAnn: The little *sparkly* things on the ceiling. I just waited for it to be over.

LCB: What kind of sexual preferences do you have?

JoAnn: The *lights out*; it has to be *dark*.

I employed the same techniques (overlapping—presented on Page 177, and changing history—presented on Page 141) with the young man and JoAnn, with equally effective results.

The important role different representational systems can play in generating conflict is evident in the following example. A couple came to me for therapy, because each believed that they were no longer loved by the other, and that their spouse was constantly expressing a lack of respect toward them. Such an environment greatly taxed any possibility for loving expressions. At the crux of this problem, as it so often is, was a difference in their individual internal processing. She represented her experience primarily in feelings. She felt everything as either concretely right or wrong. Her verbalizations were often extreme in that they were expressions of feelings rather than facts. She frequently used "always," "never," "every time." Upon investigation, I found that it wasn't that she really believed it was always, it just *felt* that way. He, on the other hand, required clarity of thought to make any decision, and a decision was a prerequisite to any action. Clarity of thought required the filling in of many details: the pros and cons of the consequences had to be looked at, etc. When all his facts were present and pointed to the same direction as her feelings there was no problem, but when they didn't the couple soon found themselves in harsh arguments. Her most significant complaint—what was most overwhelming to her—was that she felt she couldn't trust him to do something for no other reason than that she asked him. Their interactions went like this:

She: I don't feel good about it.

He: I don't see anything wrong with it. What is your objection?

She: I've thought about it and I just don't feel good about it.

He: I don't see how you could have looked at all the facts and come to that conclusion. I just really want to know what your specific objections are.

She: You just can't let it go, can you? You always have to have agreement.

He: Let's not get emotional, and it is not true that I have to get agreement. There have been times when we disagreed and I accepted it, like with having Jack over to stay last week.

She: Oh, now you want me to feel wrong.

Besides the patterns contained in these verbalizations, there were extreme differences in their tempo preferences. She placed a high value on speed, preferring things to move along as quickly as possible. She had the continuous experience of time running out and of being behind. He, on the other hand, preferred a slower, steady pace which felt secure and was also aligned with being thorough. To him, nothing should be done until it is decidedly the right thing to do—no action being better than any possible wrong action.

These mismatches were producing enormous and serious conflict in their relationship. The optimal outcome was for each to increase the range of their behaviors to include those that would pace and use the other's resources. The first step, as it is so often, was to demonstrate to them that each of their behaviors was a natural byproduct of how their personal experience was organized. The next steps were to reinforce how each of their behaviors was a tremendous resource for them, and to bring them to recognize that there was no insult or offense ever intended by the other. After that was accomplished, I assisted them in contextualizing and expanding each of their sets of behavioral choices to enable them to work and play better together. This established a context for them to learn from one another and feel valued, as well as value the other in new ways. Their relationship then became recognized and appreciated as a means of tremendous contribution to each of them as individuals.

When Lead and Primary Representational System Differ

Another important distinction is whether the lead system is inside or outside of the individual's conscious awareness. That is, whether a person can see the internally generated pictures, or feel the internally generated feelings, or hear the internally generated sounds and words that are generating an experience. Often times for people who come in for therapy, the lead system lies outside of consciousness. This was the case with the headache example discussed previously.

When the system that typically generates the experience (the lead system) is outside of consciousness, it is impossible for the individual to have choices concerning what kind of experiences will be generated: the internally generated experiences are out of control. This occurs more often when there is a difference between the lead system and the representational system than when they are the same.

As you listen to people's predicates and watch their accessing cues, you will notice that sometimes they do not match. That is, they access visually and talk about their feelings, or access kinesthetically and tell you how things look to them, or any other possible combination of systems. This tells you that their lead system is different than their primary representational system. Experientially, they access information through one system but bring into consciousness information of another modality.

For instance, a client referred to me after two suicide attempts expressed feelings of deep depression and hopelessness. Each time I asked him, "How do you know you are depressed?" or "What are you feeling hopeless about?" he would access up and left (eidetic visual) and say, "I don't know. I just feel it." In this case, his lead system was outside of his conscious awareness. He truly had no idea what was producing these feelings. By using overlapping (pg. 177), I was able to assist him in seeing his internally generated pictures. What he saw was one repetitively occurring image from his past. It was of his wife as he stood next to her hospital bed. She was dying of Hodgkin's Disease and, indeed, he had felt depressed and hopeless standing by watching her die. Not being aware of what had been generating his feelings he had been left with few choices for coping with them. Once his visual lead system was brought into his conscious awareness, the feelings were known to be a response to a past experience rather than to the present. We worked further using reframing (pg. 161) to develop his ability to access pictures which were more useful and productive to his experience.

Another client complained of feeling worthless, especially in regard to his wife. Each time he mentioned feeling worthless, he looked down and left. When asked what he was saying to himself, he said "Nothing, I just feel worthless." Somehow the feelings of worthlessness were being generated—they did not just arise spontaneously. There was nothing in external sensory experience to generate such feelings (his wife wasn't there). The accessing cue indicated there was internal dialogue outside of his conscious awareness that was generating such feelings. As the session proceeded, this proved to be true. By using the process of overlapping, this client was able to bring the offending voice and message into consciousness. (It was his mother's voice repeatedly harping about his being "good for nothing.") Once this was accomplished, the voice could be dealt with directly and separated from any association with his wife. The worthless feelings ceased and were replaced by more useful and satisfying ones.

Another case involved a man suffering from impotence. Each time he described the series of events that constituted his experience of impotency, he would look up and left and say, "I feel like I can't do it; I feel like I'm bound to fail." We discovered that he was accessing an eidetic image of his first experience of impotency, which occurred years earlier. When this picture was accessed, he responded with feelings congruent with that image. But only the feelings were in consciousness. He did not *see* the picture. Once his visual lead system was brought into his conscious awareness, he could generate eidetic pictures of times when he was, in his words, "very studly." He then had feelings about himself that were congruent with those pictures, which contributed greatly to his sexual experiences.

Problems related to jealousy typically involve a difference between lead and primary representational systems, with one of these systems occurring outside of consciousness. People often feel jealous without knowing the reason for such feelings. In such instances, accessing cues usually indicate a lead system that is outside conscious awareness.

For example, imagine a woman sitting home alone waiting for her husband to arrive. She generates internal images of her husband lingering over a conversation with another woman, or perhaps an image of him actually intimately involved with another woman. As these images occur, she responds to them with feelings of jealousy. This process is especially out of control if she is not conscious of her own internal imagery. If this is the case, then she knows only that she is experiencing extremely jealous feelings, without knowing their source. So she has no choice about the feelings because they come from outside of her conscious awareness. She can't choose to generate other, more useful images that would change her feelings. All too often this woman would respond to her husband as though the unseen images had actually occurred.

Each of these internal conflicts is an example of how internal processes can be used to impoverish rather than to enrich individual experience. These kinds of process interactions are surprisingly common. The underlying therapeutic goal in working with such internal conflicts is to make each and every internal process a resource. As a resource, each internal process contributes to the fullness of the overall experience either as a stimulus which leads the individual to the desired experience, or by adding another complementary sensory dimension to the experience.

In the case of sexual dysfunction, effective therapy is frequently a matter of teaching a client to use various externally generated and/or internally generated stimuli in all systems. The result is a move toward pleasurable kinesthetic representations, or being able to use any modality (internal or external) to generate desired feelings. So that:

Internal

visualizing sexy pictures	leads to	feeling sexual excitement
internal dialogue describing sexual feelings	leads to	feeling sexual feelings
remembering the feelings you had last time you felt highly sexually stimulated	leads to	feeling sexual stimulation

External

seeing that a partner is aroused	leads to	feeling aroused
hearing a partner's aroused breathing	leads to	feeling aroused
feeling the touch of a partner's body	leads to	feeling aroused

The techniques to accomplish this are presented in the sections on overlapping and anchoring (pgs. 177 & 131).

To summarize, besides using your senses to detect a person's primary representational system and most typical lead system, you can also discern which, if any, of their internal processes are outside of their conscious awareness. To identify when a lead system is outside of conscious awareness, observe accessing cues and listen to predicates, noting when and if there is an incongruity between the two. If there is, investigate further by asking directly or by employing some more covert means to ascertain if the lead system is, indeed, outside of consciousness. This information can indicate the best direction to proceed therapeutically, as well as establish a basis for judging therapeutic success.

Certainly, experiential goals are most easily produced when your client is facile at manipulating the internal processes inherent in producing desired experiences.

Internal Strategies

You can make even finer distinctions than a person's representational and lead system. These finer distinctions pertain to sequences of internal processes and their relationship to external behavior. Sequences of internal processes, as they relate to external behavior, is the domain of internal strategies.

Following are examples of sequences and interactions of internal processes. I'm sure you will find some of them familiar, such as the client who says:

"Well (*eyes up, right*), it looks like a great opportunity. I can really see myself getting ahead that way. But (*eyes down, right*) it just feels risky to my marriage." (*This illustrates a discrepancy between how her visual and kinesthetic systems understand "opportunity."*)

Or, (*Eyes down, left*) "It sounds logical enough, but (*eyes up, left*) I can't see it happening, and that (*eyes down, right*) makes me feel bad." (*He tells himself, but doesn't see an eidetic image of it, and feels bad about it.*)

Or, "Well (*eyes down, left*), I know I shouldn't be promiscuous, but when (*eyes up*) I see a great looking guy and I can see he wants me, (*eyes down, right*) I feel I can't say no." (*She uses her internal dialogue to tell herself she "shouldn't," but visual images determine feelings and, in her case, external behavior.*)

Or, "I (*eyes up, right*) think about all the things I should do to please him and turn him on, but (*eyes down, right*) I just can't bring myself to do them." (*In this case she thinks in constructed images, but her feelings are too incongruent with her pictures to act on.*)

In every case, the accessing cues offer a wealth of information that the words don't provide. Often, even though a person is flexible as to their lead and primary representational systems, and their internal processes are in their conscious awareness, the specific *interactions* of various systems produce conflict. For instance:

"I don't know why I'm jealous. It's just a feeling (*touches midline, eyes down and right*). (*Eyes down, left*) I tell myself there's no reason, but I just think (*eyes up and right*) of all the things she might be doing and I get jealous (*eyes down, right*)."

This example shows how systems often interrelate. He makes constructed images of what she might be doing and feels bad about the pictures even though his internal dialogue says there's no reason to. In this case, his feelings are generated from internal images, while his internal dialogue disagrees, perhaps needing some external information in order to agree with the visual and kinesthetic representations. Doing therapy with him (or any person with this type of internal strategy) would be similar to family therapy, as it is necessary to resolve differences between internal processes. They are all acting in his best interests, but they do not contain enough similar information to agree upon how those best interests will be served.

People generate their experience through simple or sometimes elaborate sequences of internal processes and external behavior. In NLP we refer to these sequences as strategies. For instance, a man might make pictures that generate feelings, then talk about the feelings to himself in words, then picture how someone would look if he knew what he was saying to himself, and so on. A past client of mine, a woman, would think of some new technique or sexual enticement she felt would be great to do with her mate. But as she thought about it (made pictures of doing it) she would say to herself that he might say suspiciously, "Where did you learn that?", and then she would feel hurt and see herself trying to explain without being defensive, and would tell herself that she had better not do the new behavior after all. She used this same strategy to inhibit any new behavior. She would imagine herself in a new dress, tell herself her husband would insult her in it, she would feel hurt and defensive and then tell herself she had better not buy it after all. It would have been difficult to persuade this woman to act out a new behavior without first changing this strategy.

Working with strategies involves understanding complex interactions of internal and external experience.[8] To give you a whisper, or glimmer, or taste, or tickle of what this means in therapeutic terms, I offer the following descriptions.

A newly-married couple came in because their love life was not as they hoped it would be. The central aspect of their difficulties was that she did not "feel" wanted or really feel loved. This was true in spite of his having married her and his many adamant verbalizations that he did indeed love her. During the session, an incident concerning the return and exchange of a wedding present was recounted. They agreed about returning the gift, but not on what to exchange it for. He offered arguments of value and aesthetics and equal rights, all to no avail. After arguing quite a while, suddenly she very happily gave in to him. This caught my interest so I pursued with her just what had occurred that convinced her to change her position so radically. In her words, "Well (*eyes down, left*), when I stopped listening to his arguments which I just couldn't accept, (*eyes up, left*) and just looked at him, I could see how much he really wanted it and I felt like it was important to him. And I just said (*eyes down, left*) to myself, 'Here is a chance to really make him happy,' and (*eyes down, right*) that made me feel good, so I gave in to him, and I could see that I really did make him happy."

Thus was revealed to me some pertinent information about how this woman generated her experience. In this context, the information concerned how she became convinced of something. The first step was when she "stopped listening." Verbally, both internally and externally, she was characteristically full of "yes-buts." So, when she stopped listening and, therefore, arguing, she *saw* him and interpreted the expression on his face to mean he really wanted it. This generated positive feelings, which generated internal dialogue saying she could make him happy, which generated more good feelings and then action. She knew she had done the right thing because she could see that he was, indeed, happy.

Utilizing her strategy, I asked him to make various facial expressions until she could identify which one meant that he loved her and which one meant that he desired her sexually. (They turned out to be the same one.) Although this seemed an awkward task, they quickly got into the spirit of it. Once the expression was identified, I sent him into the other room with a mirror to practice until he could make that facial expression at will. Meanwhile, I asked her to remember his expression when he looked at her that way, and then asked what her experience was. Of course, it followed the aforementioned pattern. She saw he wanted her and loved her and this made her feel very loved and important and desirable. She would say to herself, "I can give him what he wants," which generated feelings of arousal for her.

Bringing him back in, I gave them both instructions: Whenever she argued or stated she didn't feel loved and wanted by him, he was to stop talking and she was to stop listening. He was then to tell her, in the only way she could really understand (visually), that he did, indeed, love and want her, continuing to do so until she responded. Thus, I used her naturally occurring strategy to achieve a desired therapeutic goal for both of them.

Another couple came for help because of years of tumultuous ups and downs in their relationship. They were both highly visual but manifested the pairing principle[9] within their differing processing strategies. Their verbal labeling of his strategies for generating behavior in the world was "realistic," while hers was "idealistic."

When he became aware of any form of pain, which could be either emotional or physical, he would see, internally, what this pain kept him from doing. So, his experience went from feeling pain to an image from his past of himself happy, without pain, and then to internal dialogue suggesting ways of relieving the pain and attaining the feelings in his internal image. At this point, he would make eidetic images of any evidence he had that any of the verbal suggestions would work. If he could see proof that these suggestions would work, he would then act on them. If he couldn't find any proof in his past experience, he would decide that nothing could be done about the pain and he would just have to live with it.

This couple's biggest bone of contention concerned remarrying and again co-parenting their combined seven children. She wanted to remarry and he did not. When he considered marrying her, he would feel the pain losing her would bring and then make pictures of himself being happy with her. He would then verbalize suggestions for making this continued happiness come true. But, since the next step was eidetic images, that is, images from the past, and since all his past pictures only verified that they could not be happy living together with the children, he didn't act on any of the verbal suggestions and was resigned to staying separated from her. He complained a lot that she needed to see that being married wouldn't work out; it could only be like before, and she needed to accept that.

He used the same process to generate most of his behavior. For example, he had hated his job for years, but couldn't see how it could be different, despite suggestions from all around that he could be a consultant or do freelance work. It was only when he saw that a colleague had done just that, and was succeeding very nicely, that he believed he could do it, too. Once he verified that this possibility was, indeed, viable, he wasted no time in acting on it. All his behavior fit this pattern: future behavior being generated from past experience, which was stored in images.

Her strategy, on the other hand, began with internal dialogue which told her life could be better; then she generated *constructed* images of possible futures. For each picture, she would have a feeling response. The picture that generated the best feeling would be the one she would try to make into reality. Her internal dialogue generated suggestions as to how she could make the picture into reality and she would act on those suggestions. Her behavior was very direct and straightforward, but if she ran into too many obstacles in making her picture into reality and finally saw that she couldn't get to her desired picture, she would feel cheated out of getting what was possible. In the case of their remarrying, she generated pictures of them with their children being happy and loving, and worked towards realizing that. When he resisted, she felt he was cheating her of attaining this happiness. Her behavior was generated from her constructed images, which promised the best of all possible futures.

Their strategies led them into conflict, of course, although each was a useful strategy in some ways. His kept him from wasting time and energy chasing rainbows, and hers allowed her to frequently attain seemingly impossible goals. Their strategies, however, were also liabilities in some ways. At times, his was limiting and kept him from achieving desired goals because there wasn't a way for him to take any but the most calculated risks. Her strategy frequently led her to disappointment and disillusionment because her desired state was just too far out of reach, especially when she made images that also involved him, which required that he perform some new forms of behavior to make the image into a reality. Given his strategy, this was often impossible, particularly if the new behavior had no basis in past experience from which to be generated.

I chose to work with this couple with a conscious mind orientation. That is, I explicitly displayed to them their own and each other's strategies. Once they understood, I demonstrated to them how their conflicts were a result of their strategies and little else. Then I taught them how to use one another's strategies for more successful communication. He learned how to give her descriptions of more realistic pictures that were more easily attainable but which also generated very positive feelings for her. For instance, she would make pictures of what great fun they would have doing outdoor athletic activities together. This was fine except that he suffered from a very bad back. He would just say no, it was impossible, and she would continue to knock herself out trying to get him to enjoy athletic outings. When he didn't, she felt bad and resented him for being such a stick-in-the-mud. In her words, "If I had a bad back, I'd do anything to make it better. I'd try anything and everything. But not him. He'd rather keep his bad back." Of course, he only pursued remedies for which he had previously seen absolute proof. And since he did not search out evidence for all the suggested remedies, he really did very little about it. To work on this issue, I had him describe various scenes to her in which the two of them were very happy together in quiet, serene surroundings, engaged in activities better suited and more comfortable for his back condition. She then chose the one which *felt* best to her. In this way he learned to use her strategy to generate a desirable, yet more realistic and achievable outcome for the two of them. Meanwhile, I instructed her to offer no suggestions to him concerning possible alternatives or remedies *unless* she also provided substantial evidence of their value that he could verify by his past experiences.

In another context, she wished him to open communication channels with her daughter. His past experience led him to believe this would be foolhardy at best. I persuaded her to stop frustrating herself and, instead, use her energies to create an experience between him and the daughter in which *any* form of communication would be seen as productive to him. Once such an experience had occurred, it would become part of his personal history and evidence of future possibility. His behavior could then meet her desires. Soon, he and the daughter were both able to understand the processes of their relating and use them to bypass conflict, thereby enhancing their experience.

You can see how a rigid sequence of internal processes can influence a person's behavior. In each of these examples, I have discussed the use of the existing strategy. Another choice is to alter the existing strategy—this also would produce pervasive behavioral and experiential change. We are all subject to the experiences and behaviors our strategies lead us to. Since strategies are usually composed of rigid sequences of internal processes, the more facile we are at manipulating these internal representations, the greater our ability to generate our experience as a matter of choice. It is a means of furthering free will in contrast to having our lives happen to us.

Chapter 6: Detecting Congruity and Incongruity

As you know by now, there is much more for the receiver to perceive from a given communication than the communicator can know. The notion that there are large portions of our communicated behavior unavailable to ourselves, yet revealed to the world, can be disconcerting; especially in that no matter how carefully we might choose our words, the rest of our behavior speaks most eloquently to the knowledgeable receiver. From the point of view of therapy, this very phenomenon provides the keys to otherwise mysteriously locked doors.

Consider the following communication:

In a therapy session, when asked about his feelings toward his wife, Fred replies, "I love her. I love her a lot." His voice tempo is very fast, his volume is uncharacteristically loud, his lips are drawn tight, his body is held so rigidly that it almost vibrates, and his hands and arms are held still and tight. Fred's nonverbal messages are not carrying the most loving and tender of messages. While we can see and hear the absence of alignment in his communication, we do not yet know what it means.

Similarly, when Dorothy says, "I love making love to him," her voice intonation is a flat monotone, her mouth lines are drawn down, her shoulders shrug as she begins the statement, her body is otherwise still, and her hands lie limply in her lap. Again, we are faced with a mixed communication, with the verbal portion indicating something different than the nonverbal.

There are several theories concerning the significance of such communications, each asserting which portion should be valued or is more real than another. As behavioral communications, however, none should be denied or discounted. They are all real and are all to be valued. The relevant question is, what are all the various messages of a communication and what significance is there to each one with regard to the structure of the present and desired states?

To familiarize you further with this category of behavioral information, I would like you to recall as fully as possible the following experiences—a time when:

1. Someone you cared for gave you a present and you opened it in front of them only to discover the gift was something you disliked, found hideous, or already had at least one of and no use for. Remember what you said to them and how it felt.

2. You accepted an invitation from someone you didn't like.

3. You told someone you would do something you not only didn't want to do, but resented being put in the position of being asked to do it.

4. You told someone that you were completely sure of something that you were actually unsure of.

Contrast those experiences with memories of:

1. Telling someone about an activity you were absolutely and positively determined to carry out.

2. Complimenting a friend on some significant accomplishment he or she had achieved.

3. A situation in which you were operating at the height of your own competency and confidence.

4. Saying "I've missed you" to someone you dearly love after a seemingly long separation.

Although I am not with you as you access these experiences to see and hear with my senses the contrasts in your responses, I am sure there were subjective differences for you to detect. The first set contained the likelihood that you would have mixed feelings concerning your response—that there would be more than one subjective response to the situation. The second set was predisposed to a greater likelihood of an alignment of responses to the situations. For instance, in accepting a gift from someone you care about and the gift is somehow less than wonderful, you may want to express gratitude but feel disappointment, and you may be making pictures of having to display something you dislike or, worse, wear it. You may be asking yourself on the inside, "Whatever am I going to say?" Or in the example of telling someone that you are completely sure of something you are not sure of, you might really be wanting to believe it yourself as well as wanting them to believe it, but you feel panicky as you say it. You may be making pictures of yourself behaving very unconvincingly as the words leave your mouth.

These are situations in which you possibly would have been incongruent in your communications. That is, not all of your behavior and words gave the same message. Congruent communication, then, is when all messages, verbal and nonverbal, are aligned as to the meaning they offer. While it is critical that you be able to detect incongruent communication from clients and have effective ways to respond to them, I want to stress that there there is nothing inherently wrong with such communication. It is my hope that this is made clear to you by having you recall personal experiences in which you were apt to have had simultaneously-occurring, multiple responses. These simultaneously-occurring, multiple responses are typically manifested in some aspect of external behavior. Again, in order to detect incongruities in others' communications, you will need to have your input channels (perceptual systems) finely tuned.

For instance, Cheryl says, "I trust him, I'm sure he doesn't cheat on me." Yet her intonation goes up to a question mark at the end and she hesitates between the "I'm" and the "sure." Her palms are open and turned up, and her eyebrows are raised so high as to draw near her hairline. Her voice is a high-pitched whine. There is little in her nonverbal behavior to indicate a definiteness to her statement. She is unaware of the many nuances of her communication and their significance. If you are also unable to detect the multiple messages, and accept the verbal portion of the communication as real, a meaningful opportunity to discover the structure of the present state is lost. With Cheryl, the incongruent communication proved to be a manifestation of her genuine belief that her husband did not cheat on her, her sincere longing that he never do so, *and* her disbelief that he did not want to be with other women. The disbelief stemmed from her belief that she was ugly, worthless, and dull. Bringing her verbal and nonverbal behaviors into alignment required altering her self-concept until she could see herself as lovable and desirable. Then she could believe that, yes, it was possible that her husband wanted only her, and was satisfied with her, and did not want to cheat on her. This was accomplished primarily through the technique of *looking at yourself through the eyes of someone who loves you* (pg. 185). This intervention turned out to address the heart of all her presenting problems, and they subsequently disappeared (seemingly very magically to her). So the therapy process was brought to an efficient and effective end through (1) detecting an initally-stated incongruity, (2) discovering the source of the conflicting messages, and (3) intervening to effect an alignment in subjective experience with an ability to deliver the statement congruently.

There are several less than optimal ways to respond to incongruent communications. The first is not to detect them. In order to be sure when incongruent communication is occurring, you will need the skills you have been developing in mirroring. To further your skills, watch these items:

☐ The person's hands: How are they gesturing—with a finger pointing, palm up, clenched, relaxed, are both hands gesturing similarly?

☐ The person's breathing: Do they sigh, or hold their breath, or deepen their breathing?

☐ The person's legs and feet: Do they turn their toes in or jiggle the feet uncharacteristically (for them)?

☐ The head-neck-shoulder relationship: Is the chin jutted out or head tucked in toward the shoulder?

☐ The facial expression (especially eyebrows, mouth and cheek muscles): Do they scowl, frown, smile, pucker, clench the teeth, etc?

While you are watching for these be listening for:

☐ The tonality of the person's voice.

☐ The tempo of the person's speech.

☐ The words, phrases, and sentences used by the person.

☐ The volume of the person's voice.

☐ The intonation patterns (any hesitations, or does it go up at the end to sound like a question?).

Be sure to attend to these relative to what is characteristic to that individual's usual communication style. You want to differentiate between what is a congruent and incongruent communication style for them.

Besides not detecting incongruities, there are two other far less than optimal responses. One is to decide one portion is real and another not. The other is to decide you know what the messages mean without somehow graciously checking it out with your client.

There are several behavioral choices that will help you to

discover what the experience is that generates a mixed-message delivery. With the woman who trusted her husband and knew he didn't cheat on her, I merely leaned forward and said, "But . . ." and she tearfully replied, "But I don't know why he doesn't. Maybe it's only a matter of time until he'll just be fed up with me." This method is presented in *The Structure Of Magic II*:

This is the basis of the almost-an-incongruity experience. What has happened is that the slight rise in intonation at the end of this special class of sentences called Implied Causatives...signals the listener that the sentence is not complete—a portion of it is missing. Whenever you are acting as a therapist and have this particular experience, we suggest that you simply lean forward, look carefully at the client, and say the word but *and wait for the client to finish the sentence with the portion he had originally omitted. Thus,*

Client: *I really want to change the way that I act in public.*
Therapist: *. . . but . . .*
Client: *. . . but I'm afraid that people won't pay attention to me.* [10]

Another choice is to ask, "Is there a part of you which disagrees or objects to what you just said? Go inside and say that again and feel, listen, and look for any sense of a part that may not agree completely." (If you use this method, you can continue by using reframing, pg. 161.) For instance, in response to a question, Sue (a client) said, "Yes, I will do it," (with hesitation, plaintive tone, a sigh and a corresponding head drop). I replied, "Sue, is there a part of you which objects to your doing it? Go inside and attend to any sounds, feelings, or images that might indicate to you that some part of you objects." Sue closed her eyes, her breathing became more shallow, then she raised her head, opened her eyes, and stated that it was just that she imagined her husband being upset with her, and she felt afraid when he looked at her like that. (She was referring to her internally generated image of her husband looking at her.)

It became important to give Sue choices concerning how to respond to her husband when he was upset, choices of responses that would be satisfying to both of them. (She stated congruently that it would be impossible to behave in the world such that he was never upset with her.)

If there is a specific eye accessing cue associated with the incongruity, ask directly for the information from that system:

□ "What were you seeing as you said that?"

□ "What were you feeling as you said that?"

□ "Did you say something to yourself as you said that?"

In this way you can assist your client in bringing to consciousness possibly conflicting representations of his or her experience.

Jim: Sure, I want to do that. (*While shaking his head no and scrunching his face up around the nose and mouth, and accessing up and to the right.*)

LCB: What do you see as you say that, Jim? (*Directing his attention back up and to his right.*)

Jim: (*Eyes up right, same facial expression*) I just don't see myself doing it well. In fact, I see myself doing it terribly.

Jim's response is evidence that congruity is dependent upon Jim's seeing himself doing "it" well. It tells me to direct him to improve his imagined performance until it meets his desires. As it turned out, this step of correcting his images of his personal performance until he could see how to be successful was necessary to carry him to action. That is, he might want to do something, but he wouldn't do it until he could see himself doing it successfully.

Another behavioral choice in responding to incongruent communication concerns the use of *modal operators*. Modal operators are those words which express a person's concept of possibility or impossibility: can, can't, must, have to, want to, could, etc. The meta-model, presented in Appendix I and in *The Structure of Magic*, [11] includes ways of detecting and responding to modal operators.

Another choice is to direct the client's experience back to him or herself by mirroring, and even exaggerating, their communication. Remember the man who said, "I love her, I love her a lot," with a fast tempo, loud voice, rigid body, etc.:

LCB: (*Mirrors and exaggerates*) Yeah, I can tell you're just overwhelmed with warm, soft, tender, loving feelings towards her.

Man: (*Stops, sighs, lowers head, then softly speaks*) Well, I do love her. I just get so damned frustrated trying to get her to believe it.

LCB: Have you ever asked her to tell you the things you do that let her know, beyond the shadow of a doubt, that you love her?

Not surprisingly, he had not; he had no sure ways to let her know he loved her. This method's effectiveness depends a good deal upon the level of rapport you achieve. If your client feels understood and trusts your intentions, such a maneuver is friendly rather than offensive.

When working with a couple, you can ask one partner what

the other's communication meant to them, or what they just heard and saw in the other's communication. This maneuver leads attention away from the internal experience of the person who gave the incongruent communication, and toward the other person's response and perceived meaning. If the perceived meaning is less than desirable, you can turn back and ask what had been intended, then lead them to an expression of their intended communication that will elicit the desired response in their partner. This choice gives the perceived meaning priority over the possible internal experience that generated the incongruity. Any of the other choices previously presented can also be used in the couple context. The one you use depends on your outcome. The former choices get you more information, and direct you to interventions that will bring the *individual* to an alignment in their subjective experience. The latter focuses upon the couple *interaction* and gives you information about how miscommunication and misunderstandings are generated.

These are just a few choices of how to respond to incongruent communications in the therapy context.[12] Another choice, and sometimes the most appropriate, is to detect the incongruity and remember it but not respond to it. Instead, continue with the session and interventions and when you believe you have accomplished the desired change, elicit the statement that was previously incongruent. If it is now congruent, you have a further demonstration that the change has been achieved. If it remains incongruent you will want to investigate further, since the basis for the incongruent communication could greatly interfere with the change being fully integrated into your client's experience.

Be sure to recognize incongruity as significant behavioral information. It can point the way to what needs to be changed for a person to have their desired state. Of course, incongruent communications do not occur only in the therapy context. Your ability to detect them in consciousness will protect you from being plagued with vague feelings of confusion and uneasiness (the most typical out-of-conscious-awareness response to incongruent communications) in your personal life. I strongly urge you to identify for yourself your own incongruent communications and to use the above choices to uncover what is going on and what needs to be different. In doing so, your experience will improve and so will your ability to communicate effectively to others. The degree to which you are effective as a communicator, and successful as a therapist, rests heavily on your congruity.

Chapter 7: Establishing a Well-Formed Outcome

The behavioral information you have learned to detect assures that you are responding to sensory information rather than to your own interpretations, and protects the client from being cured of your problems. However, when you attend to such behavioral information, there is an overwhelming quantity of it presented with each interaction. For it to be useful to you and to the therapy process, it is necessary to establish a specific outcome to work toward. This reduces the complexity by providing a guideline for determining the relevancy of the verbal and non-verbal information you are perceiving. Establishing a specific outcome is the prerequisite for being able to answer the recurring question, "Is this pertinent to what we are working to achieve?" It keeps you from having to respond to every incongruity, accessing cue, meta-model violation, etc., and focuses your efforts in a purposeful way toward the agreed-upon goal. Having an outcome clearly stated also provides both you and your client with a means with which to evaluate progress.

A well-formed outcome is one that is worth attaining. Unfortunately, not all of the outcomes achieved in psychotherapy are worthwhile. Many people in therapy become overly acquainted with their limitations rather than their resources. Others become firmly entrenched in their problematic behaviors after spending much time and money discovering why they have them. Many learn to despise their childhood experiences as the root of all present difficulties, and have unpleasant confrontations with family members as demonstrations of therapeutic success. None of these represents achievement of a well-formed outcome.

There are five conditions that must be met for an outcome to be well-formed. First, the outcome must be stated in positives. Find out what your client *does want*, not what is unwanted. If you were helping someone arrange furniture and they said to you, "I don't want that chair there," you would not have the information to know what to do with the chair or what to put in its place. Like the person who doesn't like the position of the chair, most people who seek therapy know what they don't want: They no longer want to experience their perceived problem, difficulty, or limitation. For those who have not yet fully considered what it is that they *want* to experience instead, there is no basis for generating steps that would lead to a fulfilling goal, since there is no goal set to move toward. Whole portions of therapy have been accomplished simply by asking, "What do you want?" One example of this was accomplished by John Grinder when working with a woman who wanted to stop drinking. After listening to her genuinely expressed pleas for assistance in stopping drinking— about how many people she had already talked to, and how many times she had failed to stop drinking in the past—John leaned forward, took her hands and, having gotten her absolute and full attention, asked, "What will you do instead of drink?" She had never turned her thoughts or actions in this direction and the response was dramatic and effective. Changes were achieved smoothly and quickly from this point. While this is not the usual response (if it were, this book would be a short pamphlet), it does demonstrate the usefulness of stating the outcome in positives.

If a client says, "I want to get rid of depression," or "anxiety," or "blocks to my creativity," and you accept this outcome, then all the attention, focus, and energy is directed toward the *problem*, often reinforcing it and making it more than it was to begin with. This is especially true if time is spent on delving into why the client has this problem. "Why" questions will not elicit the structural information necessary to intervene and effect change. They *can* cause a person to build a belief that the problem is as much an immutable part of them as their arm or leg, and that it should (or has to) be there because of some perceived cause. (Any experience perceived by you or your client can be useful to the overall process when experienced as a choice point. The question then is how to alter the cause so that it can become the basis, or cause, of the desired state. This is the principle of changing history, pg. 141.) When a client is brought to an outcome stated in positives—"I want to feel secure" or "I want to feel competent" or "I want to be able to express my ideas in ways that can be understood"—there is a focus on a positive outcome. All resources, effort and time can now be directed toward accomplishing the new positive goal, making it much more achievable.

Positive outcomes are not automatically accomplished by eradicating an unwanted experience. In fact, if nothing is installed to take its place, the previous unwanted experience is likely to return. I believe it would be an evolutionary step if all of our processes were directed toward what we *do* want, rather than having our thoughts and efforts entangled in a quagmire of complaints. This is not to suggest that the presenting problem be ignored, but a good therapist will effectively orient both their own and their client's resources to establishing and reaching a positive outcome.

A second criterion for a well-formed outcome is that it be demonstrable in sensory experience to both you and your client. Insights can be enlightening and useful but they do not constitute an experiential change. It is not well-formed for either you or your client to think a change has taken place but have no sensory evidence to verify it. The demonstration of change may be expressed in a great variety of ways: by accessing a traumatic memory and being able to feel secure and have a new perspective on it, or confronting a loved one in a direct and congruent fashion over a deeply felt insult, or taking the initiative in creating a romantic interlude, or being able to feel loved and secure even when turned down on an important request.

Any of these could be a demonstration that the wanted and asked-for change has been achieved. It is essential to establish the kinds of behavior and/or experiences that will constitute success; they provide important feedback for both you and your client.

The third well-formedness condition is that the outcome be appropriately contextualized and specified. If your client asks for assertiveness and you agree, based on adequate behavioral demonstrations, that this would be a very useful addition to your client's experiential and behavioral repertoire, it is your absolute responsibility to establish with your client the contexts where assertiveness is useful and where it is not. Not to do so invites tragedy upon the client. A dramatic example of the results of not contextualizing change was brought to my attention when a woman in her thirties came to me for help in making changes that would assist her in establishing a lasting romantic relationship. At the time she came to me, she was a "swinger" who frequently participated in orgies and played roles in pornographic films, as well as participating in frequent, casual sexual liaisons with hitchhikers, store clerks, taxi drivers, etc. I do not mean to imply that these behaviors kept her from having a lasting romantic relationship, but they did not help. As we proceeded, I learned these were all fairly recently acquired behaviors. She had sought therapy previously for, in her words, "extreme sexual inhibitions." The therapy had been wildly successful, but never in the course of it had any criteria been established concerning the appropriate contexts (with whom, where, how) for being sexually uninhibited. In the course of our work together, and as part of the overall achievement of the desired state, we altered "sexually uninhibited" to "sexually expressive" *only* in the context of desirable relationships. By appropriately contextualizing the requested change, you assist in maintaining your client's well-being in the many situations of their life. Appropriate contextualization addresses the ecology of your clients' personal and professional lives, as well as the possible impacts that change can have upon the family system, friendships, etc.

The fourth condition which must be met for an outcome to be well-formed is that the outcome be one that can be initiated and maintained by the client. The therapist's job is to assist the client in having choice over his or her own experience so that well-being can be maintained through time without the need for the therapist's (or anyone else's) continued assistance. For instance, it is not a well-formed outcome for a woman to be able to feel really desirable and sensual only when her partner does something that elicits that state from her. Likewise it is not well-formed for a man's feelings of self-worth to be dependent upon his job or amount of salary. For well-being, self-worth, confidence, or sexuality to be dependent upon some *external* factor keeps an individual at the mercy of the environment, rather than operating from self-generated choice. Clients often ask for a change in someone else's behavior—"If only he would stop shouting," or "come home on time," or "be responsible," or "be considerate," "then I would have what I want." While this is genuinely the individual's experience, to assist them in achieving that outcome is to further entrap them in troubling cause-effect patterns with the people around them. It further reinforces the belief that their experience is dependent on the behavior of others. In fact, when the desired state is expressed in these terms, it is a sure indication that they would benefit from changing their existing cause-effect patterns.

For an experience or behavior to be initiated and maintained by the client means that he or she has the means to achieve the experience or behavior on their own. With couples, the system is treated as an individual. That is, the system must be able to achieve the desired state on its own, by choice, consistently. So it is well-formed for someone to be able to experience confidence when they want or need to by going through a sequence of defined internal processes, as opposed to needing verification from someone else in order to feel confident. It is well-formed for a couple to experience security concerning their relationship based on their consistent ability to elicit and give the appropriate reassurances to one another. (Please note this refers to security concerning their relationship and not to their individual sense of security.) It is well-formed for people to experience themselves as attractive by fulfilling their own highly valued criteria as opposed to needing to receive come-ons from others.

The fifth well-formedness condition concerns preserving the positive by-products, if any, which are somehow inherent in the present state. An example I offer to trainees learning hypnotic techniques concerns a woman who approached a colleague of mine for help to stop smoking. This was quickly achieved with hypnosis and she was very satisfied with the results. A few weeks later, however, she called and asked for therapy for herself and her husband. They were not getting along and their problems seemed to have started recently. It took a while to discover how the difficulty had begun, but as it turned out it had everything to do with smoking. For all seventeen years of their marriage, whenever one of them sat down at the kitchen table for a cigarette the other would sit down and join in conversation. These were the times they talked to one another, the kind of purposeless but essential talking that keeps two people connected and together through time. Now that she wasn't smoking, these important and frequent talks were absent from their relationship. Once this was pointed out to them, they recognized what was missing and reinstituted their talks without her needing to smoke. These talks were the positive by-product of her smoking that needed to be preserved for her outcome regarding smoking to be well-formed.

While working with a woman, Paula, to assist her in achieving and maintaining an appropriate weight, I needed to assist her in establishing useful eating behaviors in many different contexts. A difficult context for her was when she joined friends at a restaurant. Even if she had just eaten, she found she was compelled to eat again with them. Upon investigation, Paula and I learned that unless she was fully engaged in the same activity as the people she was with she felt left out and disconnected; and it was very important to her to feel connected to the people she was with. The well-formed outcome that was achieved included her being able to experience being connected to the people she was with by means other than participating in the same activity. Thus, she could be with people who were eating, or drinking, or dancing, or playing a game, and carry out personal behaviors (like telling them stories, asking questions about their interests, etc.) which were in her own best interests while still feeling connected. In this way, her sociability and personability were preserved while appropriate (for her) eating behaviors were established and maintained across contexts.

Another common example of positive by-products became obvious with Ann and John. Ann had always been nonorgasmic. This symptom elicited much attention and concern from John and their relationship revolved around what to do, what to try, what were the reasons, etc. He was very solicitous toward Ann and always a patient and considerate lover. Any well-formed outcome for Ann would need to preserve the quantity and quality of attention John was presently giving to Ann, and that they were both giving to their relationship. (Like so many people, they attended to problems and tended to ignore assets.)

These five well-formedness conditions for outcomes—(1) stated in positives, (2) demonstrable in sensory experience, (3) appropriately specified and contextualized, (4) initiated and maintained by the client, (5) preserves any existing positive by-product—are fundamental, both logically and ethically.

While the gathering of adequate information to establish a well-formed outcome needs to be thorough, there are several questions that go far in eliciting the required pieces. The question, "What do you want?" addresses getting it stated in positives (as opposed to, "What is wrong?" or "How long have you had this problem?"). "How would you know if you had what you wanted?" and "What would be a demonstration of your having what you want?" request a sensory demonstration of the desired state. The first is usually answered with an internal state response, "I'd feel great," for instance; whereas the second question is usually answered with an example in behavioral terms: "I'd look him in the eye and tell him, 'No, I don't know what you're talking about' and I would not give up until I did know what he was talking about."

Questions like, "When do you want it and when do you not want it?" contextualize the desired state. Be aware—this step typically takes some further assistance from you. It is wise for you consider several contexts, personal and professional, and ask your client how the desired state will fit in (or not) in those situations. The questions, "What would happen if you got it?" "What will you lose if you get what you want?" and "What stops you from having what you want?" satisfy several purposes. Besides identifying any possible positive by-products, they also will help elicit any existing cause-effect patterns that need to be dealt with. For example, if a woman thinks that becoming more consistently orgasmic will solve all her marital woes (a dubious cause-effect), it will be important for you to deal with that as well. These questions help point to what needs to be changed in order to achieve the desired state. If what your client is asking for does not meet the initiated-and-maintained-by-self condition, then further direction is required. For instance:

Joan: I want his ex-wife and children to disappear.

LCB: Since this is unlikely, what is it you want for yourself by their disappearing?

Joan: I don't want my husband to respond to them.

LCB: What is it that you would have if your husband did not respond to them?

Joan: I'd have him to myself. I'd know I was the most important. Number one.

LCB: Oh, so you want to have the experience of being most important to him, of being number one, even though he has an ex-wife and children.

Joan: Yes, that's what I said, isn't it?

LCB: I just want to get it straight. You want to really know that you are number one with your husband. That you are very, very important to him, and that what goes on between him and his ex-wife and children in no way undermines or threatens your marriage. Is that it?

Joan: I want them out of the picture.

LCB: So you want to see that you and he are most important to each other in all the world.

Joan: Yes.

In this way, the outcome was brought down to the confines of the couple system. From there it was further reduced to her wanting a full sense of self-worth that was independent of her husband's responses. Enlarged to the couple outcome, it involved establishing behaviors that each could do to give the other the experience of being "number one."

The following therapy transcript demonstrates the use of the kinds of questions described above in establishing a well-formed outcome. The client, Paul, is an upwardly mobile engineer working in the computer industry. He is unmarried, living alone in an apartment near his work. He holds his body very upright, sometimes with enough tension to vibrate. His tempo patterns are very rapid, and he accesses visually, both constructed and remembered, almost exclusively. Occasionally, he drops to an auditory accessing cue, but then returns to the visual cues.

Paul: I've been to therapy before, you know.

LCB: Yes, I do know that you have been pursuing personal enrichments. It can be an important commitment to yourself.

Paul: Well, I know I need it. I have done some strange things. I bought a gun because I was thinking about suicide. My parents were so upset, though, I returned it.

LCB: Are you thinking of suicide now?

Paul: No.

LCB: Great. Now that you are considering living, let's be sure to make it worthwhile. Let's take a look at what it is that you are wanting that's really going to make your life worth living.

Paul: Well, there's a lot that I should have.

LCB: What, of all that you can see that you should have, do you also want?

Paul: (*long pause*) Well, I should stop smoking, and I should exercise more, and I should finish decorating my apartment . . .

LCB: Yes, those are all there waiting for you, but what is it that you really *want* that perhaps you also should have that makes a difference concerning how wonderful your life is? As you take a good long look at your life now, what do you see that's missing? What do you see that's missing that if you were to add it to the picture would brighten up everything else? Take your time. It's worth taking the time. You are worth taking time for. (*Slowing tempo from pacing his to a more leisurely one that is appropriate to full accessing of internal pictures.*)

Paul: I just need to relax.

LCB: When is it that you want to relax?

Paul: All the time.

LCB: What is it that you will have that you don't have now if you are relaxed?

Paul: Well, important things. I could just see myself being happy and fulfilled.

LCB: Help me to get a clear idea of what you want. Describe to me what you see when you imagine being happy and fulfilled.

Paul: I see myself well-off, married, living in a nice house with a pretty and intelligent wife.

LCB: What do you see the two of you doing that completes the scene?

Paul: Well, we're just together. It's like in the morning and we're just waking up and enjoying each other, you know?

LCB: All that looks real good to you, eh?

Paul: Yes, yes, it does.

LCB: So, that is where you are headed. What is it you want now to help you get there?

Paul: To relax.

LCB: How will your relaxing help you get all that?

Paul: Until I relax I'm never going to have even a woman friend, much less a lover. No one else knows I don't have girlfriends.

LCB: So, if you can be relaxed and comfortable around women, especially women, you see such an intimate relationship as you have pictured as attainable. Is that right?

Paul: Yes, yes, if I can relax. They could get to know me.

LCB: And you could get to know them. Is there anything else you would want to add, besides relaxation, when you are around women?

Paul: Like what?

LCB: Well, confidence or curiosity, or perhaps some charm?

Paul: No, I don't want to have to be charming.

LCB: What about confidence or curiosity?

Paul: Sure, that would be great.

LCB: OK, with just relaxed I kept getting a picture of you so laid back there wasn't much going on that was leading to you showing anyone who you are. You know, letting them see you.

Paul: Yeah, I'd like confidence with my relaxation.

LCB: So, tell me how you would know that you were relaxed and confident. Oh, is it most important to have this around women?

Paul: Yes, I already have it in my work and I keep busy when I am alone.

LCB: Well, is there some situation where you definitely don't want to be relaxed and confident?

Paul: I can't think of any.

LCB: So, you can't see any situations where being relaxed and confident would get in your way?

Paul: Unless somebody was attacking me, physically I mean.

LCB: OK, so then it would be inappropriate. How about, umm, if you were undertaking some new skill that you knew nothing about, like flying or sailing, something like that?

Paul: Well, if I don't know anything about how to do it, I'm not going to feel confident, but I'd still like to feel relaxed.

LCB: Fine, let's get back to being with women. So being with a woman is where you want it the most, or rather, if you had confidence and relaxation in that context, you would be reasonably sure of having it in other situations.

Paul: Oh yeah, if I could have it around women I'd be sure I could be like that in other situations.

LCB: Great, so now, how would you know if you were re-laxed and confident around a woman?

Paul: Are you kidding? I'd feel it.

LCB: So you know how it would feel to be relaxed and confident. These are feelings you are familiar enough with to recognize.

Paul: I'd know them if I had them.

LCB: Think of a situation, a memory of when you have been relaxed or confident or both, and see what you were seeing in that memory, feel how those feelings feel, get reacquainted with them.

Paul: I have been confident. I'm confident in my work, but relaxed is a lot more vague.

LCB: Remember a time you have been lying in the sun, per-haps floating on an air mattress, or reading in a chaise lounge. Just relaxing, perhaps, with your eyelids closed, staring at the backs of your eyelids, feeling the warmth of the sun browning your body.

Paul: (*after accessing this experience*) How did you know I sunbathed?

LCB: Now, are you kidding me? I can tell a great tan when I see one. So, are you reacquainted with how it feels to be confident and relaxed?

Paul: Yeah, but not both at the same time.

LCB: We'll get to that. So, feeling those feelings while you are with a woman in a social situation would let you know that you were confident and relaxed in the ways that you want to be?

Paul: Yes.

LCB: I know that those feelings would let you know that you have what you want, but what would be a demonstration of your having what you want? What would you be doing that if I were there I could know that yes, absolutely, you were feeling the relaxation and confidence that you want to experience?

Paul: Well . . . I'd look confident and relaxed.

LCB: Yes, but what would you be doing that you are not doing now?

Paul: I'd be talking, making jokes, laughing, I could touch her, I wouldn't want to run away. It would be OK if she touched me.

LCB: So you would be talking to her, listening to her, close enough to touch, sometimes touching appropriately, and maybe she would be touching you. You both might be laughing, you would be sitting back comfortable in the chair, that kind of thing. That's the kind of thing I'd see?

Paul: Yeah, if I could do that.

LCB: Yeah, if you could do that. What would happen if you could do that?

Paul: Well, I don't want to be alone my whole life.

LCB: So, what would happen?

Paul: Well, at the very least I could date, but I really want a relationship, a lover, someone to be with.

LCB: I know this seems unlikely, but can you see any possible negative consequences to having this? Is there anything you might lose?

Paul: I'd miss a lot of TV programs. (*laughing*)

LCB: OK, I can see we are going to work our way up to flirting. Well, Paul, we have something to go after that looks like it will make a difference in your life. Even though when you first have it you will be surprised and wonder if it will be there the next time. And you'll be relaxed and confident several times before you'll get used to it, before you see yourself as a relaxed and confident person.

Paul: Well . . . maybe, I'll let you know if I get it.

LCB: When you get it. Now let's find out what's getting in the way of you realizing all that hidden potential. What is stopping you from being relaxed and confident with women now?

Paul: Are you kidding? I just go blank, I'm terrified, I freeze.

LCB: Well, that will stop you, I agree. Let's change that first. I want you to get as comfortable as possible in the chair and see yourself in one of those past memories where you froze up . . .

At this point, the outcome has been established and all the well-formed conditions met, except for the desired state to be initiated and maintained by self. This condition was met in the intervention phase of the interaction by making sure, through the use of anchoring (pg. 131), that Paul had a means to bring himself to experience confidence and relaxation when he wanted or needed to. An important shift in Paul's verbal patterns occurred while I gathered information: his shift from "shoulds" to "wants." This corresponded with a decrease in his over all body rigidity and tension, allowing him to relax more easily and naturally. I left Paul waiting in the reception area for fifteen minutes at the end of the session while I ostensibly searched for my calendar to schedule a follow-up session. This left him at the mercy of the women who run the office as well as a woman who was waiting to see my partner. Within a few minutes he was talking, making jokes, and participating fully in a conversation with all four women. This was a sensory experience demonstration that, indeed, change had taken place.

Chapter 8: Learning How a Problem Occurs

In the preceding chapters I presented information about how to detect a client's representational systems and accessing cues, and how to use them to establish rapport and gather information about their present problem state. You also have information on what constitutes a well-formed outcome, as well as how to establish one. What you still need to know is what holds the present state in place. Where in their experience do you intervene with a client to take them to the desired state? Out of all the possibilities, what, specifically, do you change to actualize that well-formed outcome? To answer that question I would now like to turn your skills toward learning the systemic nature of your client's relationship difficulties or sexual dysfunction.

As previously stated, human experience is made up of interactions between external stimuli and internal processes. In order to understand the process of dysfunction that an individual or couple is suffering, it is necessary to identify the various experiential elements which constitute the dysfunctional context. Indeed, the field of family therapy originated as a result of this necessity. Psychotherapists noticed that schizophrenics who had been cured often resumed their symptomatic behavior when placed back in their families. Further investigation proved that certain behaviors on the part of family members triggered the patient back into schizophrenia.[13] Even in less severely disturbed cases, it has almost always been found that any such symptomatic behavior makes sense when considered within the family context.

If you have worked with runaway teenagers, I'm sure your experience verifies this concept. Often times parents find their teenagers' behavior incomprehensible, while to the therapist viewing the family from a different perspective, the motivations for rebellious behavior are obvious.

I remember a case from years back which illustrates this point. A young girl, fifteen, had been absent from her high school for over two weeks. She was attending a special alternative high school for youths who had been in trouble at their previous high school and with the law. It was a very progressive school; it had three staff members and an enrollment of only forty students. This girl had always loved this school and was at the time living in the best foster placement available, so her behavior was peculiar. I had clients who attended this school and the staff asked me to look into this situation. It was a serious one, for if the staff reported her truancy she would be placed with the California Youth Authority again. I found the girl hiding out at a friend's place. At first she was completely silent and answered my questions with shrugs. With the help of her friend, I was able to slowly draw the needed answers from her. It turned out that her behavior stemmed from shyness rather than rebellion. Each morning and afternoon, a group meeting of students and staff took place at school. Its purpose was to air grievances, express appreciation and generally to reinforce positive social behaviors. This particular girl rarely, if ever, spoke during these meetings. As a result, a staff member had taken her aside and told her she would not be able to stay in the school if she did not contribute to the group by speaking and sharing of herself. This was done with the best of intentions, but it backfired completely. Rather than overcome her shyness (which she often disguised with sullen shrugs), she stopped going to school. She had rationalized that they would soon expel her anyway.

This example shows how the girl's behavior makes sense when the larger social context is understood. Usually the behaviors triggering unwanted experiences in a couple or a family are far more subtle. Perhaps you have had the experience of working with a couple when suddenly they are deep into an argument while it is incomprehensible to you what it is about and how it began. It may have been that only with a careful dissection of their respective behaviors did you learn how each time he sighed in a certain way she immediately became terribly angry.

I remember seeing a couple whose problems stemmed from just such a subtle but persistent aspect of the husband's behavior. There was very little successful communication between the two of them and they had not had sexual relations for about seven years. As I worked with them it became apparent that she was highly visual, whereas he primarily represented his experience kinesthetically. Although this produced some of their communication problems, the crux of their difficulties was occurring at a more subtle level of behavior. Each time she moved her head and eyes up and to the left in order to access visually, he would look down and right accessing kinesthetically. As he did this, he had the habit of sucking on his lips, producing a clicking sound similar to the sound a slide projector makes as it changes slides. Interestingly, it is just such a sound that consistently changes a person's internally generated pictures. If you make an image and then make a clicking noise with tongue against the back of the top teeth, typically the image disappears. This is what happened to his wife as she accessed visually and her husband sucked his lips. Each time it occurred, she became understandably frustrated and furious. For her, it was impossible to think around him. It is important to note that neither of them understood the significance of his clicking noise or the role it played in this process. Thus, each time he clicked, her thinking process was interrupted, to which she responded with anger. He then became perplexed and felt genuinely abused by her behavior towards him. This is an example of how an external stimulus (his clicking) triggered an interaction that exemplified their dysfunctional system. This particular sequence of external and internal processes occurred each time she accessed visually for more than a second or two; and, being highly visual, she did so frequently. I learned that they had remained together over the years due to communications that had occurred either by letter or telephone conversation. This made sense since both of these communication mediums made it impossible to trigger the problematic behavior.

In this case, knowledge of accessing cues and internal processes proved invaluable in determining what triggered this couple's problematic behavior. It is possible to think of such a trigger as the stimulus, or cause, and the resultant behavior as the response, or effect. Because of its importance, I would like to undertake a discussion of just how stimulus-response or cause-effect behaviors relate to an understanding of clients' sexual dysfunction.

Stimulus-Response

Phobias are very specific examples of how some external stimulus triggers internal processes that result in an undesirable experience. For example, a person may look down from a height, feel herself falling, and be overcome with terror. It's not just the looking down which frightens her, but also the feeling of falling that looking down triggers. A woman came to me because of a phobic response to having sexual intercourse in the classic missionary position (which happened to be the position preferred by her husband). Whenever he lay on top of her, she went into a panicky rage, screaming and kicking. No amount of conscious desire on her part could alter this sequence of events. The possible causes of this response were outside of conscious awareness for her, as were any internal processes that occurred in the problem context. There was only the weight on her chest and abdomen and the next thing she knew she had thrown her husband off and was panting and sweating from fear and exertion. By taking her back in time, we learned that her older siblings had once wrestled her to the floor, sat upon her, and then put a pillow over her face to stifle her screams. This became a life or death struggle to her. Long forgotten, it was only in the sexual context that she experienced a similar heavy weight on her body. When this occurred, it triggered unconscious processes that associated such weight with the previous life or death struggle.

Phobias are not only triggered by external experience, but can be set off by internally generated images, sounds, or feelings as well. For the person phobic of snakes, thinking about touching a snake will produce much the same response as contact with an actual snake. People can produce within themselves, with very little corroboration from external experience, emotional states that they may or may not want. It is important to know how they elicit such a response from themselves. Similarly, knowing how the behavior of one member of a couple elicits certain responses from his or her partner is important to understanding how their experiences as a couple are produced.

The meta-model (Appendix I) contains a linguistic method for gathering information about a client's *verbally* expressed stimulus-response or cause-effect behavior. To quote from *The Structure of Magic:*

Cause and Effect *This class of semantically ill-formed Surface Structures involves the belief on the part of the speaker that one person (or set of circumstances) may perform some action which necessarily causes some*

other person to experience some emotion or inner state. Typically, the person experiencing this emotion or inner state is portrayed as having no choice in responding the way he does. For example, the client says,
. . . My wife makes me feel angry.
Notice that this Surface Structure presents a vague image in which one human being (identified as My wife) performs some action (unspecified) which necessarily causes some other person (identified as me) to experience some emotion (anger). Ill-formed Surface Structures which are members of this class can be identified by one of two general forms:

(A) X	Verb	Y	Verb	Adjective
	(cause)		(feel	(some emotion
			experience)	or some
				inner state)

where X and Y are nouns which have different referential indices, i.e., refer to different people.
The Surface Structure presented above is of this form—namely:

My wife	makes	me	feel	angry
X	Verb	Y	Verb	Adjective
	(cause)		(feel	(some emotion
			experience)	or some
				inner state)

The other general form which we frequently encounter is that of underlying Surface Structures such as:
. . . Your laughing distracts me.
The general form is:

(B) X	Verb	Verb	Y
		(cause)	

where X and Y are nouns which have different referential indices, i.e., refer to different people.
Applying the general form to the example we have:

Your	laughing	distracts	me
X	Verb	Verb	Y
		(cause) [14]	

It is useful to challenge cause-effect statements. However, it is important to note that the existence of stimulus-response/cause-effect phenomena is not denied by the linguistic challenges. Also, ill-formedness only occurs when a person experiences *only one* possible response (effect) to a given stimulus (cause). This is where distortion occurs (not that the wife's behavior has an effect on her husband, but that he would *have to* respond in anger).

Although clients bring in many different kinds of problems,

worries, woes, hopes and dreams, an effective therapist changes the same aspect of each of them. That is, a successful therapist does not change the stimulus the world provides a client so much as how the client responds to that stimulus. Even if the therapist assists the client in changing jobs, locales, spouses, or schools, if the client does not respond to the new environment in more useful ways, the patterns that necessitated therapy will be repeated. This is especially evident in the area of sexual dysfunction where, so often, changing sexual partners does not alter the dysfunctional sexual behavior.

The problems clients bring in are examples of how they respond to the stimuli around them. Indeed, that they have come to therapy is a statement that they would like to have a different response or experience, at least with regard to some aspect of that stimuli. Often a new response to an old stimulus can generate such pervasive change that a person's whole life experience is much improved.

It might seem to many that accepting the notion of cause-effect or stimulus-response is starting out already defeated. It's true, we must respond to the stimulus, and usually that response is operative at the unconscious level. Also, that response is often predetermined by what took place early in our development when we did not have the faculties to question it. On the face of it, that does seem to leave us helpless. Certainly, these very ideas have kept humanistic psychologists at odds with behaviorists for years. It makes us seem like rats in a maze.

However, I see two crucial differences: Namely, (1) we can change how we respond to most stimuli, and (2) we can acquire several choices for responding to a particular stimulus, then choose the one most appropriate for generating the desired results in a specific context.

Most human behavior dealt with in the therapeutic context is learned behavior. In this culture, the handshake is an example of a learned response, which then occurs at the unconscious level. In fact, if the sequence of behaviors leading to the completion of a handshake is interrupted, the person involved may enter a quite altered state of consciousness.[15] Try it yourself: The next time someone extends their hand to you for the customary handshake, try to not respond. Doubtless, you will find it difficult. Answering a ringing telephone is another learned response that is difficult to override. Notice how the conscious mind makes the distinction concerning whether or not the phone is yours. If it isn't, often the stimulus-response pattern is thereby interrupted.

The process of understanding language is also a phenomenon of learned stimulus-response. Words do not have meaning in and of themselves, any more than a completely unfamiliar language carries meaning for us. Language is comprised of specific sounds organized in a sequence with specific intonation patterns. These certain sequences of sounds and intonation patterns become meaningful when they are associated with some specific sensory experience. The small child is presented with the phenomenon of a dog and as he sees, hears, touches, and smells it, he is also presented with the sounds that make up the word "dog." This process continues to occur and the two associated aspects become so profoundly linked that it becomes nearly impossible to say the word "dog" and not also think of a dog. Thus, we can generously say, "I'll give you the pot of gold at the end of the rainbow if you don't think of a big white duck."

Likewise, the child learns to associate sequences of sounds with the lack of certain sensory experiences—"quiet," for example. Words like comfort, curiosity, interest, sad, and happy become associated with certain inner states. This occurs much like the sound of the ringing bell became associated with food for Pavlov's dogs. The bell came to represent the stimulus of food effectively enough to elicit the salivating response previously only associated with the presentation of food. Since language is meaningful only by its association to sensory experience, the process of understanding language takes place when a specific sequence of sounds triggers an internal representation of some aspect or aspects of the associated sensory experience.

Similarly, as a child you learned to associate specific aspects of your family's behavior with meanings, and learned to respond appropriately. The tone of your mother's voice, the expression on your father's face, and the way a door was closed all came to influence your subsequent behavior. Can you remember how your mother looked and sounded when she was angry? When she was frightened? When she was proud? As you remembered, did you notice how your own experience changed?

It is possible to learn how to *not* respond to environmental stimuli. We label such behavior as pathological, calling it catatonia or autism, and certainly it is unusual to display no outward evidence of responding to the world around us. Even in the most severe cases of catatonia and autism it has been shown that this condition can be altered once the appropriate stimulus is found. That is, there is some stimulus, some behavior on the part of staff or therapist, which can elicit responses, though finding it can often tax both the therapist's creativity and sense of morality.[16]

I consider it to be true that the response chosen by any individual to a given stimulus is the best they have available to them, at least in its first occurrence. Richard Bandler and John Grinder expand on this belief in *The Structure Of Magic*:

Our experience has been that when people come to us in therapy, they typically come with pain, feeling themselves paralyzed, experiencing no choices or freedom of action in their lives. What we have found is not that the world is too limited or that there are no choices, but that these people block themselves from seeing those options and possibilities that are open to them since they are not available in their models of their world.

Almost every human being in our culture in his life cycle has a number of periods of change and transition which he must negotiate. Different forms of psychotherapy have developed various categories for these important transition-crisis points. What's peculiar is that some people are able to negotiate these periods of change with little difficulty, experiencing these periods as times of intense energy and creativity. Other people, faced with the same challenges, experience these periods as times of dread and pain— periods to be endured, when their primary concern is simple survival. The difference between these two groups appears to us to be primarily that the people who respond creatively to and cope effectively with this stress are people who have a rich representation or model of their situation, one in which they perceive a wide range of options in choosing their actions. The other people experience themselves as having few options, none of which are attractive to them—the "natural loser" game. The question for us is: How is it possible for different human beings faced with the same world to have such different experiences? Our understanding is that this difference follows primarily from differences in the richness of their models. Thus, the question becomes: How is it possible for human beings to maintain an impoverished model which causes them pain in the face of a multi-valued, rich, and complex world?

In coming to understand how it is that some people continue to cause themselves pain and anguish, it has been important for us to realize that they are not bad, crazy, or sick. They are, in fact, making the best choices . . . available in their own particular model. In other words, human beings' behavior, no matter how bizarre it may first appear to be, makes sense when it is seen in the context of the choices generated by their model. The difficulty is not that they are making the wrong choice, but that they do not have enough choices . . .[17]

People can add new, more useful choices of responding to almost any stimuli. In fact, they can learn *any number* of responses to a given stimulus and, as a result, be able to choose among them for the one most appropriate. This is precisely what occurs as people grow and change emotionally, enriching the interpersonal aspects of their lives.

Very often, rigid response patterns are a result of early learning. Certain stimuli send us back to a childhood state where our adult resources are unavailable. I often use the the following example to demonstrate this phenomenon in workshops. As children, most of us learned to respond with varying degrees of fear to harsh, loud voices, stern faces, and pointed fingers. Most of us learned that such a display was meant to threaten impending physical punishment and, at the very least, was a vivid display of anger. As children, emotional and physical well-being was at stake, or was at least believed to be at stake. Even some of the most competent adults still respond to a congruent display such as this with fearfulness. And, even when they know that such a display is only for purposes of demonstration, the response still occurs, being generated at the unconscious level.

So, stimulus X elicits response Y.

And, each time X occurs, it triggers Y.

Stated graphically: X ▷ Y

This common behavioral pattern shows how a specific stimuli can induce an experiential state where choices are very limited. It is rare that a loud verbal display need cause fear in an adult. Rather, any number of responses could be more useful: listening to what is being said, remaining calm, shouting back, whistling, and so on. I will be presenting a number of methods for accomplishing the relearning process that leads to a stimulus becoming a *choice point* rather than an automatic response:

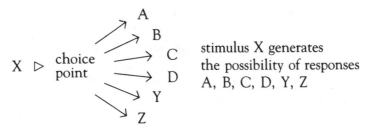

An example from the realm of sexual dysfunction can serve to clarify this concept. Mary was twenty-two years old and sought therapy because, though she desired to, she was unable to have sexual relations with her fiance. The cause of the dysfunction was traced back to an incident that had occurred in her early teens. Her uncle had sexually abused her. In itself, this was not enough to produce a sexual dysfunction, but all the terror, pain and guilt that Mary felt in the past episode had become associated with the picture or sight of an erect penis. When Mary saw an erect penis she responded with feelings of terror and revulsion. She and her fiance had attempted to overcome the response by initiating sexual relations in complete darkness. However, as soon as Mary felt an erect penis, she then generated an internal image of it and was therefore triggered into the unwanted response.

So, where the visual image of erect penis is the stimulus X (either internally or externally generated),

Y is the terror response which results from the past experience.

Every time X occurs, Y results.

X ▷ Y

This is not an unusual phenomenon. Most of us are triggered into memories by present stimuli. The smell of our first lover's cologne or perfume, or the sound of a record album listened to in the past can flood us with memories as well as the feelings congruent with those memories. Like so many of our human processes, this one can enhance our experience at times. Yet it can severely impoverish it at others.

With Mary, the feelings triggered by the visual image of an erect penis were certainly appropriate to the experience that had occurred when she was thirteen. But they were not appropriate to sexual experiences with her fiance; yet, she could not consciously control them. Similarly, a response of fear and intimidation to harsh shouting and a pointed finger is also an example of feelings being triggered that belong to the past—feelings that are not necessarily appropriate for the present. Though fear is certainly a useful response when it serves as a warning of danger, it can also be a response that limits a person's ability to operate effectively when it is triggered unnecessarily or inappropriately. Experiences that may terrify a child (usually rightfully so), need not bother the adult who, ideally, has acquired resources to deal with the world. These are resources that the child cannot know even exist.

Successful intervention in these cases requires interrupting the pattern of X triggering Y and diverting the response to a choice point where the client can choose a more satisfying response (at the unconscious level).

Thus, in the past:

X ▷ Y

triggered

You intervene to create a choice point for your client:

X ▷ C

triggers choice point C

C in turn can trigger multiple responses:

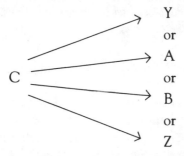

C

Y

or

A

or

B

or

Z

New responses are developed from which the client can choose. These new choices must, of course, be activated by stimulus-response as automatically as was Y. The old response is kept as a *choice*. Because it is based upon a powerful past learning, it is possible that the response would be useful at some future time. I believe all responses are useful at some time, in some context.

Once the new learning has been integrated into the client's behavior, the need for therapeutic intervention ceases. In Mary's case I used a technique referred to as a *visual-kinesthetic dissociation* (see pg. 151). As a result, Mary was able to maintain feelings congruent with her *present* experience (calm and comfortable), while recalling vividly the past experience. *Feelings* that are specific to the memory become dissociated while the person can still *visualize* the remembered experience. For Mary, the terror and revulsion were separated from her present experience and became part of the remembered picture. She could then have other feelings more appropriate to her current experience. Mary's response to an erect penis was then open to new possibilities. Mary's fiance—a very tender, loving man—was given instructions designed to guide them toward establishing positive associations for Mary with naturally-occurring sexual stimuli. And they succeeded beautifully.

Masters and Johnson are certainly familiar with the phenomenon of one intense experience influencing all subsequent similar experiences:

Frequently, one particular event, one specifically traumatic episode, has been quite sufficient to terminate the individual male's ability to, facil-

ity for, interest in, or demand for ejaculating intravaginally. Occasionally a man may lose ejaculatory facility subsequent to a physically traumatic episode, but usually the only trauma is psychological . . .

The interesting observation remains that, although there obviously are instances when primary impotence almost seems preordained by prior environmental influence, there frequently is a psychosexually traumatic episode directly associated with the first coital experience that establishes a negative psychosocial influence pattern or even a life-style of sexual dysfunction for the traumatized man. [18]

(Masters and Johnson, however, do not outline specific techniques for working with such cases.)

So when some stimulus triggers an undesirable response, you need to identify this process and then interrupt it in a way that a new, more useful response, or choice of responses, results. To further clarify this important aspect of cause-effect, I have included the following case histories of subjects who fit these patterns, as recorded by Masters and Johnson:

There are four recorded histories . . . of men with basically stable family, religious, and personal backgrounds whose initial failure at coital connection was specifically associated with a traumatic experience developing from prostitute involvement with their first experience at coition. Three of these virginal young men (two late teenage and one 22-year-old) each sought prostitute opportunity in the most debilitated sections of cities in which they were living and were so repulsed by their neophyte observations of the squalor of the prostitute's quarters, the dehumanizing quality of her approach, and the physically unappetizing, essentially repulsive quality of the woman involved that they could not achieve or maintain an erection. The fact that their own poor judgment had rendered them vulnerable to a level of social environment to which they were unaccustomed and for which they were unprepared never occurred to them. In two of these instances their frantic attempts to establish an erection amused the prostitutes and their obvious fears of performance were derided. The third young man was assured that "he would never be able to get the job done for any woman—if he couldn't get it done here and now with a pro . . ."

The following history exemplifies onset of vaginismus subsequent to episodes of psychosexual trauma. There have been three women referred to therapy so physically and emotionally traumatized by unwelcome sexual attack that vaginismus developed subsequent to their traumatic experiences.

When first seen, Unit C had been married for 18 months, with repeated attempts to consummate the marriage reported as unsuccessful. The husband, age 31, reported effective sexual function with several other women prior to marriage. The wife, age 28, described successful sexual connection with four men over a five-year period before the specific episode of sexual trauma. One of these relationships included coitus two or three times a week over a 10 month span. She had been readily orgasmic in the association.

The traumatic episode in her history was a well-authenticated episode of gang rape with resultant physical trauma to the victim requiring two weeks' hospitalization. Extensive surgical reconstruction of the vaginal canal was necessary for basic physical rehabilitation. No psychotherapeutic support was sought by or suggested for the girl following this experience.

Mr. and Mrs. C met one year after the rape episode and were married a year after their introduction. Prior to the marriage the husband-to-be was in full possession of the factual history of the gang raping and of the resultant physical distress.

During the latter stages of their engagement period, several attempts at intercourse proved unsuccessful in that despite full erection, penetration could not be accomplished. It was mutually agreed that in all probability the security of the marital state would release her presumed hysterical inhibitions. This did not happen. After the marriage ceremony, attempts at consummation continued unsuccessful despite an unusually high degree of finesse, kindness, and discretion in the husband's sexual approaches to his traumatized partner. Severe vaginismus was demonstrated during physical examination of the wife after referral to the Foundation.

The remaining two rape experiences were family-oriented and almost identical in history. In both instances young girls were physically forced by male members of their immediate family to provide sexual release, on numerous occasions, for men they did not know. In one instance, a father, and in another, an older brother, forced sexual partners upon teen-age girls (15 and 17 years of age) and repeatedly stood by to insure the girls' physical cooperation. Sexually exploited, emotionally traumatized, and occasionally physically punished, these girls became conditioned to the concept that "all men were like that." When released from family sexual servitude each girl avoided any possibility of sexual contact during the late teens and well into the twenties, until married at 25 and 29 years of age. Even then, they could not make themselves physically available to consummate their marriages, regardless of how strongly they willed sexual cooperation. Severe vaginismus was present in both cases.[19]

Problem and Desired States

Masters and Johnson have presented a detailed clinical description of the sequence and interrelationship of physiological responses involved in sexual functioning. As you have already begun to discover, the role that internal processes play in sexual functioning and couple interactions is the principal subject of this book. Sexual functioning is a sequence of naturally-occurring and interrelated stimulus-response patterns involving these physiological responses and internal processes. Sexual dysfunction occurs when some natural stimulus elicits from either partner a response that is opposed to or incongruent with the naturally occurring sequence. The present state somehow prevents the progression of the natural sequence of stimulus-response. In almost all cases the desired state in sexual functioning is a satisfying physical experience that is also emotionally fulfilling. Your task as a therapist is to remove the block of the present state so the desired state can occur.

The organization of internal processes, external behaviors and physiological responses that are experienced as a problem is the *structure* of the present state. The ability to make sophisticated distinctions in human behavior is required in order to discern what the client's internal and external behaviors and responses are, and what relationships exist between them. You do not have the opportunity to directly observe the context in which the sexual dysfunction occurs. Therefore, you are limited to what can be learned from *descriptions* of the problem offered by your client and by attending to their observable behavior and language patterns. You need to know more than *what* the problem is; you need to know *how* the problem is structured.

Your information gathering needs to be directed to discovering how external stimuli interact with internal processes to produce an undesirable experience in an individual or couple. Besides detecting your client's lead and representational systems, and obtaining a full verbal description, you can also chart the *sequence* of responses involved in the present state. By using your ears, eyes, and sometimes, sense of touch, you can learn which client expressions are linked to the events of the present state. Those expressions include voice tone, body posture, accessing cues, muscle patterns of face and body, and any particularly characteristic words.

In order to avoid "mind-reading" your clients, and thereby risking self-projection, it is important to describe these expressions in sensory-based terms rather than interpreting them. To describe an expression as "his hands gripped the chair arms, knuckles white, facial muscles tightened, breathing stopped, pupils dilated" is to describe in sensory-based terms. To say "he was afraid" is an interpretation of what these aspects of behavior might mean to you or someone else. Although this may seem a tedious distinction, it is crucial to detect the subtleties in behavior that are lost when labels are attached to categories of behavior. It is not a sensory-based description to say her voice was "enthusiastic." It *is* a sensory-based description to say her voice "became higher in tone, faster in tempo, and displayed more differentiation of intonation patterns." These are distinctions available to our senses. Labeling them with a word like "enthusiasm" leaves the door open to the interpretations of mind-reading.

I am not suggesting that you limit yourself to this one way of perceiving and speaking. I do recommend that you use all the sensory distinctions available to you, especially in the therapeutic context. Frequently, a change in voice tone or a jiggling foot is a meaningful communication. I once counseled a couple who were deciding whether or not to stay together. Every time the subject was broached, the man's left foot began to jiggle. I took this as communication, and decided to check my guess about its meaning. I began to relate stories about being in places that you can't get out of when you want to. I talked about being stuck in an elevator, waiting for bus doors to open, and missing a connecting flight because I couldn't get off the plane. All during these stories the man's foot jiggled furiously. His behavior gave me important information about his experience—information that he was not able to vocalize.

Attending to the verbal and nonverbal communication offered by your client will allow you to learn about the sequence of external behaviors and internal processes that make up the present state. You will be taking the first step in determining what sequence of internally and externally generated experiences make the problem possible. Once you have gathered enough information to know what the present state is, it is useful to elicit the state in order to verify your conclusions.

If we use Mary as an example, there is the external stimulus of the sight or feel of an erect penis, which triggers the internal process of picturing the uncle, which is represented consciously as feelings of terror, eliciting her unwanted external behavior of tightening up.

external stimulus (sight or feel of erect penis) triggers internal process (picture of uncle)

then, internal process (picture of uncle) triggers represented consciously (terror)

then, represented consciously (terror) triggers external behavior (tightening up)

Since Mary could not be presented with an erect penis, I induced this sequence by having her visualize the last time she saw an erect penis. Once she made the visualization she exhibited the same expressions manifested earlier when she described what happened when she was approached sexually. She went through the same sequence of accessing cues, voice tone and tempo changes, changes in breathing, and shifts in color and muscle patterns of face and body (tense thighs drawn close, arms tight to body). These changes in expressions were subtle to the untrained observer, and most were outside of the Mary's conscious awareness. This sequence of stimulus-response behaviors verified my understanding of her present state.

Mary would re-experience, to a degree, her past sexual experiences as she described them verbally. (It is important to remember that words are attached to experience just as are memories, and people truly experience much of what they are talking about—as they are talking about it.) This was obvious by the changes in breathing rate, facial color, muscle tenseness, change in voice tone, etc. As an example of how this works, take a few moments to think about the last time you told someone about an experience in which you had been terribly angry. Or, better yet, think of such a time now. Some of those feelings come back as you do this, and the acute observer can detect the changes in breathing, lip size, face color and tension, and voice tempo and pitch that accompany those feelings.

A trained observer can make sensory distinctions that allow subtle, nonverbal behaviors to become extremely useful communications. This is done not by labeling them, but by attending to how they relate to the process as a whole: When do they occur? What happens just before the lower lip quivers and just after? How does this behavior make sense within the context of the problem?

So you gather information about the present state by utilizing sensory experience and the meta-model to discover answers to the following questions:

□ What external stimulus triggers the unwanted experience?

□ What internal process does that external stimulus trigger?

□ What is represented in the client's consciousness?

□ How do these three categories relate to one another, and in what sequence?

□ Does the whole sequence fire off again each time the external stimulus is triggered in some way by you?

When you know the answers to these questions, and have a yes to the last one, you have what is needed to decide upon a plan of action for effecting change.

The sequence and relationship of these categories are often fixed and rigid for people. That is, something they hear (external stimulus) triggers a picture (internal process) which induces a feeling congruent with the picture (represented consciously) and their external behavior becomes congruent with their conscious representation. Frequently, a similar sequence is repeated for almost every kind of experience. For example, a person might hear a harsh voice, picture their father yelling at them, feel frightened, and act frightened. Or they might hear the description of a peaceful scene, picture themselves in that scene, feel peaceful and serene, and become outwardly calm and relaxed. In these two examples, what they are experiencing is different, but *how* they are experiencing both of them is the same.

While this phenomenon of a fixed and rigid sequence can produce useful and satisfying experiences for the person in some instances, it may not in others. Therefore, you could enhance this person's experience by helping them find new and more successful ways of responding. A more limited goal would be to keep the same sequence while changing the type of response. Although the latter will give the person the desired state, the former begins them on the road to developing a more generative personality by giving them more than one strategy for producing their experience. The techniques for accomplishing both outcomes are presented in Part III.

As you become successful at making the distinctions presented in this book you will almost always know more about your clients' continuing experience than the clients themselves know consciously. Indeed, in the course of everyday interactions I am aware of people's language patterns, accessing cues, and other nonverbal behavior in much the same way they are aware of the color of my hair. This added information greatly assists me in communicating effectively with everyone I meet, whether it's the butcher, the insurance salesman, or the next-door neighbor. If I told each of them what I see and hear that they are unaware of, it would get in the way of our communication. Likewise, it is not necessary for your client to be consciously aware of the same aspects of behavior that you must be aware of. Telling people's conscious minds about aspects of their behavior they were previously unaware of is called "meta commenting" (in therapy circles). Although a choice, it is not always the best one; it can, and often does, elicit a defensive response. A client can be unaware of aspects of their present behavior and still change in desired ways.

Chapter 9: Falling In and Out of Love

Have you ever been head-over-heels in love? Interesting way to phrase it, isn't it? Head over heels, as in somersaulting or cart-wheeling perhaps. Have you ever fallen out of love? What does it mean to fall in or out of love? It certainly is an all-too-common subjective experience. Have you ever tried to fall back in love? Did you succeed? Have you ever had someone fall out of love with you and done your best to get them back? Some of these memories are perhaps unpleasant, possibly even painful, for you to recall. Couples seeking therapy are usually engulfed in those kinds of unpleasant and painful experiences. It is the uncommon, joyful experience to guide couples in premarital or newlywed counseling where the emphasis is on how to sustain their happiness. I hope this will be commonplace in the future: people coming for guidance in how to maintain happiness, rather than how to assuage their suffering and regain satisfaction in their relationships.

You do not need to be an experienced clinician to be familiar with those signals which indicate the demise of a love relationship, whether it is your own or someone else's. Sometimes it starts with complaints, put somewhat humorously, to family and friends about the "loved one's" behavior. Or perhaps it starts with that oh-so-significant sigh as you come upon the offending by-product of some once-upon-a-time charming trait: the empty milk carton in the refrigerator, the clothes left in a heap, the millionth time you heard that same story. Other times, love is gone with little warning; some inconceivable offense is committed, an indiscretion that feels like a mortal wound from which there is no hope of recovery. Whether it leaves via the former route or the latter, the patterns which emerge are the same. At the end there are those questioning statements that ring with familiarity: "I don't know what I saw in him in the first place," "It just took a while for her true colors to show," "I was a fool (and now I'm not)," "Nothing I ever did helped," "It wasn't meant to be." Or the less personally directed euphemisms of our times, "I need time to grow to find myself (away from you)." "The relationship was too confining." (Like a neighborhood, the relationship has become something to move away from.) Or that declaration that is disheartening, all-telling, and so frustrating for both people: "I love you, I'm just not in love with you."

Whether this topic is personally or professionally familiar, or both, it is useful for us all to have an understanding of the processes of falling into, staying in, and falling out of love. Knowing more about how these processes work will allow you to assume greater control in influencing your own and (in the context of therapy) others' experience. The following is a map of the experiential journey that people typically take from attraction to separation. It is called the *threshold pattern* and it is a major tool in diagnosing the present state, and therefore, in indicating what interventions are appropriate to bringing about an achievable therapeutic outcome.

The Threshold Pattern

Attraction ▷ **Appreciation** ▷ **Habituation** ▷

Expectation ▷ **Disappointment/Disillusionment** ▷

Threshold Reached/Perceptual Reorientation ▷

Verification ▷ **Relationship Terminated**

This map can be used to pinpoint an individual's or couple's position regarding the well-being of a love relationship, as well as to designate the desired therapeutic destination. Be aware that not all people separate when the relationship is, in essence, terminated. As a friend of mine says, "The body is the last to go," meaning the heart and mind can be long disconnected even though a couple stays together. These relationships manifest night-of-the-living-dead behavior, in sharp contrast to the supportive companionship and love that typifies a relationship which remains in the habituation phase.

It is also important to know that people are usually at different places in the over-all pattern when they seek couple therapy. Because of this, it is often necessary to do certain procedures with one and not with the other in order to achieve their desired state and the overall well-formed outcome. Not all couple therapy need or should be done with both parties present.

How Love Begins . . . and Lasts

There is a special class of high context communications which my colleagues and I refer to as *behavioral complex equivalences* (behavioral referring to observable behavior, complex referring to an interconnected system, and equivalence referring to having the same significance). A behavioral complex equivalence is the meaning that a person attaches to any particular behavior. The behavioral complex equivalences that are relevant to the threshold pattern are those that convey some specific emotional quality.

Some of the possibilities of the ways in which another person can let you know you are loved, for instance, are touching you gently, saying your name a certain way, looking into your eyes, arguing with you, giving an unexpected present, leaving you alone when you are working, joining in when you are working, laughing at your jokes, or perhaps tolerating you when you are corny. These behaviors (or others that fit for you) are perceived by you as having a specific meaning. So much so, that the meaning is not questioned, but assumed to be true and responded to automatically and fully each time the behavior occurs. These behaviors are behavioral complex equivalences. While cultural behavioral complex equivalences have been documented by cultural anthropologists and other social scientists,[20] there has been little work done in exploring the significance of the idiosyncratic ones we all use to make meaning of one another's behavior.

One of the most significant aspects of behavioral complex equivalences is that people have tremendous flexibility in establishing them, allowing the same piece of behavior to be interpreted differently by different individuals. For example:

> When Jonathan interacts with strangers, or with people he hasn't known for very long, his eyes are always averted down, he shifts back and forth from one foot to the other, his shoulders are rolled forward and down, and when he speaks, which isn't often, his words are mumbled.

Two different strangers could have very different responses to Jonathan's behavior. To the first it might be interpreted as shyness (that is, it would match their behavioral complex equivalence for shyness). To the second person it might mean that

Jonathan had something to hide, hinting at possible dishonesty. Thus the first might respond by feeling protective and offering reassurances, while the second might feel suspicious and distrustful, either withdrawing from the interaction or making demands for the truth. As you read the description of Jonathan, you may have formed your own opinion about what his behavior meant— about what type of person he was (shy, bashful, unassuming, uncomfortable, socially inept, confused, stupid, disrespectful, etc.). If so, then you were responding automatically to your own unique set of behavioral complex equivalences.

The special role that behavioral complex equivalences play in relation to the attraction phase of the threshold pattern has to do with how they interrelate with the criteria (standards) that each person has regarding what makes a person attractive. Out of the endless possibilities to choose from, each of us has, consciously or unconsciously, chosen some combination of criteria that represent to us what it is that makes another person attractive. Examples of this kind of criteria are intelligence, personal power, kindness, good looks, sensuality, wealth, gentleness, sense of humor, warmth, arrogance, etc. We also have established behavioral complex equivalences for each criteria. That is, we have specified for ourselves which behaviors in others mean that they possess or satisfy that criteria. In the same way, we have also specified which behaviors not only do *not* satisfy that criteria, but satisfy the opposite (stupid, ineffectual, cruel, ugly, non-sensual, poor, harsh, stoic, cold, humble, etc.).

To make this concept more immediately meaningful to you, take a few moments and recall a person to whom you were once, long ago, attracted—perhaps someone in your early or late teens. Notice what it was that so strongly attracted you to that person back then. Do you recognize the basis of that past attraction in terms of qualities that person somehow manifested, or in how they were able to make you feel when you were near, or some combination of these? Bring your attention to even finer detail by discerning the distinct behaviors that conveyed those messages. Once you have explored this to your satisfaction, leave your past and come back to the present. Identify someone whom you find very attractive today. Again, what are the qualities they manifest that attract you and what are the specific behaviors which convey those qualities? This behavioral and cognitive pattern—the formulation of and automatic response to behavioral complex equivalences—is the truth behind the saying, "Beauty is in the eye of the beholder."

Attraction   I can think of no better way to introduce you to the stages of the threshold pattern than by telling you about David and Sue. In the beginning, David found Sue to be just the woman he wanted. Her soft voice and slow way of speaking, even how she paused and thought a bit before she spoke, was so demure, so appealing. She had a full, luscious figure but dressed conservatively, not calling attention to herself (unlike some flashy types of women that he didn't care for). He especially enjoyed the way she asked his advice and opinions on so many subjects. It made him feel respected. It also let him know that she recognized his intelligence. He was thrilled when she touched him, which she did often, almost always holding his hand or pressing close to him whenever they were together. She was great to be with—undemanding and nonaggressive. There were only good times, no unpleasant confrontations. David found Sue to be pretty, intelligent, demure, and sensuous. And fortunately, Sue found David tremendously attractive. He was strong and smart, and knew the answers to everything. He really spoke to her and wanted her to hear what he had to say. He was so definite and sure of himself. She thought he was sexy the way he stared into her eyes, and his eating and exercise habits verified that he was responsible and disciplined. Also, he wasn't demanding of her; she could sit quietly and felt no need to perform for him.

While David and Sue were finding each other irresistible, there were others who couldn't imagine what they saw in each other. Some found Sue dull, boring, and complacent, and David a pedantic know-it-all. But David and Sue had on those rose-colored glasses that bring everything wonderful into view. Once enough of their respective criteria for attraction had been met, they saw each other through love's eyes only. Not unlike the eyes a mother has for her children, we tend to see our loved ones as special creatures above and beyond other mortals. We experience them through a special filter made up of our belief that they are lovable, desirable, worthwhile, etc. They are fulfilling all of our contextually important behavioral complex equivalences. It is a fun time, full of intensity and excitement and romance.

Appreciation   The next phase, appreciation, is reached if the attraction is enough and is maintained long enough (that is, if the behavioral complex equivalences continue to be fulfilled long enough) for a steady relationship to form. So now David and Sue are a couple, perhaps seriously dating, living together, or even married. Regardless of the formality of their commitment, they experience themselves as a couple and are delighted to be to-gether. Of all the possibilities of experience that they could notice and respond to in one another, they perceive those which meet and fulfill the desired states of mind and body that are held most dear. Their filters freely let through all the examples of being loved and of their mate as being lovable. It is only natural that they feel loving since they are paying attention to the things that add to their experience. They don't take one another for granted, but genuinely appreciate each other instead. This phase can be based on a wide range of illusion or varying degrees of knowledgeable understanding of each other's wants and needs. The extent to which it is based on knowledgeable understandings is the extent to which it can be depended upon to last. (Of course, some relationships last a long time even though they ride on illusions; they usually end up being unfulfilling, however.) A knowledgeable base, in this case, refers to knowing one another's significant behavioral complex equivalences and having the will-ingness, capability, and desire to fulfill them. For instance, how do you know that you are loved? How do you express your love? How do your loved ones really know they are being loved by you? Is it via the same way that you express your loving? Are you sure? Or have you just assumed it is? If you were to list the significant experiences you believed necessary to establishing and maintain-ing a fulfilling primary relationship, what would they be? Would your list include respect, trust, love, support, regard, challenge? How about others? If you placed respect on your list, what does your mate do that gives you the experience of being respected? What about disrespect? What gives your partner the experience of being respected? Is it asking the other's opinion, or sharing personal insights, or following advice given, keeping secrets, disagreeing with you, challenging you, expressing criticism? At first it may seem obvious to you, but there is an infinite variety to what people find significant and insignificant. I once achieved a seemingly miraculous outcome with a couple by getting him to lower the toilet lid after he urinated. After falling through the seat once too often in the dark of night, she had come to the conclusion that the toilet seat was in every way the ultimate manifestation of his disregard and disrespect for her. She had begun to see him through a filter that painted him as a real woman hater.

Until the significance of seemingly random behaviors is known, there is little opportunity for two people to consistently fulfill one another's wants and needs. Also, knowing the meaning or intention of our partner's behaviors offers greater possibility for appreciation and understanding. It is important to know that he cleans the kitchen because he is feeling loving, not because he feels guilty; that her voice sounds harsh when she says no not because she is angry, but because she hates to say no to him and really wants to give him what he is asking for. This kind of knowledge has been treated as if we are supposed to know it automatically, as if we are born with it. Everywhere I go I see and hear people tragically at odds with one another over misunderstandings involving behavioral complex equivalences.

There are basic steps for achieving and maintaining a state of appreciation in a relationship. One is to know what you want and need in a relationship. Another is to know what specifically fulfills those wants and needs. A third is to be able to elicit those fulfilling behaviors, lovingly, from your partner. These steps apply to each person in the relationship. Underlying these steps is a requirement of requisite flexibility of behavior so that you are flexible in having many ways to have your wants and needs fulfilled, as well as flexible in your behavior when it comes to fulfilling your partner's wants and needs. Assisting couples who come to you for therapy in actualizing these steps (as well as the ones discussed later in this section) constitutes a well-formed meta-outcome for couple work.

Habituation   The phase of habituation can be a very positive one, provided it cycles back to appreciation and includes an occasional trip back to attraction. Habituation is the experience of becoming accustomed to something. If you have been in a room for a very long time, you may no longer notice every nuance of color, texture, or shape that is part of it. It is no longer new or precious, but it is familiar, and you may have come to depend upon that familiarity to free your attention for other things. The same process occurs in relationships. We fall in love in a flurry of intensity, glow with appreciation, and become comfortable and secure with familiarity and dependability. How wonderful this phase is depends to a large degree on whether the individuals are seeking security or adventure. If they are adventure-seekers, habituation can equal boredom. If they seek security, habituation can equal commitment and safety. For better or worse, they are now used to each other. The glasses are not so rosy but the blush has not disappeared.

Sometimes a couple will seek therapy at this time. It is not difficult to detect that what was once a source of great delight has fallen unnoticed. It can be dangerous if one person decides to bring the edge back by making the other jealous, or treats the experience as the beginning of a long and dreary haul. A useful response is to redirect their attention to what there is to appreciate, as well as lead them to new discoveries of how to entice and please each other. If what you perceive going on has more to do with apathy than hostility, prescribing romantic interludes can go a long way to making a significant difference. It is an important time for you to initiate a renaissance in their relationship, not to invent problems for them. There is a task I have found useful to give couples having an unpleasant time in this phase. It involves getting them to commit two weekends over the upcoming two months to carrying out the following instructions. Each is to design and plan a complete weekend of activities for the two of them to participate in. Each is to do all of the planning and arranging alone, so that the whole weekend experience is a surprise to the other. The only constraint is to stay within an agreed-upon budget. Each is to design the weekend to fulfill their own fantasies of how he or she wants to spend time with the other. The weekend is then a learning experience for the other concerning their partner's previously unexpressed or newly formed desires. In the follow-up session I usually can concentrate on how to integrate into their everyday lives those aspects of their weekends they both enjoyed, and how to bring a sense of humor and adjustment to any aspects that fell short of their desires. While this has frequently proved to be all the therapy a couple needed, I must caution you: This is an inappropriate intervention for couples who are in any of the subsequent phases of the threshold pattern, as it then becomes a ripe opportunity for disappointment or the expression of hostility.

How Love Begins to End

Expectation   The difference between duty and pleasure often rears its ugly head in the phase of expectation. You probably know the couple that lived together and then got married only to start bickering over seemingly petty things. She had been a single parent and, at first, when he got up in the morning and took the child to school she appreciated it. After they were married she expected him to do it. Maybe she used to feel loved when he did the grocery shopping and cooking, and now it's something he *should* do as his duty as a husband. Before, the backrubs she gave him were really special; now he just knows how long it has been since he has gotten one. Before, her ability to budget and save money was proof that she was smart; now she just damned well better keep it up and not jeopardize their future. Expectations are the big set-up for the big fall known as disappointment.

It is easy to slide from habituation to expectation. What was once appreciated goes unnoticed. Then it shifts to becoming the way it "should be" rather than the fulfillment of an important desire. This phase is signaled by there being more complaints than compliments. The filters are shifting to notice what is not there, rather than what is there. Remember David and Sue? Once it was meaningful that David came home on time, but now it is only meaningful when he doesn't. If he remembers all the holidays but fails to deliver anything on Valentine's Day, and that is what stands out the most to Sue, she has reached the stage of expectation. Of course, expectations are brutal to the sexual expressions in a relationship, whether they are about how often, or how long, or what kind. A transition from romance to duty is only as far as "want" is from "should." The most significant aspect of this phase is that the filters have shifted to notice when highly valued behaviors are *not* there, instead of when they are. Without realizing it, the couple has come to disregard, and therefore jeopardize, what was once so precious to them. It is one thing for Sue to expect David to have all the answers to her questions. If he is *supposed* to know the answer, however, she will notice and respond when he doesn't more than when he does. With one couple, where the woman was expecting much and appreciating little, I led her through a process so that every time he left their house she would consider that it might be the last time she saw him. (When I took her through this process of considering his mortality and the unknown timing of death for each of them, I had information that he was fantasizing walking out the door for good.) As a result, she made sure their partings were loving ones, and she was happy to see him when they were together again. Frequently at this phase of expectation, the most effective intervention is to get each person to once again treat the other as a lover instead of a spouse.

It seems natural for us to develop expectations in our lives. Imagine your response if you went to wash your face and no water came out of the tap. What is your response when the electricity is out for more than a few minutes? How about when your car breaks down? Whereas it is appropriate to take such things for granted and expect them to be there when you want them to be, it is not useful to place such expectations on a mate. It can turn a ripe and lush romance into a sour and bitter job.

Again, the behaviors which let you know the expectation phase has been reached are those which indicate that a person is noticing when something desired is *not* there, rather than when it is there. There are more complaints than compliments. In the phase of expectation, the *absence of desired behaviors* is in the process of becoming the behavioral complex equivalence for being not loved, not cared about, or not wanted.

Disappointment/Disillusionment Disappointment/disillusionment is only a short step from expectation. Once the absence of highly valued behaviors comes to mean the negation of important behavioral complex equivalences, the filters are adjusted to let in other offenses. In this phase people often complain that their mate just started new bad habits when, upon investigation, it is discovered that he or she has been doing that very behavior all along. The difference is that now it is experienced in a different, less flattering, light. Attending and responding to the absence of fulfilled desires, rather than to their fulfillment, leads to the experience of being not loved, not respected, etc. Unfortunately, people often respond to feeling unloved by proceeding to determine for themselves that the offending partner is really unlovable, uncaring, disrespectful, and so on. We are quite capable of finding what we are looking for, creative species that we are.

So with the filters reset, the examples that form the basis of disillusionment and dissatisfaction begin stacking up—sometimes quickly, sometimes slowly. They may be small wounds that continually are inflicted, like being stoned with grains of sand. Sometimes it will be one glaring experience that violates an essential behavioral complex equivalence, like infidelity or violence. This phase is often characterized by a see-saw effect that is often experienced as confusion. The most significant sign that a person is still at the phase of disappointment/disillusionment, and not over threshold, is that they can still remember the past as wonderful, and typically long "for it to be like it used to be." Even though most of their present experience is negative and brings them consistently to dissatisfaction, their memories serve as rich sources of yearning and possibility. As long as you can catch them at this point, it is not too arduous a task to redirect the focus of their attention, thus readjusting their filters.

Two things need to occur in order to succeed at redirecting their focus of attention at this point. First, the client needs to experience motivation to recapture the joys and fulfillments of the past. Second, it is necessary for the client to make a firm commitment to be responsible in the future for eliciting from their mate the behaviors that the client desires. Directing them to re-experience all of the joyful and fulfilling experiences of the past will not only help install motivation, but will also help restore the belief (which at one time was automatically assumed) that it is both possible and desirable to receive what they want and need from the other person. Emphasis on the future negative and traumatic consequences of separating or divorcing will also help in establishing motivation and commitment. By making sure that the client has a repertoire of ways to elicit the desired responses from the other person, you make it possible for the client to assume control in creating the experience they desire. This new response of motivation and commitment to actively pursue desired responses will lead them to again notice when the highly valued behaviors *are present*, taking them back to appreciation.

Falling Out of Love

Threshold/Perceptual Reorientation ▷ **Verification**   Unfortunately, it is common for at least one member of a couple to have gone over the edge and reached threshold before they seek therapy. This makes it more challenging for everyone. The threshold point is the moment in time where a belief is built that the relationship is over, that it is not worth having, and that the partner cannot and will not provide the desired and necessary fulfillment of highly valued behavioral complex equivalences. Once threshold is reached, a person's memories change—a person dissociates from the past pleasurable experiences and fully associates into past unpleasant memories. They might know the good times happened, but they are unable to feel them. They are outside of the good times and inside all the bad times. Their filters are not just adjusted to notice presently offensive experiences, but they have been focused onto the past and future in a way to make the unpleasant more real and significant than the pleasant. The rose-colored lenses are smashed and a very grey pair take their place. It is here that you hear, "It's too late, there isn't anything to do now." "Now I know him for who he really is." "Sure, she used to do nice things—but she didn't mean them."

A sad, disheartening experience to have, it is also a terrible one for the partner who is not over threshold. It is not a misperception on their part that nothing they do can make a difference. Everything is perceived by their mate as an example that somehow verifies the existing belief that they are really some monstrous creature or that the relationship is beyond repair. Often times, this experience occurs unexpectedly. People sometimes stack up small experiences and respond only when they reach a threshold. Like the straw that broke the camel's back, they become outraged and furious over a seemingly insignificant incident. This only serves to further confuse and confound their spouse. Also, if one is over threshold and the other not, the former is apt to sabotage, however innocently, your efforts to achieve reconciliation. This is why it is important to concentrate your efforts on bringing them back to the other side of threshold before you proceed with couple interventions (see threshold neutralizer, pg. 202).

Once the threshold point is reached and a belief is formed that is diametrically opposed to the sustaining of the relationship, verification proceeds and current experience is viewed through this new perceptual filter. Behaviors are experienced as the fulfillment of highly valued *negative* behavioral complex equivalences: the mate is obviously stupid, dishonest, ugly, etc. Even if it is not taken this far, the existing filters verify, through repeated detection, the uselessness of continuing the relationship. Interestingly, people often stay together for their lifetimes, without seeking therapy, even though they have gone over threshold. I once did family therapy with a family whose problems revolved around what to do with a set of aging and ill parents who despised each other and were prone to screaming and violent arguments. I have seldom witnessed such venomous insults thrown back and forth as the ones hurled by these two elderly people.

As you gather information to develop a well-formed outcome, and as you become acquainted with the behavioral information that evidences the present state, be sure to attend to those signals which indicate what phase of the threshold pattern each person is experiencing. Pay special attention to the responses elicited by pleasant and unpleasant memories. Can they re-experience past pleasures as they recall old and better times, even if only briefly? Do unpleasant memories constitute what is real? What happens when you direct them to possible futures rich with fulfillment? You will need to calibrate to the difference between their being *discouraged* concerning the future, and their being *repulsed* by a continuation of their relationship.

There are many ways to gather this information. I often have my clients play a card game. I give them each eight cards, four red and four black. They are to give a red card to their partner each time they feel hurt, offended, or misunderstood by some behavior (regardless of whether their partner is speaking to me, directly to them, or even if they are not saying anything). They are to give their partner a black card each time they feel cared for, complimented, understood, etc., by anything their partner does. The cards provide an undeniable source of feedback concerning the responses they are eliciting from one another. I usually stop them at each card play to explore what, specifically, was experienced as offensive or caring, both for their education and mine. This game is a behavioral metaphor for the premise that *the meaning of the communication is the response elicited.* It is a positive step to engage them in considering the possible responses their communications are apt to elicit from each other.

If I am working with a couple but seeing them one at a time, I might use the following technique. I first direct them to think of a place where they would love to spend a leisurely weekend. Once they have identified a place, I ask them to think of three people whom they regularly spend time with, one of them being their spouse. I then direct them to consider—one at a time—going to that place with each of those three people. (While they imagine this I have the opportunity to calibrate to their responses, attending to indications of one projected experience being better or worse than another.) Then I ask them to consider going there alone. Then with someone different than any of the first three. In this way, I can graciously gather information concerning significant outside relationships. Now I direct them to review their imagined experiences of these weekends and to rate them from the most appealing to the least. If their spouse was not at the top of the list, I can learn who was and what about them makes them the most desirable to spend the weekend with. This is valuable in determining what behaviors could be useful for the mate to manifest if he or she is to move up on the list. While these are two possible ways to elicit information, be assured that no matter what you do your clients will present you with behaviors that, as long as you remain attentive, will give away their location within the threshold pattern.

Wherever their location, the desired state lies within the realm of appreciation, with regular journeys into attraction for enticement and spice, and into habituation for security and dependability.

In summary, there are four qualities that are needed to build and sustain relationships with a high level of love and appreciation. The first quality is to know what you want and what the person you care about wants. Ask yourself what makes you feel loved, wanted, cared about, and respected. Find the answers in non-equivocal sensory-rich detail. Don't assume they are the same for your mate. Ask. Discover what makes them feel loved, wanted, appreciated, cared about, and respected.

The second quality is to have the willingness and the flexibility of behavior to express and manifest your partner's important positive behavioral complex equivalences in the way they need them to be expressed, as well as having a variety of ways to elicit from your partner the behaviors and responses that you desire.

The third quality is to have the sensory acuity to notice those cues that would indicate whether you or your partner had slipped out of the desired positive states of attraction, appreciation, and habituation.

The fourth quality is to have the skills and commitment to lead yourself or your partner back to attraction, appreciation, and habituation if it should ever be necessary.

As long as these four qualities remain present, two people can stay in the state of incredible wonder and appreciation, with the comfort, security, and richness that characterize a fulfilling and mature relationship. These qualities establish and help maintain a solid foundation, enabling a couple to prevail with intensity and passion over any of life's obstacles.

III Techniques to Replace Problems with Fulfillment

Chapter 10: Anchoring

Once you understand your client's present state and know what set of experiences would constitute the desired state, your task is to evolve your client *from* the present state *to* the desired state. It's important that you have available a number of effective choices to accomplish this change. With a number of choices, a method can be chosen for its appropriateness both to the client and for the specific problem content.

Just as a carpenter carefully selects the right saw for any particular job, and the seamstress chooses from a wide variety of needles—some for silk and gauze, some for crewel or leather—an effective therapist must decide which intervention or combination of interventions best suits the needs of each particular client. There are many different ways to effect change. My purpose in offering you the following interventions is to provide you with a variety of effective tools, each one tailored for use with certain specific types of problems. Having a large repertoire of techniques will allow you to do appropriate and effective change work, transforming your client's experience from a set of limitations to a set of choices.

A basic premise of my work is that people have all the resources they need to make the changes they want and need to make. My job is to assist them in accessing and organizing their resources to make those desired changes an accomplished fact. Regardless of whether or not this basic premise is true in actuality, when I structure my behavior *as if* it is true the results provide ample testimony to its usefulness.

The resources I am speaking of here lie in each of our personal histories. Each and every experience we have ever had can serve as an asset. Most everyone has had an experience of being confident, or daring, or assertive, or relaxed at some time. Each of those experiences is a possible resource. My task is to make those resources available in the contexts in which they are needed. Bandler, Grinder, DeLozier and I have developed a method called *anchoring* which does just that.

In the same way that certain external stimuli become associated with past experiences (thus recalling the past experience), you can *deliberately associate* a stimulus to a specific experience. Once this association has taken place, you can then trigger the experience at will. It works in the same way that language does.

For instance, if I ask you to remember a time when you felt very confident, a time when you felt truly satisfied with yourself, my words send you on a search through your past experiences. As you access various memories congruent with being confident and satisfied with yourself, various aspects of those experiences come into the present experience. Similarly, you are probably familiar with how you can become angry again by remembering an argument, or frightened again by remembering a terrifying movie or incident. By bringing up a memory (an internally generated experience), we re-experience many of the same feelings that occurred when that memory was formed.

Anchoring uses this natural process by making a deliberate association between a stimulus and a specific experience. Examples of this, with which everyone is already familiar, are our responses to hearing the national anthem or seeing our flag, or perhaps our response to being given the "finger." The Russians may have understood this principle when, after the Revolution, they kept all the melodies of their national songs and merely changed the lyrics. The melodies were already associated with patriotic responses, so merely changing the lyrics made the new associations nearly automatic. As a further example, have you, as an adult, visited a grammar school and been flooded with memories and feelings that were a part of your childhood? Can you remember the first time you were passionately kissed, really recalling the fullness of that experience and all the feelings associated with that kiss?

These are all examples of some aspect (some stimulus) of your *present* experience recalling or triggering you to a *past* experience such that your feelings become congruent with that previous experience. I have learned that by deliberately inserting some discreet new stimulus while a person is fully in touch with an experience, that new stimulus then becomes associated with the recalled experience. That new stimulus could be a sound, a touch, a specific visual input, or even a smell or a taste. If the timing is good, re-inducing the same exact stimulus brings back the feelings of the recalled experience. This procedure is called *anchoring*. The specific inserted stimulus is referred to as the *anchor*. The anchor then can be used to trigger the associated experience again and again. For instance, if you and a partner were feeling especially romantic while a particular piece of music was playing, when next you played that same music you would again be flooded with those romantic thoughts and feelings. "Your song" would be playing. Anchoring allows you to deliberately set such feelings in any chosen way and have them available whenever they are wanted or needed.

Being able to identify when a person has accessed an important experience is essential to effective anchoring. In a previous section, the connection of external stimuli with relevant experiences was discussed. That discussion accentuated the importance of recognizing specific expressions. Since you cannot know exactly what internal state a person is experiencing by their expression, you must depend upon your senses to detect the external expressions of an internal experience and be able to tell one experience from another. With anchoring, the specific areas that are useful to focus upon—because they change radically enough to be easily detectable—are voice tone, skin color, lip size, facial muscle tone, skin temperature, breathing rate, and breathing location (from upper or lower chest). By eliciting various intense responses that correspond to different internal states, you can recognize and differentiate a person's various expressions.

You can elicit various intense responses simply by asking someone to access a series of past emotions, such as when they were last angry, or frightened, or passionate, and then watch and listen for changes. The more you practice the more you will be able to detect the important differences. A person's lips may become thinner, face color paler, and breathing more shallow when remembering a frightening experience; whereas lips typically are fuller, color flushed and breathing deeper with a softening of facial muscle tone when accessing passionate memory feelings. Your eyes and ears will become increasingly accustomed to detecting such minimal distinctions the more you do this. Should you detect no change or very little change in your subject's responses, check two things. First, are your own voice tone, facial expression and words congruent with the response you are asking for? The more expressive you are, the more expressiveness you are apt to elicit. Your own behavior needs to be congruent with the response you are asking for. If you are asking for a passionate memory, ask for it with an appropriate voice tone and facial expression: perhaps a throatier, lower, sultry voice with a wink. Your success with anchoring is very much dependent upon your own flexibility of behavior since you will often be using your own expressiveness to elicit desired responses.

Second, check whether your clients are remembering the asked-for past experiences by *being* in the picture, or by *seeing* themselves in the picture. Remember that seeing themselves in the picture is a constructed image, and so can often be detected by noticing your clients' accessing cues. If you are not sure whether they are seeing themselves in the picture or not, then ask them directly. It is crucial to discover this because if they are seeing themselves in the picture they will not be re-experiencing the past feelings; they will, instead, be experiencing feelings *about* the past experience. To exemplify, I would like you to picture yourself on a rollercoaster and see yourself in the first seat going up that first big hill, so you are *watching yourself* sitting in the rollercoaster. Then bring your own body into the picture so that you can feel yourself sitting in that seat looking up, feeling the rollercoaster pulling you higher and higher to the peak of that big hill, where you can see *all* the way down. Then feel your stomach rise as your body drops, listening to your own scream as you race towards the bottom. Obviously, there is a big difference between the two images. The difference is crucial. If your client is watching himself in that past experience, you will not be anchoring the powerful feelings which would be occurring if he was inside his picture. If you discover that, indeed, he is watching himself, merely ask him to step inside the picture and feel what he felt then, hearing the sounds which occurred then, and seeing just what he saw in that past experience.

Once you can elicit and detect various expressions, you can anchor them. That is, while observing a full expression (an external representation of an internal experience) that would be useful to have access to for therapeutic purposes, you can supply a stimulus to which the expression becomes associated. (This might be a touch on the back of the hand or a snap of the fingers.) With proper timing, firing off that stimulus will bring back the same expression, which means it will bring back the associated internal state as well.

Many therapists already use this process by using a special voice tone and tempo when doing guided fantasy or hypnosis.

This voice tone becomes an anchor for the altered states that are experienced when it is used. In Gestalt chair work, too, each of the two chairs becomes an anchor for a different emotional state and a client changes radically as they move from one chair to the other.

In order to anchor a response successfully you should follow three rules:

☐ Have your client access the desired experience (or induce it) as powerfully and fully as possible.

☐ Insert your stimulus at the moment of fullest expression or most intense response. Timing is crucial!

☐ Be sure your stimulus can be reproduced *exactly*. Repeating the stimulus will bring back the internal state fully *only* if it is repeated exactly. Although I may describe establishing an anchor as touching a client's knee or shoulder or the back of a hand, I want you to know that in actuality it is a far more specific touch. I repeat those touches exactly, even as to pressure. You can and should test these guidelines in your own experience, both to verify them and to discover what, if any, leeway exists.

Using anchoring as described here gives you access to a client's various experiential states. A common complaint about working with mentally disturbed people is that they change who, what, and how they are with great rapidity. As soon as a therapist is headed in a useful direction with such a client, the end experience is that the client goes somewhere else. Anchoring can serve to steady the client's emotional state, allowing the therapist the opportunity to arrive at a desired goal.

Desirable sexual experiences can also be anchored. Couples often already have useful anchors available to them. One man always knew he was in for a fantastic evening if his wife put on a specific nightgown. Seeing her in that nightgown aroused him immediately. Thus, the nightgown served as an anchor that triggered a state of arousal in him. Another couple had set up cues to one another concerning their sexual desires—cues based upon which side of the bed they got into. I have discovered that women frequently use a specific nonverbal behavior, a directed touch, which signals their mate that they are ready or eager for penile entry.

In cases of sexual dysfunction, too, there are anchors that trigger the unwanted experience. Often the anchor is outside of the person's conscious awareness, and they are aware only of the resulting unwanted experience.

A young woman, Melissa came to me for therapy because of sexual dysfunction. She became absolutely petrified when men approached her sexually. When asked to merely describe her experience as a man approached her, she became terrified. So, I anchored this response. Then, while using that anchor to trigger the same set of feelings, I asked her to go back through her past and to describe other times when she had those same feelings.

The point was not to gather information concerning how it was possible for her to be frightened when men approached her; it was to get an experiential answer to the question, "What stops you from being comfortable when you are approached by men?" The precise steps to this method of gathering information are:

1. Identify the expression (the external cues) that indicates that the client is experiencing the unwanted state.

2. Anchor this state with a touch that can be repeated and sustained.

3. Hold the anchor and, as the client experiences the unwanted feelings, instruct them to travel into the past to find other times they have had the same feelings.

4. As the client moves further back into his or her personal history, use overlapping (pg. 177) to help them recover the full details of the individual past experiences. (This allows them to have more choices than if the full details are left out of conscious awareness—see "When Lead and Primary Representational System Differ," page 66) Listen for information revealed by the client's description of these experiences that would be relevant to the present state.

5. Bring the client back to the present, making sure they are comfortable and secure. Ask what was learned from this journey into the past.

Using the technique of anchoring this way allowed me to take Melissa back through her personal history to a long-forgotten childhood incident: a time when it seemed her mother had induced a male friend of the family to demonstrate seductive behavior toward Melissa. As he did so, her mother had forcefully impressed upon her the warning that a man who behaved in such a way intended to hurt her very badly, and that this behavior meant that the man was dangerous and she was to run as fast and as far away as she could. Once this material was available to Melissa's conscious mind, it was quite easy for her to leave her mother's well-intentioned message behind. Melissa now believed that she no longer needed the protection such a message was intended to provide and that she could, in fact, protect herself from dangerous men in other ways. Using anchoring, we then accessed experiences from Melissa's past that provided more appropriate resources for realizing her present desires.

Anchoring with Couples

Anchoring can also be used to make desired responses more available to members of couples. When a couple comes for therapy, their whole history of mutually-shared experiences is available as a resource. The fact that they are a couple indicates they wanted each other at some time in the past, that they perhaps loved each other, and that they had dreams about a good future. At the very least, they have gotten through some hard times together.

Anchoring allows me to access and employ these past experiences to build a better relationship for them now. And, if they are seeking therapy, now is just when re-experiencing the feelings that brought them together can be very useful.

For instance, with a couple who came to me for counseling, each time she would give him her sexiest come-hither look he thought she looked funny, even ridiculous. Her come-hither look was definitely not eliciting the response she desired from him. Her tendency was to find and respond to men who *would* respond to her come-hither look as she wanted them to. Yet she loved her husband and stated she would be content if only he would respond in a manner that validated her sexuality. One choice at that point would have been for me to teach her to stop giving him that come-hither look, and then to find some new behavior that would better provide what she wanted. But changing external behavior is often a long-term goal, one that takes time and strong motivation on the part of the individual to achieve.

Another alternative, easier to effect, was simply to ask him to remember a time when he really felt she was sexy—perhaps when they first met or during their courtship, I didn't know when for sure, but surely there was a time when he just couldn't resist her attraction. I chose this method and used my analogue behavior— voice tone, body posture, etc.—to help him remember a time when he really desired her. When I observed changes in his breathing, skin color and lip size, and heard changes in his voice tone and tempo, that indicated that he was indeed remembering such a time—and when I was certain that he was remembering it well enough to be actually re-experiencing those feelings of desire—*at that moment* I inserted a discreet and covert cue (an anchor) into his experience. Since the timing of my anchor was concomitant with his remembered feelings, each time I used that anchor he would again have that same experience. In this case, the anchor was a touch on the shoulder which, since I touch people frequently as I talk to them, could be gracefully repeated without distracting from the particular experience.

I then *tested* the anchor by touching his shoulder just as I had before and checking closely to be certain I was getting exactly the same response as the original expression (facial tension, lip size, breathing patterns, etc.). After ascertaining that the anchor worked, I triggered the anchor each time she gave him her come-hither look, which I had her do repeatedly.

By doing this, I was working to associate his experience of desiring her (which I could bring back by touching his shoulder) with her come-hither look. Thus, I obtained the response that she wanted from him and associated it with *her* behavior. Of course, another choice would have been for her to merely touch his shoulder when she wanted him to know how much she desired him, thus giving him an opportunity to respond. My preference, though, was to access the desired experience in him as a response to her *naturally-occurring* behavior.

Anchoring also proved useful in working with a woman who participated in a workshop in Tucson. Her problem was that although she loved her husband dearly, she was not sexually attracted to him. Much older than she, he did not fit the Adonis image she found stimulating. This problem had caused trouble for quite some time in their otherwise very happy relationship.

Since this woman generated her body feelings primarily from internal images—that is, she used a visual lead to a kinesthetic representation—I merely asked her to imagine the perfect male image and then signal by nodding her head when she had it. As she visualized various male bodies, the color of her skin flushed, her lips swelled, and her breathing became deeper. As she began to nod, I reached out and touched her lightly on the right shoulder as I said, "Excellent, I'm sure he's very beautiful." I had thereby associated a very specific touch on her right shoulder with the experience she had while visualizing the perfect male physique. She was not aware of this consciously. Shortly thereafter, as we continued our talk, I again repeated the touch on her right shoulder to determine if the anchoring was successfully done. It was; the same expression that had occurred came back again. I then asked her to visualize her husband standing naked before her and to nod when she could see him clearly. As she began to nod this time, I said, "Good, now continue to look at him and notice how your feelings change as you see him in a new way." As I said these words, I again repeated the touch on her shoulder, triggering the response she desired to have with her husband. Her breathing became deeper, her skin tone flushed, and her lips swelled as they had done before. I repeated this process twice more while we were together. When her husband came to pick her up at the end of the day, I took advantage of his presence by instructing him privately in just how to touch her on the shoulder when he wanted her to know that he desired her. As he tried it in my office, I watched closely to make sure the anchor worked when he touched her. (I needed to make sure that her response was to the touch, and not in part to me.) The touch on the shoulder would not be needed for very long because the experience of being aroused by the visual experience of her husband would generalize. In the meantime, his special touches would continue to be meaningful. In this way, I used the process of anchoring to locate the desired experience (one of being aroused) and then associated it with the context in which this woman wanted to experience it.

Besides Touching

Thus far in my presentation of anchoring I have primarily discussed the use of kinesthetic anchors. Because touching is a natural aspect of my own communication pattern, this form of anchoring is easy for me to use. There are, however, other advantages to using kinesthetic anchors. One is that they can be held, and thus the effect sustained more readily than visual or auditory anchors. In terms of teaching the process in seminars, my specific touching can be made obvious to the audience, therefore facilitating the teaching process. Also, when transferring the use of an anchor, a touch can be repeated by another person with greater accuracy than a voice tone or visual facial expression. This increases my client's ability to use that anchor effectively.

However, there are special properties of visual and auditory anchors which make them preferable to some people and in some contexts. Richard Bandler uses, almost exclusively, changes in his voice tone and tempo as auditory anchors. Because such shifts are subtle to all but the most trained ear, these anchors remain far outside of conscious awareness. The ability to purposefully alter voice quality comes easily to Richard, whereas I have spent much time learning to bring such subtle aspects of my behavior under my own conscious control. I was impressed by the usefulness of such an ability years ago during a session with a couple. Richard and I were working with them together and I noticed that he was using the husband's tonality and intonation patterns in his own voice to anchor the wife each time either of us elicited a powerful positive response from her. Thus the husband's naturally-occurring tonality and intonation patterns would and did continue to elicit positive responses from his wife. In this way a general and pervasive mood change between them was accomplished.

Auditory anchors can run the gamut from these kinds of subtle voice changes to pencil tapping, chair squeaking, music, or even clock chiming. The importance is the timing of the anchor and being able to repeat the same auditory stimulus at will.

Likewise, there are special properties that make the use of visual anchors most appropriate for certain people and certain contexts. In situations of potential violence a visual anchor is more appropriate than a kinesthetic one, since getting close enough to touch could be dangerous. While working with a woman whose husband was prone to violent reactions, I taught her how to take an impressive karate stance. (Her husband was not participating in therapy.) I then gave her instructions that should a violent situation seem imminent, and if she could not get away or feel as if she could not adequately defend herself, she was to take that stance. Such a situation did arise and she did take the stance. Her description of her husband's reaction was that he stopped cold, looked confused, and then burst out laughing. I did not know he would have that specific response, but I was going by the rule that new and different behavior will elicit new and different responses. Because this stance elicited such a useful response from her husband, I instructed her to use it whenever tensions began to mount. Thus it became a useful visual anchor which elicited humor from her previously angry husband.

So anchoring in any modality can be useful. You can determine the advisability of using a particular anchor by answering these questions: How appropriate is the anchor to the context? How easily can it be repeated? Can it be done as a naturalistic behavior and thus be integrated into everyday interactions?

Chapter 11: Changing Personal History

Our personal histories are our memories of past experiences and, as such, they can be changed. The benefits of being able to alter your memories, and therefore your history, are demonstrated by the work I did with another client, Chuck. Chuck believed he was a complete failure with women, especially in the sexual context. Judging by his behavior, it was easy to concur with his belief. He had been in therapy for two years and had been referred to me by his male therapist, a psychologist, who thought I would be especially effective in helping Chuck with this problem area.

Chuck was completely certain about his likelihood of failure with women in almost any situation, but he was acutely certain concerning sexual encounters. He stated that his certainty was based on past experience and that he could not imagine things ever being different or better in the future. As we talked, I learned that Chuck's behavior was generally predicated upon past events. He used eidetic (past) images to guide his present behavior. What he did well in life, he did very well—over and over again. He used these eidetic images as a lead system and then represented them kinesthetically as feelings about what he was going to do. So, whenever he came into contact with a woman, he accessed visual images from past unsuccessful experiences with women (the only kind he had) and felt sure he was going to blow it again. And, of course, he did. In order to quickly change his habitual behavior with respect to women, I needed to alter these past eidetic images. To accomplish this I employed *changing history*, a technique which utilizes anchoring. The partial transcript which follows illustrates the use of this very important technique:

LCB: Chuck, can you tell me again how you feel when you approach a woman?

Chuck: Well, sure. If anything I'd like to forget it. But I just feel really shitty, you know. (*As he answered, I watched closely to see if the same expression that he had before re-occurred when talking of women. Part of this expression was an up and left accessing cue.*)

LCB: (*When the expression was fully there, I touched him on the right knee.*) Good, it's important that you remember that feeling just now.

Chuck: Oh, yeah. Why?

LCB: You'll understand very soon. Now, take that feeling, (*I touched him again on the right knee and held it there, watching the expression come back*) that "really shitty" feeling, and tell me what scene from your past comes to mind.

Chuck: Well, it's a time from a couple of years ago when I was out with this woman. I, uh, made a pass at her. Wow! It was a real disaster!

LCB: I believe you. Now, what I want you to do is take that same feeling and go back in time. Back through your past and find other scenes in which you had this feeling.

Chuck: (*Closes eyes*) Okay.

LCB: That's right. And just go back and I'll stop you from time to time.

As Chuck searched through his past on the pathway provided by this particular feeling, he remembered other experiences for which this feeling is representative. So while other content portions of the experiences changed—like who was there, how old he was, what was said by whom, etc.—the feeling portion of the experiences remained constant. While he was doing this, I watched for subtle exaggerations of the expression: greater intensity of skin color, deepening of lines in the forehead and around the mouth, tightening of the lips, and changes in breathing. These exaggerations indicated that he was remembering especially intense experiences during which this unpleasant feeling occurred.

Holding the anchor constant keeps the feeling constant, and therefore insures that the search through time is done on the pathway of a specific feeling. When I saw an exaggeration, I said to Chuck:

LCB: There! Stop there. Take a really good look at that scene. Does it make sense to you in relationship to your feelings? (*With my other hand, I mark out this specific experience with a touch on his other knee so I'll be able to come back to it later.*)

Chuck: Yes, yes it does.

LCB: And how old are you there?

Chuck: Oh, I was sixteen then.

LCB: Good, good. Now continue traveling back through time just as you were.

Chuck: Okay.

Again, I wait for the exaggerations. The moments slip by until there is a very gross exaggeration of his expression:

LCB: Stop there. Take a really close look at that scene. Tell me, how old are you?

Chuck: I'm about six (*voice quality is higher, more childlike than before*).

LCB: And what's happening to you there, Chuck?

Chuck: I'm in parochial school. God, I hated school and I'm in trouble with the nuns. I don't know what for, but I really remember that somehow this was the first time I ever realized that nuns were women. I don't know what I thought they were before, but this is the first time I knew they were women.

LCB: (*Again, I marked this with a different touch on the knee, making it possible to facilitate his going back to this experience; then I take my hands from his knees.*) Now, Chuck, I want you to come back here. Open your eyes and see me. Hi. That was quite a trip you took. Are you all the way back here now? Can you feel the back of the chair?

Chuck: Yeah, sure I'm here.

LCB: Good. What I'd like you to do now is to think about what resource you would have needed in those experiences in order for them to have been good ones, so that they would have been experiences that you felt really satisfied about.

Chuck: What do you mean by resources?

LCB: Like being confident, or assertive, or relaxed. If you had been able to be assertive, say, then you would have acted differently and those experiences might have happened in a way that satisfied you instead of giving you that shitty feeling.

Chuck: Well, what I needed was for the women in those experiences to like me.

LCB: I agree; but what could you have done to get them to like you?

Chuck: I don't know.

LCB: Do you get along well with men?

Chuck: Yeah, pretty good.

LCB: What resource do you have in dealing with men that makes it so different?

Chuck: I don't know. I guess I'm just relaxed. Yeah, just real relaxed. I don't worry about what's going to happen. I just feel like it doesn't really matter.

LCB: Good, good. That's what I'm after. Chuck, go ahead now and remember a time when you were really relaxed in the way you just described, a time when maybe somebody else would have been nervous but you were really calm and relaxed (*as I said this, I calmly leaned forward so I could reach his arm to anchor this experience*).

Chuck: Sure, I got one.

LCB: Good (*touching his forearm*). Tell me about it.

Chuck: I asked my boss for a raise and I was just as calm as could be. It didn't really matter what he said. I had nothing to lose so I felt really relaxed.

LCB: Great (*taking hand from arm*). A lot of people couldn't have done that. You know those feelings of being really relaxed? (*I touch his arm again and I can see the relaxed expression come back.*)

Chuck: Yeah.

LCB: Well, what I want you to do is to take *these* feelings of relaxation back to those other experiences. So, starting with the most recent one that you took a close look at, I want you to take these feelings with you and notice how different everything is. (*These feelings are kept present by keeping my hand on his forearm, thus using the anchor to fire off relaxed feelings.*) Notice how you behave with *these feelings* and how differently those women respond.

Chuck: Okay.

LCB: Good. When you've gone through that first experience and are completely satisfied with it, and only when you are completely satisfied with it, I want you to nod your head. Now, go ahead.

Chuck: (*Time passes, and Chuck nods.*)

LCB: Excellent, and now I want you to go back to that time when you were sixteen (*I trigger the anchor on the knee with my other hand, which marks out that experience*), and do it over again as you did with the last experience. And, again, when you've gone through it completely and are completely satisfied with it, just nod.

Chuck: (*Again, time passes and Chuck nods.*)

LCB: Excellent. Now, I want you to do the same thing with the last experience (*I trigger the appropriate anchor*), the one where you were six and were dealing with the nuns. Just do the same thing that you did before.

Chuck: (*Time passes, and Chuck begins to frown slightly.*)

LCB: Oh, oh. What's happening?

Chuck: I'm not sure, but I just can't make this one okay. It's better than it was, but I still feel a little shitty.

LCB: That's okay. It just means you need some other resource. (*I release the anchors by removing my hands*) After all, sometimes a six-year-old boy needs all the help he can get when it comes to getting into trouble with the nuns. Come back and let's figure out what else you need to take back there with you. (*Chuck opens his eyes and returns to the here and now.*) Now, what do you think the six-year-old needed?

Chuck: Well, they made me feel like I was really bad. Really bad and dirty.

LCB: But you know better than that now, don't you?

Chuck: After two years of therapy, I should hope so.

LCB: Good. Now tell me about a time when you did something wonderful, maybe something nice for someone else that made you feel like a *really good* person.

Chuck: Hmmm, let's see (*eyes up and left*). Well, I, uh, helped my next-door neighbor fix his car. I don't even know him, but he was having lots of trouble and I could see him out the window and I just went out and gave him a hand. It took the whole afternoon, but I feel like that was a real nice thing to do. (*As he describes this incident, I again anchor him on the forearm with my other hand.*)

LCB: Makes me wish you were my neighbor. Now, you know those feelings of feeling really good about yourself, really knowing you're a good human being (*I trigger the anchor*)?

Chuck: Yeah.

LCB: And those feelings of being very relaxed? (*I trigger the relaxation anchor, so I now have both hands on his forearm, simultaneously firing off both resource anchors.*)

Chuck: Yeah.

LCB: Well, take *all* these feelings back and revisit the nuns, and just nod when that experience has happened in a way that really satisfies you.

Chuck: (*Chuck closes his eyes. A few moments pass, and he grins broadly and nods his head.*)

LCB: (*I let go of his arm*) Great. Really makes a difference when you can take your resources where you need them, doesn't it?

Chuck: It sure does. Those experiences just seem kind of funny to me now.

LCB: Do they? Good. Then go back and remember them again and find out for sure.

Chuck: Okay (*closes eyes, sits quietly for a few moments, then smiles*). Yeah, they weren't any big deal.

LCB: Excellent. Now, when is the next time you're going to make contact with a woman? Other than me, of course.

Chuck: (*Laughs*) Oh, you don't count. You're a therapist.

LCB: Thanks a lot. But when will you make contact with a woman that will be somehow meaningful?

Chuck: Well, I won't, unless I make one happen.

LCB: When is your first opportunity to do just that?

Chuck: Well, I could approach Sally. She's a girl at work that's single and attractive.

LCB: Great. What I want you to do is to imagine how you'll approach her, but be sure to take that sense of relaxation and those good feelings about yourself along, okay? (*I am now using no anchors in order to learn if the changes that have occurred concerning past perceptions will generalize into future imaginings.*)

Chuck: Okay (*closes eyes, sits quietly, gives a half-smile and chuckles*).

LCB: How'd you do with Sally?

Chuck: Well, pretty good. I didn't make like Paul Newman or anything, but I didn't feel scared about talking to her.

LCB: Fantastic. That deserves a handshake. So, you really felt okay about talking to her. That's just great. (*We ritualistically shake hands. Thus, shaking hands can also be an anchor for this successful internally generated experience and can be triggered in the future by a handshake.*)

From this point, it was easy to assist Chuck with future projections and role playing in order for him to be relaxed and comfortable about relating to women. By taking resources and incorporating them into a context where they are needed, it is possible to change a person's history. In a sense, Chuck's history had stopped him from expressing new behaviors. Until his history was subjectively changed, he could only continue to live out a predetermined present and future with regard to women. Our personal histories are sets of perceptions about past experiences and, as such, can be altered. Chuck used his memories of the past to anticipate and even program himself for the future. To a large degree this is true for all of us. With Chuck, changing the past with respect to women, in a way that resulted in good feelings and a sense of satisfaction, also allowed him to change his present and future behavior. Just as only one trauma easily generalizes to many associated contexts, I have found that only a few important past experiences need be changed for generalizations to occur in connection with other related past experiences as well. Changing history produced an alternate set of eidetic images for Chuck to recall when he thinks about relating to women. Usually only one added resource is needed to effectively use changing history. In Chuck's case, his experience with the nuns was so powerful that a second resource was needed.

The tremendous effectiveness of changing history was discovered when I paid attention to how people can distort their internally generated experience and then act on the distortion, forgetting that they created it in the first place. For instance, jealousy is an experience almost always generated as the result of a person making constructed images of a loved one with someone else, and then feeling bad in response to the picture they have themselves created. This picture and feeling are then acted upon just as though they had been experienced externally. In fact, it is sometimes impossible to convince the jealous person that his or her imaginings did not actually take place. Once a constructed image is made, it can be stored and recalled as an eidetic image. Because of this, a person must remember in some system other than visual if he or she is going to know that they created it.

Changing history is a utilization of this same process. The fuller and richer in detail the internally generated history change is, the greater the possibility of it being given equal validity with the "real" history. Because of our ability to store experiences and draw upon them as resources, the changed history becomes an accomplished experience and thus can serve as a foundation for the future. The steps for the changing history technique are:

1. Anchor the unwanted or unpleasant feeling.

2. Use this anchor to assist the client in going back through time, finding other times when he or she felt this way.

3. When exaggerations of the expression are noticed, stop the client and have them see the full experience, noting their age when the experience took place. Establish an anchor for each experience so you can get back to the specific experience if needed (these anchors can be auditory or kinesthetic).

4. Once the client has identified three or four such experiences, release that anchor and bring them back to the present.

5. Ask the client to identify the resource they needed to have in those past situations for them to have been satisfying experiences. Be sure the resource is one which influences the client's behavior and subjective experience. Many people, like Chuck, think everything would be fine if only the other people were somehow different. The point, however, is for the *client* to have been different and thus to make new learnings by eliciting different responses from the other people involved in that past experience. Once the needed resource is identified, assist them in accessing an experience where they genuinely exhibited that resource fully. Anchor it.

6. Using the resource anchor, have the client go to each of the already identified past experiences and change them using the added resource. You can use the anchors which designate each of the three or four experiences to assist the client in going directly to them. When they are satisfied with the changed experience, have them nod and then proceed to the next one. (If your client is not satisfied with the new outcome produced in the old experience, move back to step 5. Get another resource, or a different resource more appropriate to the specific past experience, then proceed to step 6 again.)

7. Have the client remember the past experiences with no anchors to discover if, indeed, those memories have subjectively changed.

8. When past experiences have been changed, have the client future-pace the changes. That is, have them imagine the next time a situation similar to the past ones is likely to occur, suggesting they take the needed resource along. Use no anchors. This is a way of testing for whether the changes have generalized and been fully integrated.

This technique gives you a way of knowing what result you are going for, a way of getting that result, and a way of testing for the attainment of that result. It is best to use kinesthetic anchors with this technique because they can be held constant, as opposed to auditory anchors which are difficult to sustain and visual anchors which are ineffectual if the client's eyes are closed. If you are working with a client who cannot "see" pictures, then use the process of overlapping (page 177) to bring visualizations into consciousness before proceeding with the changing history technique.

Changing Personal History with Couples

This same procedure is also useful with couples. If both persons keep bringing up a bad experience—an argument, a situation where they hurt each other's feelings, or a time in which one of them was especially offended—use changing history on it. It will take care of the pain it is bringing them now, clean the slate for the future, and educate them concerning what to do next time the same kind of situation arises. Since they already have the significant incident identified, you can lead them right to it. (Actually it is often difficult to lead them *away* from such memories until you effect some positive change regarding it.) Once they are both accessing their memories of what happened, have them identify for themselves what they most wanted to have happen, and what resource(s) they needed to manifest in order to have brought about a more satisfying resolution to that past experience. Do not have them describe what took place, as it is very unlikely that they will completely agree—and arguing is what you are leading them away from, not to. Be sure to emphasize that this process is about each of *them* being different, not their partner. Assist them individually in accessing the resource and taking it back to the past incident. When each of them is satisfied with their internal representation of the past, you can have them apply the same resource to other similar bad times to check on the usefulness of their chosen resources. The next step is to identify a present area of conflict that resembles the past incident. Use the resource anchors and set them loose with one another to bring the present conflict to a mutually satisfying resolution. If there is no present conflict (some people just fight about the past, making the past their present conflict), have them re-enact the past one, using the resources to bring it to a mutually satisfying conclusion in the present. Certainly, you can do both if you want to. If at any point they are doing badly, stop them. Ask each person what other personal resource would help. If you perceive that one (or both) of them are further into the threshold pattern than the stage of expectation, leave out the enactment in the present until you have evidence of mutual commitment toward making their relationship better. Otherwise, the unconscious commitment is to build a case for the negative rather than for the positive, and their partner's behavior will be experienced only through that filter. The steps prior to enactment are useful regardless of where in the threshold pattern they are. The emphasis on their own behavior, and their ability to influence the quality of their experience, empowers them and directs them away from blaming their partner.

Chapter 12: Visual-Kinesthetic Dissociation

Sometimes clients who seek therapy are suffering from the results of a severely traumatic past experience. Their response is so intense, when anything associated with the trauma occurs in their present experience they become overwhelmed by feelings that are pertinent to the prior episode. In short, they have a phobic response.

This was the case with the woman mentioned earlier, who had a phobic response to the sight of an erect penis. The case histories presented by Masters and Johnson cite a gentleman who walked in on his wife completing intercourse with her lover; he was thereafter impotent with her. Each time he began to make love to her, he would visually flash back to that unfortunate incident and again feel as he did then.

All phobic responses have this same form: An external stimulus triggers feelings associated with a past or, sometimes, a future projected traumatic experience. This is not only the case with phobic sexual dysfunction, but is also true for phobias concerning heights, darkness, closed-in places, and so on. Often the past incident is unavailable to the client's conscious awareness. In such cases, going back through time (as in the changing history technique) and then overlapping (pg. 177) from feelings to visual and auditory modalities can bring the past experiences into consciousness.

Occasionally, it is difficult to find a subjectively positive experience powerful enough to counteract the overwhelming terror or grief typical of phobic responses. When this occurs, simple anchoring techniques are not sufficient. It then becomes necessary to find a way to take as much of the intensity out of the trauma as possible.

One way of successfully doing this is to assist the client in disassociating from the *feelings* connected with the trauma. Specifically, the three-place *visual-kinesthetic dissociation* technique is applicable in such cases. This technique takes advantage of some of the unique aspects of internal visualization. If a person visually recalls an experience as though they are in it, they have the feelings contained in the experience itself. But when people *see themselves* going through an experience, they have feelings *about* what they see.

While my colleagues and I were investigating the relevance of accessing cues to human behavior, we discovered that some people remembered their past pleasant and unpleasant experiences in different visual ways. Unpleasant past experiences were remembered in constructed images (that is, they saw themselves in the picture and thus had feelings *about* the past experience) whereas pleasant past experiences were remembered as eidetic images (they were in the picture and directly re-experienced the pleasant feelings from the past). This natural unconscious sorting process allows the individual the luxury of re-experiencing past pleasantries and dissociating from past unpleasant feelings, while still keeping all of those experiences available to the conscious mind. In this way, the conscious mind can learn from past traumas without re-experiencing them. People whose unconscious processes make the aforementioned distinctions recover fairly easily from unfortunate or unpleasant experiences. Because they can think back to them from a dissociated point of view, the pain is lessened and the perspective is clearer.

Phobic responses occur when people actually re-experience the unpleasant feelings that were present during the trauma. The technique of three-place visual-kinesthetic dissociation employs the process described above and enhances it with added dissociation and anchoring. The technique involves having people watch themselves from a third position, which allows them to watch themselves watching themselves going through the traumatic experience. In this way people can remain comfortable while still remembering the experience because the kinesthetic (feeling) portion is dissociated from the visual memory. Since the two-place dissociation that is naturally occurring in some people is sometimes not enough to keep the phobic client from collapsing into the reality of the trauma, the use of the third place is added as insurance against the occurrence of this undesirable possibility.

I have used this technique hundreds of times and for just as many different kinds of traumas. One woman, who had witnessed the death of her young daughter and was still immobilized by grief two years later, was able to put the experience behind her and go on. A man whose first sexual experience had been painfully traumatic found it to be something he could smile at rather than something that continually inhibited him.

I used this technique with both members of a couple seeking counseling after an experience that had been traumatic for both of them. She had had a double mastectomy and when she first exposed her naked body to him he could not hide his shock from her. Taking each of them through this process greatly assisted them in re-establishing the tender sexuality that existed before her surgery. Following is a brief description of the use of this technique with a particularly difficult and dramatic case.

I was called in by the police to work with a woman, Jessica, who had been the victim of an especially brutal rape. She was unable to give the authorities any information concerning her assailant because any reference to the incident triggered such a psychotic episode that sedation was required. She also reacted violently to being touched or handled by male hospital personnel, making it difficult for the staff to care for her physical needs. She refused to allow her boyfriend to visit her and became extremely upset when he came anyway.

Jessica had been in the hospital a bit more than three days when I came to work with her. During our first two sessions, one in the morning and one in the evening, I concentrated on establishing trust and rapport with her, and immediately began establishing powerful anchors with her for safety and comfort. Using hypnotic techniques, I was able to assist her in recalling times of safety and security from her childhood and I anchored those experiences. She would sometimes say she didn't know if she could hold on, so I established her holding on to my arm as an anchor for feeling safe and for staying in the present experience.

Since I already knew that I would use the three-place visual-kinesthetic dissociation technique with her, I needed to be a powerful anchor myself as well as to have access to her own strong feelings of comfort and security. Only with these would I be able to keep her from accessing the feelings associated with the experience of being raped, which belonged in the past and not in her present experience. After our third session, I believed the necessary trust and the appropriate anchors had been established. Under the circumstances, we were doing very well. The fourth session proceeded as follows:

LCB: Jessica, you trust me, don't you?

Jessica: Yes. Yes, I trust you.

LCB: Good, because I'm going to talk to you and I know that since you trust me, you'll be sure to hear what I say. Jessica, you're here with me in this room. And just you and I are here. You're sitting comfortably in the bed and I'm beside you. Can you feel my arm? (*Jessica reaches for my forearm.*) Feels good to hold on to someone, doesn't it?

Jessica: Yes.

LCB: You remember how safe you can be as long as you hold my arm? (*Jessica nods yes.*) Jessica, something happened to a *part* of you a few days ago. (*In this case I used the description of a "part" in order to further dissociate Jessica from the incident.*)

Jessica: (*Jessica begins to tighten and show a fear response.*)

LCB: Just hold on, Jessica. You're here now. Here with me, very safe. Take a breath and look at me. (*She complies and visibly relaxes.*) What happened, happened to just a part of you, not all of you. Do you understand? Just a part of you. And you're here now. (*Jessica nods and continues to hold onto my arm.*) That part of you needs your help, Jessica. It needs you to make some learnings so it can be okay again. You're here now and safe with me, and you can be very strong and even very solid. But, right now, that part of you isn't and it needs you. It will be hard for all of you to feel as good as you can feel until that part gets the help she needs. You know I'm right here, don't you, Jessica? Will you begin with me to help that part of you?

Jessica: (*Jessica nods her head yes.*)

LCB: Excellent. Now, Jessica, the last time this part of you was just fine was right *before* something bad happened to her. What I would like you to do is to see that part of you—her—out in front of you. But see her the way she was *before* anything bad happened. Just nod to me when you can see her out in front of you.

Jessica: (*Jessica's pupils dilate, facial muscle tone relaxes. She is still holding on. She nods.*) Okay, I can see her.

LCB: That's very good, Jessica. How does she look? Does she look okay to you there? (*indicating by gesture the* *location of the visualization.*) Can you see how she is dressed?

Jessica: Yes. She's wearing jeans and a blue T-shirt.

LCB: Good. Now keep her there and you feel yourself holding my arm.

Jessica: Yeah.

LCB: Now, Jessica, I want you to begin to float outside of your body to just in back of yourself—so that you can see yourself sitting here next to me. See yourself holding my arm and watching the part of Jessica that needs help out in front. So you float outside until you can see Jessica next to me watching the younger Jessica out in front. You'll be watching yourself watching yourself. When you can see yourself here with me, nod your head.

Jessica: *(Jessica becomes completely still, her breathing is more shallow, and her hand rests lightly on my arm. She nods.)*

LCB: *(I reach over with my other hand and place it atop her hand in order to anchor this third-place dissociation.)* That's very good. Now, you can begin to help *that* part of you that's *there* in front. The slightly *younger* Jessica over *there*. Slowly watch as the scene begins to transpire. Let *that* part of you show *you* what happened so *you* can know how to help *her*. Making sure that *you remain comfortable* watching Jessica *today* watch the *younger* Jessica go through *that* experience that happened *then*.

As Jessica proceeded to visualize herself in the past experience from the third place, I watched closely for any sign of her becoming associated with the experience (that is, having the feelings of being raped instead of the feelings of being safe and comfortable with me in the present). During the next few minutes I repeated these suggestions and instructions several times:

LCB: *You,* Jessica, feeling comfortable *here, now,* as you watch yourself watching the *younger* Jessica over *there,* going through *that* experience. And *you're* learning. Learning what that *younger* Jessica will need from *you.*

Whenever I observed changes in breathing or tightening muscles indicating she was collapsing into the the reality of the rape scene, I used the anchor on her arm to help her stay in the third-place dissociation and repeated the directions, emphasizing those words which reinforced the dissociative process: *her, there,* the *younger Jessica* (anything before the present is younger even if it refers to only four days previously); *you, here, now, Jessica of today, safe,* and so on.

As she proceeded, Jessica's eyes welled with tears and soon they streamed down her face.

LCB: That's fine, Jessica. Watch yourself here with me, crying for her. She deserves your tears and when *that* experience is over and *that younger* Jessica from *then* is quiet, nod your head.

Jessica's tears were a response to what had happened rather than a re-experiencing of the assault. Jessica continued to cry silently, her eyes open and pupils dilated, staring straight ahead at the scene before her. After a few minutes passed, she nodded.

LCB: Very good, Jessica. And I know you've seen a lot and I know you've learned a lot. Now, I want you to float back into your body—here, next to me—feeling your hand on my arm reminding you of safe feelings of now. When you are back inside, just nod again.

Jessica: (*Jessica nods.*)

LCB: All right, Jessica. You've just watched the younger you go through a dreadful experience. She needs a lot from you. Soon you'll go to her, take her in your arms and hold her, reassuring her that you're from her future and that it's going to be all right. There are other people who will help, and you can reassure her that she will feel safe again. Jessica, she needs to know that you love her and care about her. She needs to know that she is going to be okay, and, especially, that you appreciate her. She went through a very horrible experience and you can appreciate her for doing the very best she could. Are you ready to do that, Jessica?

Jessica: (*She nods, and is now beginning to sob. She reaches in front of herself, arms outstretched, and brings them into herself, rocking and sobbing.*)

During the following sessions with Jessica, I used the same three-place dissociation to help recover important information for the police concerning the assailant. She improved very quickly and her boyfriend proved to be helpful and supportive. Our final sessions were used as premarital counseling for them.

The steps for three-place visual-kinesthetic dissociation are:

1. Establish a powerful anchor for solid comfort.

2. Holding the anchor, have the client visualize the younger self out in front in the very first scene of the traumatic incident, making it a still-shot. Thus, they are sitting there, next to you, seeing their younger self before them.

3. When they can see the younger self clearly, have them float out of their body so that they can see the first self sitting there next to you watching the younger self. There are now three of them: the visual perspective remains from the third place, the actual body in the second and the younger self going through the trauma in the first place. When this three-place dissociation is accomplished, anchor it.

4. Now have the person run the experience through, making sure they remain kinesthetically dissociated from the traumatic incident by the use of anchors and by the use of verbal patterns which separate out the three places—*him, there, the younger you, that experience, what happened then, you, here, today, watching yourself,* etc.

5. When the experience has been completely seen, have the person float back from the third place into the second place (so the visual perspective is being integrated with the actual body position of the client).

6. Have the present-day person go to the younger one (the one who went through the traumatic experience) and reassure the younger self that they are from the future, and have them give the younger self needed comfort and appreciation.

7. When the present-day person can see that the visualized younger self understands, have them integrate by bringing that younger part back inside their own body.

The following diagram will help clarify the steps involved.

You anchor the client (2) to feel secure in the present. Then the client visualizes their younger self (1), then floats out of their body to the visual perspective of (3). Anchor this dissociative state. From (3) the traumatic episode is run through, after which (3) integrates back to (2). Then (2) comforts and reassures (1) and finally (2) brings (1) back into (2), and only you and your client are there.

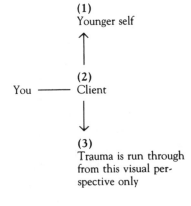

(1)
Younger self

↑

(2)
You —— Client

↓

(3)
Trauma is run through from this visual perspective only

If at any time your client should collapse realities and begin re-experiencing the feelings contained within the past trauma, stop. Bring them back to the present completely, re-establish the first powerful positive anchor and begin again. In a few cases, I have had to stop and start this process two or three times before the person was able to remain dissociated enough for the whole process to be completed.

This process first carefully dissociates the client and then fully integrates the dissociated parts of the person. This is an effective method for dealing with those cases that involve a very powerful past experience that negatively influences a client's present experience. Typical comments made by clients about this process are "It brought things into perspective," "I can remember the incident, but I'm not overwhelmed by it anymore," and "I thought I just wanted to forget that awful thing ever happened, but now I think it's good; I learned a lot from it."

Associating into Experience

The inverse of the process just described is useful for clients suffering from *loss* of body sensations: For example a woman who feels nothing in her entire pelvic region or a man whose impotence stems from experiencing only numbness in his penis. With cases such as these, I have found it very effective to have the person visualize themselves clearly and to have their visualized self be quite obviously enjoying the sexual experience. When they can really see themselves responding with full sensation (in the man's case, seeing himself with a full erection), I then have the person feel himself or herself floating over and into their own visualization. Thus, they associate into the kinesthetic portion of the desired visual experience by *stepping into the picture.*

The process of association, then, is the inverse of the visual-kinesthetic dissociation process. Clients visualize themselves in a scene and adjust the picture until it is just right for them. They then step into themselves in the picture in order to feel the feelings which are congruent with the projected experience.

This is also an exquisite technique for accomplishing self-image changes and for preparing a client to express new behaviors. It is also an educational tool. When leading seminars, I often ask participants to picture themselves interacting in their idea of a perfect relationship. When they have such a picture, I ask them to step into themselves and notice how it feels. Does this indeed feel like a perfect relationship, or should they change their image of what such a relationship is like? If it does feel like the perfect relationship, I have them memorize how they are responding and behaving toward the other person. They can then use this memory in making ongoing evaluations of their behavior. This helps insure that they continue to manifest the qualities and characteristics which they have identified as integral to making their desired future a reality.

Chapter 13: Reframing

The belief that underlies the process of *reframing* is that every behavior (internal and external), every symptom, and every communication is useful and meaningful in some way. Inherent within the structure of reframing is the belief that people have all the resources they need to make any desired change. This may or may not be true. What is important is that when I organize my behavior as though it were true, positive change becomes easier to accomplish. Remember that we humans never experience the world directly, but instead create maps or models of our world experience such that the only reality we ever know is a subjective reality. Adopting the above belief provides you with a terrific advantage. Since subjective realities can be altered and reorganized, we are given the opportunity to mold our realities in useful and beneficial ways.

So that this may be clear to you in a concrete way, I would like to present a typical example of how I use this belief to produce change in my clients' subjective realities. During a seminar in New York, a couple asked for help with a very specific and somewhat unusual problem. It seemed that the carpeting in their house was plush and showed every footprint. Now this was, of course, not a problem in and of itself, but the woman was compulsive about vacuuming the carpet so no footprints showed. Since every time anyone walked on it there were footprints, she did a lot of vacuuming. This drove everyone crazy, and was a source of tremendous tension between her and her husband. Every time she looked at the footprinted carpet, she felt bad and could not feel good until she had vacuumed it. After listening to this description, I asked myself how footprints on the carpet could be experienced as a positive occurrence by this woman in a way that she would not feel the need to constantly vacuum. The answer made my task an easy one. I asked her to close her eyes and see her carpeted home—to see that the carpet was perfect, not a single strand of it out of place. And as she was enjoying seeing the carpet so perfect, I told her she could become aware that there was also complete silence in her house; and as she listened to the silence, she could realize she was *all* alone. Her loved ones were gone and she was *all alone* with her perfect carpet. It was only now, I told her, that she would finally realize that every footprint that appeared on that carpet was a sign that her loved ones were near, and that she was with her family. So each time in the future, whenever she would see a footprint on the carpet, she could feel the closeness of her family and the love she felt toward them. Like Mother's Day presents saved year after year, each footprint could be looked upon warmly. After all, I said to her, whose small or large foot had stepped there for her to see?

By doing what I did, I reframed "footprints on the carpet" to trigger warm, loving feelings rather than compulsive cleanliness. As strange as this may sound, it worked with her and, really, it makes more sense to feel good about footprints than it does to feel bad about them.

Besides this type of reframing, there are step-by-step explicit techniques of reframing that have been developed by my colleagues and me to accomplish positive change. These techniques can be integrated into a client's behavior so that he or she can accomplish personal change without need of a therapist. While other therapeutic and conflict resolution methods work with the *content* of individual problems, these explicit reframing techniques work to reorganize a person's internal processes into integrated *process-oriented resources* that can be applied to any type of internal conflict. This is accomplished by providing for the maximum employment of resources and a free flow of communication within that person. We refer to such a reorganized person as being *generative*. They are capable of generating new behavior and even a new reorganization of self should the need or the desire arise.

In comparison with other therapeutic models (which for the most part are implicitly methods of organizing human beings such that the complexity of behavior is reduced so the therapist can more successfully cope with it), reframing is a method of organizing the organization of human systems. Therapeutic models that are concerned with accomplishing a particular change or resolving a particular conflict ignore the possibility of constructing a generative system that can resolve future conflict and induce future change on its own. With reframing, a particular change is achieved or a particular conflict is resolved by a process that can be generalized to other contexts and integrated into the ongoing behavior of the human system, whether that system is an individual, a couple, or any other type of human systemic organization.

Six-Step Reframing—Separating Intention from Behavior

There are essentially two types of reframing: *six-step reframing*, which separates intentions from behaviors, and *contextual reframing*. Six-step reframing, the process of separating intention from behavior, is comprised of six explicit and sequential steps:

1. Identify an unwanted behavior. Identify a specific unwanted behavior or symptom. The behavior may be any physiological symptom or any action that your client cannot keep from exhibiting. It could be any behavior that prevents or inhibits the client from acting in a desired way.

2. Contact the part that generates the identified behavior. This step begins the building of a bridge between conscious and unconscious processes. The client uses internal dialogue to ask, "Is the part of me that generates this behavior willing to communicate with me?" The client then pays exquisite attention to any response—any sounds, pictures, feelings, or words. You also watch for any noticeable behavioral response of which your client may be unaware.

If the response is other than words, be sure to make the communication as unambiguous as possible. This can be accomplished by establishing an intensifying of the response as a *yes* and a diminishing of it as *no*. For instance, a brighter picture or a louder sound or a stronger feeling would indicate an affirmative response. If the behavior is a symptom, using it as a means of communication is most effective; if the symptom is numbness, for example, have it spread to indicate *yes* and diminish to indicate *no*.

3. Separate intention from behavior. Once communication has been established, the task is to discover the intention behind the behavior. Thus, have your client ask, "What are you trying to do for me?" Again, the answer may come in pictures, words, or feelings. If only feelings occur, and it's impossible to make sense from them, use overlapping (page 177) to build a more complete representation.

Sometimes the answer will seem to be an undesirable intention, like "I'm trying to kill you." or "I'm keeping you from having sex." When this happens, take another step back by having them ask, "What are you trying to do for me by killing me?" This allows you to obtain a more useful answer, such as "I'm trying to save you from this miserable life that just keeps dragging on." or "If you have sex, you'll get hurt and that will be bad." In this example, this extra step back revealed the intention to be one of protection. Always continue to step back until a positive intention is discovered.

4. Find three new ways to satisfy the intention. This is most commonly done by accessing the person's creative part (or clever part, or intelligent part, or scheming part, etc.) and having it generate three new, more satisfying ways to accomplish the intention. If the person doesn't have a creative part, build one. This can be done by having them remember a time when he or she has been creative and then establishing an anchor that gives access to that creativeness (the creative part). If they claim to have never been creative, ask if he or she knows of anyone considered creative. If yes, have them imagine that person, visually and auditorily, and then have that imagined person generate three better ways to satisfy the intention. (Of course, the answers are still generated from the client's own internal processes, but this technique can serve to bypass feelings of "I can't do it.") The least desirable choice, but still a choice, is for you to suggest possible alternatives.

5. Have the originally-identified part accept the new choices and the responsibility for generating them when needed. You now have your client ask the original part if it agrees that the three new choices are at least as effective as the original, unwanted behavior. If it says "yes" (using the pre-established mode of communication to insure continuity), have them ask if it is willing to accept responsibility for generating the new behaviors in appropriate contexts.

If it doesn't agree that the new choices are better than the original behavior, have your client ask it to go and work with the creative part to come up with better ones. If it won't take responsibility for generating the new behaviors (this *very* rarely happens), access a part that will.

6. Make an ecological check. For the final step, instruct your client to ask on the inside if any part objects to the negotiations that have taken place. If there is an affirmative response, be sure to establish that it is a *yes* response by following the procedure described in step two. If there is an objection, cycle back through the process by identifying the objection, separating intention from objection, and so on through the rest of the steps. When there are no objections during the ecological check, the process is complete.

If, as sometimes happens, the part that generates the unwanted behavior refuses to communicate in consciousness, the following steps, which bypass the client's conscious awareness, can be substituted for the ones listed above:

Step 2. Even a no response is a communication and can be used. So presuppose that contact has been made and proceed to the next step.

Steps 3 and 4. Ask the part if it knows what it's doing for the person. If it answers *yes*, have it go to the creative part on its own and get three new ways to do it better. Just have it signal in a specific way when it has accomplished this.

The rest of the steps require only a yes/no response and the conscious mind need not know the specific content of the new behaviors. Since changes in six-step reframing come about without conscious intervention, this experience often provides the client with a foundation for greater respect and appreciation for his unconscious processes.

In rare cases, a part may respond negatively, saying it doesn't know what it does for the person. After you have asked it if it's sure of this, you can then directly ask it to *stop* generating the undesired behavior. In all my experience with six-step reframing, such a response has only occurred once. The part said it had forgotten what the intention was. It complied with the instructions, though, by stopping the unwanted behavior (bed-wetting).

Contextual Reframing

The second type of reframing is *contextual reframing*, which presupposes that *all* behaviors are useful in *some* context. With this technique, the task is to identify the context in which the behavior is appropriate, and then to attach the behavior to that context. The steps are the same as previously outlined, except step three becomes *establishing the useful context,* and step four is necessary only if the part generating the behavior doesn't know of any appropriate context. When this occurs, the creative part can be called upon to generate possible appropriate contexts. In step five, the part accepts responsibility for generating the behavior *only* in the appropriate contexts.

In the following transcript I demonstrate the use of a combination of these reframing techniques with a client, Tom, who suffered from impotency.

LCB: Now, Tom, I know that the part of you that is keeping you from responding is trying to do something positive for you. So, what I want you to do is go inside and ask what that part of you is trying to do, paying close attention to any words, pictures, sounds, or feelings that occur.

Tom: (*Closes eyes momentarily, body pulls back as if avoiding being struck.*)

LCB: So what happened?

Tom: I asked the question, but nobody answered.

LCB: Oh yes they did; what happened?

Tom: Well, I saw my mother just like she was when . . . well . . . you know. (*Tom was seduced by his mother while still in his teens and was unable to perform adequately. This inadequacy has continued to the present.*)

LCB: And . . .

Tom: And nothing . . . I had the same feeling I always do when I remember my mother that way.

LCB: And you don't think that picture and resultant feeling had anything to do with the question you just asked?

Tom: Well, when you put it that way . . . but my mother is dead and gone. What's that got to do with me now?

LCB: She's dead and gone, but the picture isn't. Now, go inside and ask if that part of you will tell you what it is trying to do for you. If the answer is yes, have it show you the same picture again. If no, have it do something else.

Tom: (*Closes eyes, manifests same involuntary pulling back.*)

LCB: Good, the answer is yes.

Tom: How did you know?

LCB: It was easy. Ask it to go ahead and tell you.

Tom: (*Closes eyes for a few moments and then opens his eyes but sits quietly for a few moments more.*)

LCB: Well?

Tom: It says it's trying to protect me from my mother.

LCB: Do you agree that you needed protection from your mother and perhaps things connected with your mother?

Tom: Yes, sure.

LCB: Like what?

Tom: She was a dreadful bitch. Castrating. She would've destroyed me.

LCB: Oh, so you agree that you needed protection from her.

Tom: Yeah, but . . . but how's not being able to get it up going to protect me from her? And she's dead now.

LCB: I don't know. Can you *see* how it may have protected you from her then?

Tom: Hmmmm (*eyes up-left, right, left*). Yeah.

LCB: Like it or not, there are parts of you that believe you still need protection from being destroyed or castrated or however you want to talk about it, right?

Tom: Yeah, but not like that.

LCB: I want you to go to your creative part and ask it to suggest three *other* ways to protect you.

Tom: My creative part?

LCB: Yes, I know you have one. Just go inside and give it a chance to do its thing. It may respond in pictures, words, feelings, or such, and you may not understand, but just pay exquisite attention to your experience.

Tom: (*Closes eyes for awhile; nods head once, twice, three times; smiles.*) Okay, I got it.

LCB: What have you got?

Tom: Well, I asked inside like you said and at first nothing happened. Then I started seeing these short movies. I saw myself punch her out, really smack her up the side of her head. Then another picture of me walking out on her. Right out the front door. Then, best of all, I just laughed in her face. Ha, ha, ha, ha.

LCB: Great. Those sound like much better choices. By the way, who was in your pictures?

Tom: Why, my wife (*pause*) of course. Wow, my wife.

LCB: Hmmm, how 'bout that? Well, never mind that now.

Let's go on. Now, I want you to ask the part of you that made you impotent in the first place if it agrees that these are more useful ways of protecting you. Pay attention to your experience. If the answer is yes, have it show you a picture of your mother again.

Tom: (*Closes eyes*) It said yes. Can't we give it another way to say yes? That is so unpleasant.

LCB: Of course. Ask it to say yes another way. Perhaps a warm, tingling sensation along your midline.

Tom: (*Closes eyes, opens eyes, smiles*) Okay.

LCB: Now ask it if it is willing to generate those new behaviors for you whenever they are needed. Since it is the part that generated the original problem, it already knows when you need those behaviors. Right?

Tom: Right.

LCB: Wrong.

Tom: Huh?

LCB: Wrong. Unless you consider sexual encounters as the time to smack your mate, walk out on her, or laugh in her face. (*Moving from separating intention to behavioral reframing to contextualizing the new behaviors.*)

Tom: Oh, yeah. But it would have been good to do with my old lady—I mean, my mother.

LCB: Yes, but that was then, not now. How can you tell when it's time to protect yourself from those things your mother tried to do to you?

Tom: You mean did to me . . . I don't know.

LCB: Go inside and ask your creative part to show you when you need to use those behaviors.

Tom: (*Closes eyes for awhile, facial expression changes, color becomes redder, frowns, lips tighten, opens eyes*) Okay.

LCB: Okay. So, how do you know when it's time to use those behaviors?

Tom: (*Eyes down, right*) When I feel pushed. When someone is trying to take advantage of me. You know, when they're trying to hurt me, make me do something I don't want to.

LCB: When they're trying to make you do something you don't want to do. Okay. So, go back and ask if that part—the first one—agrees that when you feel that way, *pushed,* that it's time to generate the smacking, walking out, or laughing behaviors.

Tom: Okay. (*Closes eyes*) I can't remember what to ask it.

LCB: (*Repeats directions given above.*)

Tom: (*Closes eyes, smiles*) It says yes. I think it understands this better than I do.

LCB: Let's hope so (*smiling*). It's the one that really counts. So, ask it if it will generate the new, more useful behaviors at the appropriate times instead of the old one. You know the old one—impotence.

Tom: Okay. (*Closes eyes*) It answered with the warm feeling. What if I just get that warm feeling and it doesn't really mean anything?

LCB: Distrustful S.O.B., aren't you? Ask it a question you know it will answer no to and find out what happens.

Tom: Okay. (*Eyes up, left; then closed, taking on Tom's usual go-inside posture; eyes open, laughs.*) Well, it sure didn't give the warm, good feeling; that's for sure.

LCB: Oh yeah, want to tell me what you asked it?

Tom: No (*reddening*). I think I'll keep it to myself.

LCB: Well, do you believe it now? Ask if there is any part that has any objection to the negotiations that have taken place.

Tom: Okay. (*Closes eyes*) I got a queer feeling.

LCB: Ask if the queer feelings means there's an objection.

Tom: (*Closes eyes*) I got the queer feeling again.

LCB: Wait a minute. Ask if all your parts are satisfied with what took place.

Tom: (*Goes inside, smiles.*) I got the warm, good feeling.

LCB: Ask it if that means yes to give the same answer.

Tom: (*Closes eyes, smiles.*) It or they did.

LCB: Good, we have to be careful about keeping yeses and nos separate. Well, this means it's *time* for you to have a *coming out party* if you know what I mean (*laughter*). But I want you to wait for at least a week while your parts *get used to the changes*. And, no matter how much you *respond*, to wait until you can *wait no longer*. For *you* are now going *to begin* to learn new, more delightful ways of responding to sexual stimuli. With no need for the old ways, they will be replaced. But we'll talk about that then.

With Tom, reframing served to allow a much-despised behavior make its usefulness known to him. Tom's impotence could then be seen by him as being useful in protecting him from what his mother might do to him. Although he still needed protection at times from people other than his mother, he was able to find that more useful behaviors were available to him—more useful behaviors that were presented by his own internal resources. Still, the *timing* for such behaviors was not yet appropriate; the new behaviors needed to be the result of appropriate stimuli. So this transcript demonstrates an integration of the two processes of reframing: separating intention from behavior, and finding the appropriate context.

When reframing is done with a more-than-one-member human system (a couple, for instance), it follows the same steps already presented, but it uses the other member(s) of the system as creative resources. The following partial transcript of a counseling session with a couple illustrates the use of reframing in this therapeutic context.

LCB: Tony, what would you like changed with your wife and you to make you happy?

Tony: I'd like her to stop her bitching and nagging me all the time.

LCB: And you, Nancy, what would you like changed?

Nancy: Him.

LCB: Yes, but what, specifically, about him? Pick something to start with.

Nancy: His constant moping and whining. I can't stand it.

LCB: Okay, you want him to stop moping and whining and he wants you to stop bitching.

Tony: So we trade?

LCB: I don't think that would work for very long. Tony, I want you to really think about this very carefully. What is it you would really like Nancy to do when you're moping around? Now, really think about it and tell me when you have an answer. While he's doing that, I'd like you, Nancy, to do the same about your nagging.

Nancy: Oh, that's easy. I want him to get off his ass and do something around the house.

LCB: So, what you're really after with all that nagging is to get a helpful response out of Tony. Is that right? (*Intention separated from behavior.*)

Nancy: Yes.

Tony: Well, what I really want is some support from Nancy—for her to understand how tired I get and not to pressure me.

LCB: So, when you're moping about what you're really after is some support? (*Intention separated from behavior.*)

Tony: Yeah.

LCB: How, specifically, would you like Nancy to support you?

Tony: You know, maybe put her arms around me, pamper me a little, make me feel appreciated.

LCB: So, if she came and put her arms around you and pampered you, talked to you—nice things like that— you would feel supported by her. Right?

Tony: Yeah, I would.

LCB: Well, what I know is that right now the way you let her know that you want her support is to mope around. And your moping around just makes her want to nag and bitch at you. Right, Nancy?

Nancy: Right.

LCB: Now, wanting to be supported is fine, and getting that wanted support is important. But you've been doing just exactly the right thing to get nagging and bitching and just the wrong thing to get supported, at least by Nancy. So, congratulations, you now have the perfect way to get Nancy to bitch at you.

Tony: Oh, thanks a lot.

LCB: Would you like some ways to actually get from Nancy what you *do* want?

Tony: Of course, but I'll be damned if I know how.

LCB: I believe you. But there's someone in this room who could tell you exactly how to get the support you want.

Tony: So tell me already.

LCB: Oh, I don't know, but *she* does. Nancy, what is it that this man could do that would get him the needed support? Only you know. (*Nancy is used in the same manner as a creative part.*)

Nancy: Well, I never thought about . . .

LCB: Now's your chance. You can tell him how to act instead of that moping. He was just moping to get your attention, but the attention he got wasn't the kind he wanted. So, what could Tony do that would get you to put your arms around him, pamper him a little. You know, that sort of thing.

Nancy: Well, if he was just nice to me.

LCB: Let's be more specific. Can you remember ever feeling like you wanted to do just what it is he wants?

Nancy: Well, sure, I must've sometime.

LCB: That's right. And what did he do to get you to feel like doing that?

Nancy: I'm not sure he ever did this, but if he would just come and put his arms around me and tell me he's dead tired or wiped out and that he needs me, I'd fall all over myself pampering him.

LCB: Great. Listen to that, Tony. There's your answer. Can you do that? Put your arms around her and tell her you're dead tired and that you need her?

Tony: Sure, I can do that; it just never occurred to me, that's all.

LCB: Do you know when you need that support, Tony? I mean, do you have a way of telling when it's time to get yourself some support, instead of time to mope? (*Establish context to generate new behavior.*)

Tony: Oh, yeah. I know that. I can really feel it when things are slipping out from under me. That's when I need support.

LCB: That's beautiful. So, do you both think this new arrangement is better than the old one?

Tony: Yeah.

Nancy: Yeah.

LCB: Good. Now, about that nagging . . . (*The reframing process continued, with Nancy using Tony as the creative part.*)

Communicating with a Symptom

As I mentioned before, it is possible to use reframing to rid a person of problematic symptoms by establishing communication with the symptom. In the following example, Carol came to therapy seeking help to alleviate recurring headaches. Probably everyone suffers from headaches now and then, but Carol's headaches formed a significant pattern. They occurred when she was in a situation that involved being alone with a man, and disappeared when this situation changed. Except in this particular context, Carol was calm and adroit in social situations.

Knowing that such a systematic behavioral pattern constituted a meaningful communication from her unconscious processes, I chose to use reframing with Carol. I began by giving her these instructions:

LCB: Carol, can you remember the last time you were alone with a man?

Carol: Yes (*her eyes drift down and right, her forehead and temples obviously contract as the muscles around her eyes tighten*).

LCB: And, as you remember, do you also re-experience some of the headache?

Carol: Yes. God, yes; I do.

LCB: Good. Look at me and tell me when it's gone.

Carol: (*She complies; in a few moments her muscles relax and her forehead again becomes smooth.*)

LCB: Carol, I want you to use your internal dialogue and go inside and ask, "Is the part of me that gives me the headaches willing to communicate with me in consciousness?" Then I want you to pay attention to any feelings, pictures, sounds, or words that occur—any response whatsoever. Go ahead.

Carol: Okay (*her eyes go down and left, and then again the same facial muscles contract*).

LCB: Good. I can see that it responded.

Carol: Well, I got a twinge of my headache if that's what you mean.

LCB: Excellent. You couldn't ask for a better response. (*It's preferable to use the symptom as the vehicle of communication. It provides assurance that communication has been established with the appropriate part or unconscious process.*)

Now, we must make sure that we understand that part of you correctly. So, I want you to go inside and say, "If this feeling in my head means yes, and you are willing to communicate with me in consciousness, then intensify the feeling; if no, then make it go away." Okay. Do you understand?

Carol: Yes, I do. (*Carol closes her eyes and soon the same mus-*

cle contraction occurs. These muscle contractions now serve as a visual means for me to know what answers Carol is getting, while she is experiencing the same phenomenon kinesthetically. Shortly, Carol opens her eyes.) It intensified the feeling.

LCB: That's good. Now we have a way of explicitly communicating with that part. Go inside and thank it for communicating with you.

Carol: (*She complies.*)

LCB: Now go inside and ask it if it would be willing to tell you what it is trying to do for you by giving you the headaches.

Carol: (*Carol nods, and exhibits her going-inside behavior. Again, her facial muscles contract.*) I got the pain again, so I guess it is willing to tell me. It's hard for me to believe it's doing something good for me.

LCB: I believe you. But I know that it is. All your behaviors are meaningful in some way. Go inside and say "thank you" again and ask it to go ahead and tell you what it is trying to do for you. It may tell you in words or pictures—whatever.

Carol: Okay. (*Closes eyes for several moments.*) Hmmm.

LCB: Did you understand its answer?

Carol: Oh, I understand it. It said it's protecting me because I can't say no, especially to men.

LCB: Well, did you know that before?

Carol: No. No, I had no idea. Actually, because of the headaches, I've never even had to say no.

LCB: Well, then, it's done a very effective job, hasn't it?

Carol: Yeah, I guess so.

LCB: Do you agree that its intention is positive? Do you want to be protected from the consequences of not being able to say no to men?

Carol: I'd rather just say no.

LCB: Could you?

Carol: Well . . . I think so.

LCB: So, *you* think so, but *that part* of you apparently doesn't agree.

Carol: Well, actually, I really do have trouble saying no to people, especially men.

LCB: So, perhaps you do need that protection, at least until you learn how to say no.

Carol: Yeah, I do need it. Before I got the headaches, I, uh, got myself into a lot of trouble. I agree it has a good intention.

LCB: You just don't like the way it's been satisfying that intention, right?

Carol: Yes.

LCB: Until you're adept at saying no when it's necessary, would you like to continue to be protected from the consequences of not being able to say no?

Carol: Yes.

LCB: Go inside and thank that part of you for having protected you these past years.

Carol: Okay (*Closes eyes*).

LCB: Now, do you have a part of you that you consider to be your creative part?

Carol: Yeah, yeah I do.

LCB: Good. I want you to go to your creative part and ask it if it would be willing to generate three other ways to satisfy the same intention while you're learning to say no.

Carol: Okay. (*Closes eyes, smiles.*) It says yes.

LCB: How did it say yes?

Carol: It spelled Y-E-S in bright rainbow colors, just the way a creative part should.

LCB: Great. Ask it to go ahead.

Carol: (*Carol shuts her eyes and leans her head back. She nods once, twice, then three times.*) Okay, I've got them.

LCB: Do you want to tell me what they are?

Carol: Sure. One is only to be alone with men I want to say yes to. Two is to make myself ugly so he won't want me anyway. And three is to occupy him in activities that lead away from sex instead of toward it.

LCB: Okay. Now, take those three new choices to the part that gives you headaches and ask it if it agrees these will work at least as well as the headaches.

Carol: Okay. (*Closes eyes for several moments, then her facial muscles contract.*) Ouch! It says yes.

LCB: Good. Ask it if it will generate the new choices in the needed context.

Carol: (*Closes eyes; facial muscles contract and then relax.*) It

175

said yes and then the headache disappeared.

LCB: Great! So much for the headaches. Now, ask inside if any part objects to the negotiations that have taken place.

Carol: (*Closes eyes*) Yes. I get a printout that says YES.

LCB: Ask what the objection is.

Carol: It says in big, bold, block letters, LEARN TO SAY NO!

LCB: I agree fully. Go inside and reassure that part that that's exactly what you are going to do, and since it has no trouble in raising an objection it can be very helpful in that process.

Carol: Okay. It says OKAY in big, bold, block letters.

LCB: Good. Ask if there are any other objections to the negotiations that have taken place.

Carol: (*Closes eyes; opens eyes*) Everything seems fine. I feel great.

Carol learned to identify an unwanted behavior (headaches) as a way of satisfying a positive intention (staying out of trouble). She established communication between her conscious verbal processes and the unconscious processes generating her symptom. In later sessions, I assisted Carol in accessing and organizing her responses to enable her to say no gracefully in appropriate contexts. Also, we employed reframing with other content so that the process itself could be integrated into her behavior. Soon she was able to do it on her own, obviating the need for a therapist.

Sexual dysfunction often is a manifestation of incongruity between conscious and unconscious behavioral processes. Reframing brings these processes into alignment by establishing a meta system that is directed toward the well-being of the entire organism. This meta system is a verbalizing part that can contact and communicate with all other parts at the conscious or unconscious level. It does not take sides, and it does not label behavior or parts as bad or sick. Instead, it simply acts as a negotiator to bring various factions of an individual or a couple into alignment. In this way, all of the inherent resources are used to achieve the goals agreed upon by the entire system (person, couple, or family). Once all the steps of reframing are learned and integrated into a person's natural behavior, that person can accomplish any number of desired changes on their own.

Chapter 14: Overlapping

A fundamental method of evolving a client is to assist them in generating rich, full, vivid internal experiences involving all sensory modalities. Besides producing a profound altered state experience, this develops their abilities to use their internal processes as the resources they are: the tools required to generate needed experiences. *Overlapping* is a technique used to accomplish the construction of such experiences. Overlapping begins with a verbalization congruent with a client's primary representational system, and then continues by adding the other sensory modalities one at a time. This is done verbally, using the natural points of intersection that exist between the senses.

For example, if you are a highly visual person, this process begins by your making an image of, say, a tree or grove of trees. Once you can see the trees clearly in front of you, noticing the varying colors and shapes of leaves and branches, then you can begin to observe the beginnings of movement, the gentle swaying of the leaves and branches. As you watch the leaves and branches swaying, you can begin to hear the sounds of the breeze as it blows gently through the trees, rustling the leaves. And, as you listen to the sound of the breeze whispering past, you can begin to feel its coolness as it brushes past your face. With the coolness of the breeze across your face, you can smell the freshness of the breeze as it wafts the fragrance of the trees to you.

Beginning with the visual experience—the image of a tree—and then overlapping sensory experience at natural points of intersection, you are able to expand the original representation to include all the sensory modalities of a vibrant, internally generated experience. If you can see the wind moving the leaves and branches, then it's a short step to hearing the sound of the wind. Hearing the wind, surely it's also possible to feel it blowing across your face. And, if you can feel the breeze, it is only a small step to smelling the freshness of the breeze and the fragrance of the trees which you can see so clearly.

Our senses work together in this way to create whole experiences. Starting from any of the sensory modalities and progressing through the natural points of intersection, a full, rich experience can be quite easily constructed. Our senses work this way *naturally*. It would be odd, indeed, to see a drop of water on your arm and not simultaneously feel its wetness and perhaps hear the sound of falling rain and smell the dampness in the air. When you use overlapping, it is helpful to the process to use evocative words that are appropriate to the sensory system being described. Below are the words I used in the preceding example.

Visual	Auditory	Kinesthetic	Olfactory
see	hear	feel	smell
clearly	sound	coolness	freshness
image	rustling	brushes	fragrance
colors	listen	catch	
shapes	whispers		
watch			

To use overlapping effectively, you need to describe the underlying characteristics of each modality. Here is a brief list of sensory-specific characteristics for each system:

Visual	Auditory	Kinesthetic	Olfactory/Gustatory
color	tempo	weight	odor
brightness	volume	temperature	concentration
saturation	pitch	density	essence
location	location	location	texture
texture	timbre	texture	fragrance
clarity		movement	moisture
shape		shapes	taste
movement			temperature

Although overlapping representational systems is a technique that is effective in and of itself, it is often an integral aspect of communication patterns designed to enrich a person's experience. It is especially useful with clients who are unable to focus their consciousness on the kinesthetic portion of experience in the sexual context.

In order for the natural sequence of internal and external processes which make up the successful sexual experience to take place, the kinesthetic portion of experience—i.e., body feelings—must be in consciousness. By beginning with whatever is in consciousness and then adding the other modalities, body feelings come into awareness and can be emphasized.

Overlapping can be a valuable way of assisting those people whose internal processes interfere with their ability to sense, partially or completely, the intense pleasure of the sexual experience. Overlapping brings portions of experience that were outside of conscious awareness into consciousness, and also serves to align the internal and external processes so that the experience becomes congruent.

In teaching the very highly visual person to use what he or she sees to lead them to their feelings, I have used overlapping in these ways:

"Look at him. Do you see him clearly? Good. Now, as he leans closer and you see that very special look in his eyes, you can begin to wonder, really wonder. And as he comes even closer, until you see his shoulder as his face is next to yours, you can begin to hear his whisper. As he whispers, you can feel his breath as it brushes your ear, perhaps tickling it slightly. His words and his nearness change the rhythm and rate of your breathing."

"As you see her hand reaching over to you and then lightly touching, you can feel the temperature of her skin as it rests next to yours."

"While you listen to the tone of your voice, you become aware of the feelings behind it."

"As you see her look at you in that very special way, you can tell yourself how much she wants you and then feel how good it feels to be desired."

"As you hear the changing rhythm of your breathing, your excitement grows."

"As you watch yourself reach out and caress her, and notice when your skin meets hers, you become aware of the texture of her skin. And as you move your hand and feel the changes from one place to another, you can watch the expression of her face."

These are examples of giving instructions that use the principle of overlapping. For those clients who have not had a successful sexual experience or who are terribly shy or inhibited, I have found it useful to lead them through guided fantasies of sexual experiences using overlapping and remaining maximally vague. This allows them to be free to internally generate an experience most satisfying to them. The art of remaining vague and yet specific enough to generate a rich guided fantasy is learned through studying language patterns, particularly those found in *Patterns of the Hypnotic Techniques of Milton H. Erickson, M.D., Volume I* by Bandler and Grinder. By remaining vague while directing verbalizations toward positive experience, I can assist a client in accessing a fantasy from their own internal resources rather than from my internal experiences. For instance, I might say, "And there can be a certain sense of satisfaction in knowing what you know." Now, "certain sense of satisfaction" doesn't specify what kind of experience that might be, and "knowing what you know" does not specify the experience of knowing, also leaving unknown what is known.

This method is especially effective with clients who typically say, "I just can't *see* myself doing that," when they are asked what stops them from having the kind of sexual experiences they desire. Such a statement tells me that their behavior would likely change if they *could* "see themselves doing that." Since seeing yourself doing something is inherently an internally generated experience, it is quite appropriate to use guided fantasy—making sure to employ the principles of overlapping to insure a rich and full experience.

Clients can be taught how to use their own internal processes to enhance their sexual experience. Once you learn how a client generates body feelings (that is, whether they do so directly, or from words, or pictures, or sounds), you can teach them how to use that information. As an example of this, I mentioned earlier a female sex therapist who complained of experiencing orgasm only with the use of a vibrator. Upon investigation, I learned that when she was making love her internal voices began to fret at her, saying, "He's getting tired, you'll never make it," and similar suggestions. When this occurred, she became worried and anxious, which diverted her consciousness away from the current sexual experience.

It was important to her lover that she have an orgasm with him, and she also wanted this very much. But, because of the anxiety produced by the voices, they would repeatedly begin their lovemaking from the original excitement phase, until the voices' description of his being tired and even bored finally were indeed true—they became a self-fulfilling prophecy.

Although there were many choices of intervention in this situation, I chose to teach her how to use her internal voices to describe her current external experience: to describe where he was touching her, the warmth of his hands, the tenderness or strength of his touch, the sound and rhythm of his and her breathing, the beating of her heart. As she learned this, I also taught her how to use those internal descriptions to bring her closer to the experience she desired. That is, I taught her how to verbally make a present experience lead to a desired one: "As I feel him moving with me, I can feel myself becoming even more aroused; breathing more and more rapidly; coming closer and closer to orgasm." These verbalizations imply that *since* she feels him moving with her she is becoming more aroused and *since* she is breathing more rapidly she is coming closer to orgasm.

Because this woman's emotional states were derived primarily from her internal dialogue, this method allowed her to feel desirous, aroused, excited, and even orgasmic. It brought external sensory experiences and internal processes into alignment in such a way as to produce her desired outcome. Later, I was pleased to learn that as she continued to use this process, the internal voices began to drop outside of her conscious awareness, leaving the fullness of the kinesthetic pleasures to occupy her attention. She also reported that she was able to induce other desired experiences—such as alertness, confidence, and a sense of calm—by employing her internal voices in the same manner.

I have also found overlapping to be useful in assisting clients in identifying with their partner's experience. Both men and women have frequently asked what I thought their partners would like of them sexually. It's almost always true that once they have had the internally generated experience of being their partner, they have come up with appropriate and creative behaviors on their own. By "being their partner" I mean imagining what they would like to experience *from themselves* sexually. This involves imagining what the other person is experiencing; that is, putting yourself in their place.

To use overlapping in this way, the client imagines stepping into their sexual partner's body. Beginning with the most typical representational system, the client uses the overlap principle to develop the full experience. They see themselves from their partner's perspective, reaching out, hearing the sound of their own words, the tone of their own voice, the touch of their own hands and body. Such an experience gives the client a source of feedback as they fully imagine themselves from their partner's perspective. During the course of this experience, clients typically alter and adjust their own imagined behavior, making it more appealing from this new perspective. Of course, the client must use the direct sensory feedback offered by the partner in the actual sexual context to know whether his or her behaviors are indeed eliciting the desired response. Follow-up reports from clients have indicated that their partners are usually delighted with the new behaviors.

This technique proved to be exceptionally effective with a woman who came to me specifically for sex counseling. She complained that she always had to take the initiative with her husband sexually, while he remained passive. Furthermore, he refused to join her for counseling and seemed content with how things were. During my initial session with this woman, I used overlapping to produce for her the experience of being her husband. As him, she very much enjoyed the sense of being so desired, and reveled in her own advances. The following week I received a call from her cancelling our next appointment. When asked the reason, she said everything was fine. She elaborated further by telling me that she had so enjoyed identifying with her husband that she shared the experience with him. She then asked him to imagine being her, which he did, and then to pretend *behaviorally* to be her. At first it seemed silly and funny for him to act like her, but she had responded so favorably that he had played the same game again later in the week. They were now taking turns being each other, alternating between being passive or taking the initiative. This woman surpassed even my expectations by creatively using her therapy experience to elicit the response she most desired from her husband. Since that time I have instructed clients who come without their partners in this and similar methods of eliciting desired behaviors on their own. When doing this, I always use overlapping to induce the client into a state of partner identification first, allowing this experience to serve as a foundation for their own subsequent actions.

Similarly, for some people, touching their mates while simultaneously imagining how this touch feels on their partner's skin is highly stimulating. This technique is especially appropriate with couples when one member has an aversion to oral sex. By imagining how their oral manipulation of their partner's genitals must feel, it can suddenly become very exciting. In questioning clients who very much enjoyed performing cunnilingus or fellatio, I found that this was in fact the strategy often used by them.

Besides being useful in the context of sexual expression, overlapping is a means to introduce useful experiences otherwise unavailable to the client. It is a frequent problem in couple therapy that one or both persons feels unloved and unlovable. This places a heavy burden on the partner to continually and dramatically demonstrate their love. This will wear on even the most loving individual. The well-formed outcome in this case should include the experience of being lovable as an internally generated ability, rather than as a continued dependency on another person. The next chapter outlines a technique that does much to accomplish this outcome.

Chapter 15: Looking at Yourself through the Eyes of Someone Who Loves You

Imagine, for the time being, that you are an author. You are writing a book in which you, yourself, are a character along with many of the people who have played parts in making your life what it is today.

It is time for you to identify someone in your life who you know loves you. It is not important that you love them, but critically important that you know that he or she loves you. Search through the people in your life until you have found that person, the person you know loves you.

You are sitting at a desk or table filled with a typewriter, papers, pen, etc. Across from you are windows, or perhaps sliding glass doors, looking out to the outside. There, occupied in some endeavor of their own, is that special someone who you *know* loves you. It has come to that time in the book you are writing to describe this very character. You sit back, looking at them, musing to yourself as you let the possibilities form of how to describe this person in words—how to capture and express in words that which makes them unique, the words which would allow a reader to see them as you do. So you describe to yourself the idiosyncratic gestures, words, looks, and behaviors that make this person who they are: their humor, passion, intellect, foolishness, blind spots, strengths and weaknesses; the small and the global that coalesce into making that person unique in all the world. You listen to your own description, feeling the feelings that come and move through you as you are watching them on the other side of the glass.

As your description draws to a close, you quietly change positions and perceptions. You float out of your place there at the table, you float outside and enter into the person on the other side of the glass—becoming that person who loves you. From there, your eyes look up from the activity in which you have been so engrossed, and you see yourself sitting there working on a book. You see yourself through the eyes of someone who loves you; seeing for the first time what someone who loves you sees as they look at you. Listening closely, you hear your own gestures, words, and looks described by someone who loves you. Seeing yourself through the eyes of someone who loves you, you recognize qualities and attributes which were unknown, or viewed as faults by your own eyes. Viewing yourself through the thoughts, perceptions, and memories of someone who loves you, you find yourself to be someone to love—someone who enriches another by the simple act of being yourself. You hear and see what it is about you this person cherishes. Holding close all that is worth knowing, you slowly come back into your own being, remembering who you are to someone who loves you.

This technique is a special form of dissociation. It brings someone outside of themselves while influencing their perception of self. It has been universally useful for developing appropriate criteria for self-evaluation, and particularly appropriate in dealing with states of depression, loneliness, and self-deprecation. It also has been consistently powerful in use with couples. It provides each person with a means to internally generate the experience of being loved, alleviating the perpetual necessity for external verification from their loved one—something which often drags a relationship down. It is also useful for creating an internal state of feeling lovable from which an individual naturally expresses more loving and relationship enhancing behaviors.

This is a technique to use on yourself and to use on others. Be sure to attend closely to your client's responses as you progress. There are seven steps to this technique:

1. Establish the experience of being an author.

2. Have your client identify someone they *know* loves them. If there is no one presently, orient them to a time in the past when there was someone they are sure loved them. If they claim there never was any such person, assist them in creating such a person, taking care to create someone your client will appreciate.

3. Establish the position of sitting looking out the window at the person who loves them.

4. Have your client describe to themselves the essential characteristics, large and small, that they recognize that make that

person special to them (to the client).

5. Have them float out to and into the body of the person who loves them—use your overlapping skills and anchor this dissociated position tonally. If it becomes difficult for them to maintain, establish a kinesthetic anchor. If it is difficult for them to see themselves, use overlapping and then anchor the state. (Use the same steps that you would take for V-K dissociation, except they will be seeing themselves through the eyes of someone who loves them rather than through their own eyes.)

6. Have them describe to themselves what they love about the person they see. Reinforce this special perceptual state with verbal patterns ("seeing yourself through the eyes of someone who loves you"). Direct their consciousness to aspects of self they would be unaware of through their own eyes.

7. Reassociate them back into their own body, bringing along that which is valuable, i.e. *feeling lovable.*

Chapter 16: Therapeutic Metaphor

A discussion of methods for evolving clients from the present state to the desired state would be incomplete if it did not offer an explanation of the use of *therapeutic metaphor*. Therapeutic metaphor is a special technique of storytelling that provides a person with important unconscious or conscious learnings that instigate new productive behaviors.

The art of therapeutic metaphor was richly developed by Milton H. Erickson, M.D. He was a wizard at both the construction and delivery of therapeutic metaphors. The book, *Therapeutic Metaphors*, by David Gordon, is an excellent presentation of the techniques of therapeutic metaphor construction. I recommend reading it. I would like to offer here just the barest essentials of metaphor construction, along with a few examples, so that you can understand the general process and begin to develop your own skills.

In order to be effective, a metaphor must:

1. Be isomorphic to the problem content. To be isomorphic is to be of the same or similar structure. Sticking to a diet is isomorphic to staying within a budget—the two situations have similar components.

2. Supply a vicarious experience in which a person has the opportunity to operate out of a different set of filters, providing access to previously unrecognized choices.

3. Supply a solution, or set of solutions, in the isomorphic situation that can be generalized to the problem, thereby leading the client to make the appropriate changes.

Since it is a non-threatening, often covert method of dealing with subjects that are not easily addressed between people, metaphors can be extremely effective with problems that are not easily remedied by other techniques.

The basic steps for constructing a metaphor are:

1. Identify the problem completely.

2. Define the structural parts of the problem and the pertinent "characters."

3. Find an isomorphic situation. (David Gordon recommends you practice making analogies, i.e., "You know, life is like wine, with proper handling it can get better with age.")

4. Supply a logical solution. Determine what learnings would be useful and then find contexts in which these learnings would be evident.

5. Couch this structure in a story that is either entertaining or disguises the intent (so as to avoid client resistance).

The following case history is a pertinent example of the use of metaphor to assist a client in accomplishing personal change.

An attractive woman named Dot came to me for counseling. She wanted help in learning to control her promiscuous behavior. She was married to a fine man (her description) and had two lovely children, but participated in extra-marital relations whenever and with whomever possible. She wanted to stop this behavior. I used the following elements of her description to create a therapeutic metaphor. Like so many attractive women today, Dot was also concerned about being overweight (which she was not) and so I used that content to make the metaphor appear like a more natural extension of our therapeutic interaction.

Problem Description	Therapeutic Metaphor
Dot's promiscuity is leading her to lose her husband and her self-respect.	A woman on her way to obesity.
Dot cannot resist the temptation of other men.	A woman who cannot resist gooey desserts and rich food when eating out.
Dot finds extra-marital sex more exciting.	This woman loves to eat out.
Dot is unsatisfied with her marital sex relations.	This woman merely picks at her own homecooked food.

Each extra-marital experience produces more guilt and brings her closer to losing her husband.	Each eating out experience produces more fat.
Dot's guilt becomes so painful she *has* to do something about it. She cannot sleep nights, etc.	The fat lady *has* to do something about her habits. She can no longer fit into any of her clothes.
Dot has never developed satisfying sexual behaviors with her husband.	The fat lady had never learned to cook pleasing food for herself.

Each of the elements in the constructed metaphor so far are isomorphic (that is, they have a one-to-one relationship in structure) to the presented problem. They pace the presented problem in that the form of each is the same. The next step is to move from pacing the problem to *leading* to a behavioral solution.

The desired response is for Dot to change her behavior in a way that resolves the problem. The story, then, must somehow provide for an appropriate behavior change from the obese woman, since she represents Dot metaphorically.

Problem Solution	Metaphorical Solution
For Dot to apply energy to developing stimulating and satisfying sexual experiences with her husband.	The woman applied herself to rearranging the kitchen. She began reading cookbooks to decide upon desirable dishes and began experimenting with creating healthy and satisfying meals.
For Dot to find necessary satisfaction at home.	Over time, more quickly than you think, she found there was nothing in restaurants that could compare with her own home creations and she lost the desire to gorge herself elsewhere, finding satisfaction at home.
For Dot to take pride in her marital relationship as well as finding sexual satisfaction with her husband.	Now slim, this once-fat woman takes great pride in her culinary skills as well as in her trim figure.

These, then, are the elements of a therapeutic metaphor designed to elicit a specific outcome. Anchoring and various other nonverbal and verbal techniques are used in this process of story-telling to help make it work. As I related this story to Dot, I made it genuinely interesting to ensure that she would identify with the subject. She then experienced the emotions along with the subject, enabling me to anchor (kinesthetically, visually, and auditorily) the internally generated experiences appropriate to making the change. I also used overlapping to make the metaphor more rich and compelling.

A couple, Don and Iris, sought marital counseling to improve a relationship that had been deteriorating for some time. Don was six years older than Iris. They had been married for six years and had two children, ages four and two. Although Iris had been a slim, attractive woman during their courtship, she had gained about fifty pounds since then. This weight was gained during each of her pregnancies and had not been taken off afterward. Don found her appearance disgusting and had not initiated sexual contact with her for several months. Since he worked in a management position with a large firm, there were some social commitments that went along with his job. He chose to deceive Iris about these, preferring to attend such functions alone rather than risk embarrassment about her appearance.

It was Don who had made the decision to have children, and he had convinced Iris that it would be a good idea for them. But as she gained weight during her first pregnancy, Don began working overtime more and more. Even at the time of counseling, Iris' weight fluctuations were directly representative of how much time Don spent with her, and her overeating binges occurred on evenings when he was away working overtime. Although it was not evident that he was having, or had ever had, an affair, it was obvious the thought had crossed his mind.

Don was meticulous about his appearance and talked about how he saw himself. Iris, on the other hand, talked about how her life was empty and how she needed something to fill it up. Don typically represented his experience as visual; Iris, as primarily kinesthetic. They were both congruent about loving each other, although Don almost shuddered when he would look at Iris. Both described their previous sexual experience together as "idyllic." With two small children at home, Iris was extremely dependent upon Don for everything beyond her mothering role.

For both Don and Iris, the desired state was for her to lose weight, thus reviving his physical desire for her. For Iris, Don's desire (or lack of it) very much controlled the condition of her subjective experience. The more he moved away from her, the more she ate to fill the empty aching within her and, as a result, the further he would move away.

Since an increase in Don's attentiveness towards Iris would have greatly facilitated her weight loss, improving her overall happiness and self-esteem as well, I might have simply told him how his actions worked, and depended on his good intentions to remedy the problem. But the good intentions he had were not succeeding. Somehow, his experience of being with Iris, as she was, needed to be enhanced. I was certain that if Don could be warmly supportive of Iris, even protective, she would respond by losing weight and by "being more her own person" (her own words). However, her present appearance prevented either of them from eliciting the desired response from the other.

Therefore, keeping in mind both the short-term goal of increasing Don's attentiveness towards Iris as well as the more long-term goal of strengthening a mutually nourishing relationship, I decided to use therapeutic metaphor with them. In constructing it, I used information gathered from them concerning their behavior and incorporated specific verbal expressions used by Don to make it yet more effective.

In the metaphor designed for Don and Iris, which follows, Don is cast as Uncle Ronnie while the land and the artichoke plants represent Iris. The basic relationship of a farmer who nurtures and elicits a response from the land is kept constant throughout. Metaphorically, this relationship is congruent with Don and Iris' relationship. The story was told as follows:

"You say your father was a rancher of sorts. My Uncle Ronnie is a rancher. I mean, that's what they're called in California, no matter what they grow. He wasn't always a rancher, though. No, before that he had a career in business and he was good at it, too. Real up and coming fellow. But his dad—my granddad—had this big, beautiful piece of land out on the coast of California. Well, Ronnie knew someday it would probably all be his. He kept an eye on it as time went by."

"But his business career took a lot of his time. You know how that is. Finally, the time came when his father called him out to California and told him things were just too heavy for him and that he needed Ronnie to take things over. The way it looked to Ronnie was that this could be a great opportunity. Financially, he could make something of the place and it was such a beautiful piece of land—he couldn't resist."

"For a while he simply enjoyed his new position as a gentleman rancher. But then he decided it was time to get down to business. His father had grown mostly crops of cut flowers. Very beautiful. But not that productive to Ronnie's way of thinking. After investigating various possibilities, he decided that growing artichokes would be the better use of the land. They were hardy, perfect for the climate, considered a delicacy of sorts, and got a high price."

"So, he had the fields of flowers plowed under and he sowed seeds for artichoke plants. He felt this was a wise and provident move on his part. But artichoke plants take some time before they really produce and Ronnie was an impatient man. His interest began to wander. One day as he looked out over the fields, they seemed quite ugly to him. He would tell himself that this was more practical, but still he missed the lovely flowers. More and more, he stayed away from the land and left the tending to others. Of course, the land suffered. The hired hands didn't care as much for the land; after all, it wasn't theirs. And the land showed the results of Ronnie's neglect."

"Ronnie told me that one day he went out to the fields and looked around. He was appalled by the lumpy mounds and the unattractive artichoke plants, their leaves sticking out all over. He said to himself, 'My God, what have I done? This is awful. I don't even want to call it my own. I should have left it alone. I wish I'd never touched it.' "

"But, he had. And what was he to do with it now? True, it was now producing artichokes and there was a good market for artichokes. But the land needed more of his own personal tending and attention if it was going to be really productive. Deep down inside, he knew this was true."

"As he walked back to the main house, he reached out and picked an artichoke, carrying it with him. While sitting at the kitchen table pondering his problems, he began to really study that artichoke. It was kind of ugly. All those bulging, inedible leaves on the outside. He found himself wondering why anybody would be tempted by such a thing."

"But then he began to gently peel the artichoke. And, as each layer came off, he became more and more enthralled with what lay underneath. Why, it was beautiful! The smooth, tender inside leaves led him to the heart of the artichoke. Of course, that's what tempted people to buy and to grow artichokes. They knew about the lovely and succulent heart that lay within."

"As he now looked out the window, he began to see a sea of artichoke hearts across his fields. He laughed because, instead of a lot of ugly lumpy sticky plants, he could now see a lot of plants working very hard with all those outer layers protecting the precious inner heart which, after all, is what everyone wanted of them. Those thick, spiney outer layers kept the heart of the artichoke from anyone who wasn't willing to take the time to get at the treasure inside."

"Something about this touched Ronnie, for he appreciated the idea of being vulnerable. And what's more, the artichoke couldn't peel itself. It couldn't expose its inner treasure without him. These were his fields, his plants, and he suddenly felt the strong desire to tend and care for them, to insure their growth and productivity. He would make sure that the plants and the fruit were cared for tenderly lest the precious heart be bruised."

"Now, of course, my Uncle Ronnie is tremendously successful as a rancher and is very proud of his land and what it bears. He says of the early days that he nearly lost sight of where he was going because he let himself wander when things weren't looking good. And that wandering cost him the extra time and trouble it took to bring things back into shape."

"Once he took a closer look at what he had, he gladly gave all he had to offer rather than take a chance on losing everything he'd always wanted. Naturally, the land responded by making him a very rich and proud man. Everyone could see he had something of value."

This metaphor worked very well to elicit the desired responses. Don became more attentive to Iris. He began to encourage her and even participate in a weight loss program with her. His words were that he had an "investment in his marriage" and he would have to "put some time and energy into it if that investment were going to pay off."

The special advantage of metaphors is that people *respond without trying*. Their conscious processes do not interfere and, while knowing that something happened, they really are not sure just what (or how) it happened.

Had I chosen a different desired outcome, the metaphor would have been constructed differently. If the desired response was for Iris to become more assertive and independent, the metaphor might have had the land go wild from neglect, becoming overrun with strange and beautiful plants until Uncle Ronnie no longer knew his way through his own land: "And it was like a virgin frontier to be discovered and perhaps tamed and cultivated once again. But, alas, the land would have none of his taming and cultivating, for it had outgrown him and, if anything, would instead tame and cultivate him to suit its own needs."

Such a metaphor would certainly have elicited a different outcome than the previous one. It was my opinion that a really assertive and independent response from Iris, at this time, would have been destructive to their relationship rather than beneficial. This opinion guided my behavior in constructing a metaphor that would elicit a *useful response*. When using therapeutic metaphor, do be sure to keep the desired outcome firmly in mind throughout both the construction and telling of the metaphor.

The following case histories, together with excerpts from therapy transcripts, further demonstrate the effective use of therapeutic metaphor.

Bud was suffering from impotency. He had no history of erections sufficient for coitus or ejaculation. At age fourteen he was seduced by his aunt who lived with him and his mother. This aunt repeatedly humiliated him because of his inability to perform. There had been no father in the home since Bud was twelve, and the sexual incidents were never revealed to his mother. Although Bud had been married six months, the marriage remained unconsummated. His description of his wife matched that of his aunt exactly, but Bud gave no indication of being consciously aware of this similarity. He had pictures of both his wife and aunt in his wallet and the physical similarities were striking. His aunt had died a few years before he came to see me for help. The metaphor I used was constructed using these components:

Problem Description	Therapeutic Metaphor
Aunt is threateningly aggressive.	Church is burning.
Bud is impotent as a way of protecting himself, even now that his aunt is dead.	Firemen can't get any water pressure from the hydrant to save the church, the church burns down.

Problem Solution	Metaphorical Solution
Bud's unconscious needs to realize that impotence is no longer needed as protection.	Firemen find a way to open the hydrant valve.

Bud needs to separate his feelings about his aunt from his wife.	Firemen notice sparks from the church igniting the house next door.
Doing this will allow Bud to be potent with his wife.	Firemen put out fire in the house with no problem.

"My mother told me a story that her sister had heard from a neighbor in Wichita, Kansas, concerning a fire. It seems the town's largest and most important church had caught fire. No one knew how it had started, but the firemen were summoned to put it out. Upon arrival, it was plain to see she was ablaze from bottom to top. And the heat she put out! The firemen were irregulars, not well trained, and scared as hell. Seems all the regulars were away at the annual firemen's picnic. Untrained as they were, the firemen did their level best, but hardly knew where to begin. With a great sense of urgency, they hooked their hose to the hydrant, uncoiled it, and approached the burning church. It was their intention to enter once the hose was working and to save what they could."

"But, alas, no water filled the hose and they dared not enter without it. You, being a fireman, can imagine how frustrating this was. The firemen grew desperate and frantic, wasting time with their frenzy while the church burned away."

"It was only when they had accepted defeat and had turned away that the needed actions became obvious. Approaching the hydrant with curiosity, the frenzy gone because the church could not even hope to be saved, the firemen easily found the way to open the valve, releasing water long held under pressure in the hose. But, dammit, it had come too late."

"However, as they turned back to watch the church crumble into dying coals, they noticed that the house next to the church had caught fire from flying sparks and embers—and there was life inside it. The church was gone; there was nothing to be gained by directing efforts there. Upon hearing the cries of those inside the house, the firemen rushed with their hose to quench the thirsty flames. Entering with the hose at full power, they thoroughly put out the blaze, leaving not even a tendril of flame to flicker on."

"They were tired and satisfied firemen as they withdrew from the house. All of the lives had been saved, and the only sign left of the fire were the smoky sighs escaping through open windows."

> "The church had burned to the ground, but even the regular fire-fighters had agreed that she was beyond saving even from the beginning, and they had been right to attend to the house next door. Before leaving, though, the firemen checked the hydrant once more, making sure all connections were as they should be . . . in case they ever needed to come again."

Several years ago in a seminar, a young man, Allen, pleaded for help with a very personal problem. Though I told him that the seminar was not the place to seek private consultation, his insistent and persevering pleas induced me to give him a few private moments.

His very urgent and pressing problem was that of premature ejaculation. He had suffered from this for several years without previously seeking help for it. But now he was in love, truly in love, and it was terribly important that he be a great lover for this new woman. Because of my knowledge of Allen's conscious and unconscious behavior in the context of the ongoing seminar—and also because the evening's subject would be therapeutic metaphor—I decided to use just that as a covert intervention with him.

To his conscious mind, I merely consoled him, saying that not much could be done for premature ejaculation. My suggestion was to reframe the behavior toward his new woman, telling him to say she was so enticing, so exciting, that he simply couldn't control himself; that his premature ejaculations were just a response to her sexual prowess. Allen was stunned by this suggestion, but politely accepted it, and he even began to plan just how he would phrase his post-coital remarks.

During the evening training session I induced a light trance state in Allen and told him several stories, all of which were constructed to elicit a specific response. One story, which exemplifies the others, follows. I'm sure the intended response will be obvious to the reader, although it was not at all obvious to the others in the seminar. In fact, the majority of those in attendance believed it to be a trance induction with the desired response being a deep trance state.

> "There are many ways to go many places. For the man who has worked hard all year there is but a brief two-week vacation. A brief two weeks in which he must cram all the vacation pleasure of a year. What frustration to cram a year's pleasure into two weeks! Often he might pick a destination to reach in order that he might spend his vacation time there. Once picked, he

might locate the destination on a map and, on that map, he might choose the quickest route possible to reach his chosen destination. He might even find a shortcut, so much does he desire to reach his chosen destination. And that might be all very well."

"But that is how he spends *all* of his life—by deciding where it is that he is going and taking the shortest possible route in getting there. What of others who may wish to journey with him? What of the unforeseen adventures and delights ignored by setting his sights only upon the destination point? And this man, why this man would even take the same shortcut to the same destination year after year. That is, until one year."

"And a good thing, too. That year a friend was going to that same destination point. The Grand Canyon. That's where they were both going. And that's where they both had been. But the friend drove. And the friend was in no hurry to get there. The friend did not even have a roadmap or a route, but nonetheless was completely sure of arriving at the desired place and was content to take all the time in the world to get there."

"At first, the man was impatient. But then he became intrigued and even beguiled with what this very odd way of traveling had to offer. For they did whatever fancied them at the moment. They took side trips where they were surprised and delighted with what they found."

"And no matter where they went, the closer they came to the Grand Canyon. Sometimes when a side trip would be especially delightful to the man, he wouldn't want to leave. His friend would persuade him to move on by reminding him, 'You can come again and again to a favorite place. And you can leave it, knowing you can come again whenever you like.' Only then would the man move on. They were both surprised when they reached the Grand Canyon itself. So engrossed were they in each phase of their journey, their arrival was an unexpected extra pleasure."

"His friend traced the way they had come in the warm earth: 'You can come this way and you can come that way or that way. There are as many ways to get there as there are pleasures to have. They can all take you there. Some quickly, some slowly. It matters not. It only matters to be where you are when you are there, instead of where you are going before you get there. When you are where you are, nothing will be missed.' "

"And, year after year, the friend and he traveled to places

known and unknown, and they did so comfortably and with great pleasure."

This metaphor proved to be effective in altering Allen's sexual behavior. He later reported having no difficulty with premature ejaculation over the next several weeks. His learning behavior also changed in response to this metaphor, so that rather than using methods he was well acquainted with, he began to explore various aspects of the processes we were working with in the seminar. As he did so, his enjoyment increased along with the expression of his creativity.

Allen was never consciously aware of any sex therapy taking place. When I next saw him he smugly remarked that there had been no need to worry, he had found other ways around the problem. I replied that I believed him absolutely. He paused, looked at me out of the corner of his eye, began to speak, then checked himself. He shrugged his shoulders and said, "Feels good, you know."

Chapter 17: Re-evaluating Relationships

It took me and my colleague, Michael Lebeau, a very long time to develop effective interventions for people who had gone over threshold. It is not difficult to persuade someone to go through the motions of giving their relationship another chance, but it is something else entirely to intervene such that they can see their partner through unprejudiced eyes. As you recall, when a person has gone over threshold they have a firm belief that their partner is somehow significantly unsuitable to be in love with. Threshold can occur in any type of significant relationship. It can be in relation to trust or respect, rather than love. People even go over threshold concerning their jobs. It is the pattern underlying most experiences that contain the phenomenon of being fed up, of quitting, or disowning. The *threshold neutralizer* and *relationship evaluator* are effective for these situations.

Michael and I developed these two interventions to address three different aspects of the threshold pattern. The threshold neutralizer is appropriate for those situations in which two people have already separated. It assists each of them in remaining separated in a healthy way (if remaining separated is the appropriate outcome). It can also serve as a preparation for the relationship evaluator, which is a technique that, depending on the circumstances, either motivates individuals to fully re-engage in making their relationship work, or allows them to be assured that their decision to separate is a proper one based on a realistic, appropriate, and thorough evaluation.

Threshold Neutralizer

When a person is over threshold they are associated into their past painful memories concerning their partner, and dissociated from any past pleasure. Their pain and dissatisfaction is attached to and associated with their partner. The purpose of the threshold neutralizer is twofold: one, to separate the pain and dissatisfaction from the partner—without dismissing that it has occurred—and, two, regain access to any past pleasant memories. To illustrate the usefulness of this latter outcome, I would like to tell you about Maria. Maria is a resourceful and lovely woman who was training to be a therapist when I knew her. In the course of training her, I became aware that she almost never accessed any past memories. She did not use her past for examples that would have made her therapy more effective. I learned she had been divorced for one year and that accessing memories of the previous five years was distressing for her because her ex-husband was a part of them. The unpleasantness was so strong and so pervasive that even her memories of the birth of her son were spoiled because her ex-husband had been present. She had never thought to ask for help concerning this, thinking it was just how things are when you get a divorce. Going through the threshold neutralizer did not make her want to go back to her ex-husband, but it did give her access to all the important and beautiful experiences they had shared during the years they had been together. Her therapy improved too, partially due to having greater access to her own personal history. But much more important, her work as a therapist improved because she now had a compelling personal experience of the possibility and value of bringing change to situations she had never thought to question.

Todd and Ann came in for therapy after having been separated for three months. Todd very much wanted to get back together. Ann felt guilty about leaving and hated living alone, but really didn't want to move back in with Todd. They had lived together for almost four years and, according to her, all four years were awful. Todd invariably disagreed with this but Ann had many, many specific memories of just how bad it had been. I gave Todd the task of identifying how he had changed during those years and how he wanted to be sure to change over the next two years, and then I escorted him into another room so I could spend time alone with Ann. I asked her if she was happy to see Todd again:

Ann: No, not really.

LCB: What would happen if you were home alone, just hanging out on an afternoon off and there was a knock at the door. You are not expecting anyone, and you answer it. As you open the door, there stands Todd.

Ann: Oh God. Why? Why is he standing there? (*Her expression was something like what you would imagine someone would look like if they had just stepped in a pile of dog excrement, barefooted.*)

LCB: I don't know why he's there. Let's forget him for now and just pay attention to you. I know this is a difficult time for you. Whether you remain separated from Todd or go back together, it will be in both your best interests for you to be feeling good about yourself. If you go back to him out of feelings of guilt, you will be cheating yourself and Todd. The same would be true if you were to go back because you were afraid or felt insecure about going into the future on your own. Todd and you each deserve to have a relationship in which you are loved, wanted, and really cared for.

Ann: I just don't know if I can ever feel that way about Todd again. I've tried, you don't know . . .

LCB: Well, I don't need to know everything to believe you. I can see and hear your sincerity. Right now it would be best for us to pay attention to you and how you are doing with yourself. I would like you to tell me what you most appreciate about yourself. What are the qualities or attributes that you cherish? Take a few moments and give yourself a gift by appreciating something about who you are. (*pause*) And you can relax into that feeling of self-appreciation even more. Perhaps you are seeing yourself from a past experience where you really demonstrated some highly valued quality; or perhaps seeing just what you were seeing and feeling in a cherished memory, getting fully in touch with what it is to appreciate yourself. Appreciate yourself in a way that will sustain you and assure that your qualities will be expressed throughout your future. Know yourself in the past, the present, and the future, from an appreciative point of view.

This appreciation of yourself is yours. It is not dependent upon anyone, and can't be taken away from you by anyone but you. It is worth holding onto. It is worth taking with you as you look into your past, your present, and your future. With self-appreciation you can see mistakes and successes while still caring for yourself. With appreciation you can encourage yourself and others.

Feeling this rich and full feeling, carrying it with you, I want you to begin to turn the clock back, though you will stay here with me. I want you to recall an image of how Todd looked to you in the beginning. Just a still shot. The only thing that is important, for now, is that you can still feel those feelings of self-appreciation as you see him. Hold on to feeling good with yourself at the same time seeing him as he was in the beginning.

Now, you know all that has happened between you and Todd. But from this point of view, see him separate from you, as a separate person, as another individual moving through the world. That is, over there, separate from you, just another person. While you continue to feel those feelings of self-appreciation, take a look at Todd—getting to see him independent from your shared times together—not as your man, or your ex, but as another person on this planet. He must have been seen as special to you for him to have been so important in your life. Good and bad, his qualities, style, and attributes once attracted you, and were cherished by you. Think of him as someone you met and got to know only briefly. You may or may not see all his talents, the little things that make him who he is, separate from you. Feel those feelings of self-appreciation while you see him as another person. Identify with what it was that drew you to him in the first place. Not now, but in the first place.

When you have taken a look at Todd from those eyes so that you can see him clearly as another person, keeping your own sense of self securely in your own hands, pick some one pleasant memory, some past experience that was good for you that you shared with Todd—some experience where together there was more than there would have been if either of you were alone. Explore that memory, perhaps as if a long, long time had passed—enough time to be able to reminisce and feel nostalgic over an old, good time with someone you then cared about. You cared enough to have such a pleasant experience to place in your memories. This is your memory, no one else's. It would be a shame to lose the precious memories that are yours.

Always continue to feel your own sense of appreciation for yourself as you are reminiscing through a past experience, or more than one, that you shared with him. Feel how much of that experience comes back to you. And sense it is yours and you can come to it anytime, leisurely, taking all the time you need to hold onto feeling yourself whole, secure in your sense of self, appreciating who you are and who you are becoming. Slowly return now to the present, to this room, and to talking to me here, comfortable and relaxed about how you are feeling. (*Ann sits quietly for some time, looking out the window and around the room before she speaks.*)

Ann: I really wasn't expecting that.

LCB: How was it?

Ann: Great. I can't remember when I've felt so relaxed or when I've felt that good about myself. It's as if I'd forgotten that I really am a good person. I'm responsible, and fair, and lots of things that I'm glad to be.

LCB: Remember that no one can take you away from you. After all, you really are the only person you have to wake up with every morning. Isn't it nice to be with someone you appreciate?

Ann: Yes, yes it is. I never thought of that.

LCB: What was it like to take that kind of look at Todd?

Ann: Well, it was different. I had trouble at first, but as long as I could feel good about myself I could see him as, you know, a person. Not someone who was part of me. It made me realize I had been thinking of him as some kind of disease that I might have to spend the rest of my life with.

LCB: What about the memory that you recalled? Where were you together?

Ann: Oh, it was great. I hadn't thought of it in forever. It was from the very beginning. On a walk in the woods. It began to rain, he was always so romantic.

LCB: If you were home alone on an afternoon and Todd stopped by, how would you feel when you saw him at your door?

Ann: (*pauses, accesses*) Oh, I don't know, kind of mixed, I guess. I could be happy to see him, it depends on what he wants.

LCB: Well, that is always important, what he wants, and he may want more for the two of you than you do for some time. As you see him there, (*gesturing to where she has made a picture of him*) can you see if he expects anything?

Ann: No, I don't think so, not anymore, he doesn't. He just wants me.

LCB: That can speak highly of him, don't you think?

Ann: (*laughing*) Yes, I guess so, but it's hard to see him want me and not give in.

LCB: Well, he deserves to be wanted, too. I'd like to spend some time with Todd now while you go back over this experience. We'll talk more before both of you leave.

Ann: Thank you.

This is the kind of success the threshold neutralizer brings. It opens previously closed and locked doors, but does not necessarily put people on the same side of the door to live happily ever after. Ann and Todd did not go back together, but they did become very close friends. Each has since begun a new relationship. Todd did so first, which caused Ann some distress, which she came to see me about. She was concerned that it meant she really did love him and wanted him back. Together we discovered she just didn't want to give up her greatest fan. Certainly, Todd had some difficult times over their break-up, but he used them as an opportunity to become more of who he wanted to be. After all, if he was being all that he wanted to be, and she still didn't want him, he could be grateful for the freedom to find someone right for him.

There are six steps to using the threshold neutralizer:

1. Establish a baseline. Have your client imagine unexpectedly meeting the person with whom they are over threshold. Pay close attention to their response since you will use this same imagined meeting as a test later. The degree to which there is a more positive response is the degree of success.

2. Access a state of self-appreciation in your client and anchor it tonally and kinesthetically. Use the kinesthetic anchor with the instruction to "hold on to those feelings." You want your client to be experiencing this state of self-appreciation throughout the entire process. Being able to feel good about themselves when seeing the other person (and remembering a past memory) separates the bad feelings from being attached to all aspects of the other person. Being able to maintain the self-appreciation gives them more of an experience of choice concerning what to experience when they are around the other person.

3. Have them picture the other person in a still shot as they looked when they first met. While the your client is looking at that picture, reinforce the self-appreciation anchor and when you can see that they can do both (see the other person and feel self-appreciation), direct them to view the other as separate from them, an individual, furthering the separation of the other person from their pain and dissatisfaction. Then, have them recall what drew them to that person in the first place: what qualities, attributes, style, etc.

4. Once they have done this, direct them to access a past, pleasant memory they shared together. Assist them in recovering the fullness of that experience, reinforcing the notion that it is their memory and not to let anything take it away. Continue to use the self-appreciation anchors.

5. Graciously bring them back to the present, instructing them to bring the feelings of self-appreciation with them.

6. Have them again imagine a chance encounter with that other person (if they are still living together, make it a surprise meeting). This gives you something to calibrate to other than the ingrained responses of their usual meeting times. So have them come home early, or run into each other grocery shopping— something that lies outside the ritualized schedule and provides you with the opportunity to see if they are appalled or delighted, or something in between, at this unexpected meeting. Ask your client how it is different than when they first imagined it.

As with all the techniques, only continue on to the next step when the preceding one has been successfully completed. If it is not going well, stop and shift to the three step visual-kinesthetic dissociation technique, having your client see their partner from a dispassionate point of view. From the dissociated position, they may be better able to see their partner's frustration, pain, etc., separate from its effects upon them. Then start again with the threshold neutralizer.

Relationship Evaluator

The relationship evaluator is a process that assists one or both members of a couple in identifying and evaluating their criteria (standards) and behavior in connection with relationships. This process includes an evaluation of whether or not each can get their wants and needs fulfilled by the other. Depending on the outcome of the evaluation, they will either come to the conclusion that they are no longer appropriate for each other (allowing them to be assured that a decision to separate is a correct one), or they will be motivated to positively re-engage in satisfying and receiving satisfaction from the other.

This technique is designed to assist the individual in evaluating needs and wants and establishing specific intentional and behavioral guidelines concerning how to reach and maintain fulfillment in the context of personal relationships. You will recognize that it is lengthy and brings up much material for further exploration at each step. Frequently I use two or occasionally three sessions to take someone through this procedure thoroughly. It has always been worth the time it took.

In presenting the relationship evaluator, I will offer you the sequence of questions/directions that constitute each step. Since each step elicits a wealth of material, no actual transcript is offered. Rather, it would be useful for you to take the time to answer each question and follow each direction in connection with someone with whom you have gone over threshold in the past. I've offered examples of simple answers for the first few questions for you to contrast with your own. Following these questions and directions is a step-by-step summation of the entire procedure.

> What is it you really want from a relationship now? What do you want now, not necessarily from your existing relationship, but from an ideal relationship?
> (e.g., Companionship, a partner and a friend, someone I can trust to stand by me, not someone I always have to entertain or please, but someone who will go for it *with* me.)
>
> How does this differ from what you wanted in your past? Go back to several years ago and, looking through younger eyes, see what it was you wanted then. What attracted you then, what filled the needs that you had back then?
> (e.g., Then I really wanted to be taken care of—I didn't believe in myself enough to think it could be otherwise. Also, I wanted to be entertained and stimulated.)

And then go from there to here and off into your future. Go forward in time to discover what you will be wanting and needing in the future that differs even from now.

(e.g., Well, it's more difficult to know for sure, but it feels a lot like what I want now only deeper. I'm more aware of wanting affection. I want to be sure that there would be lots of affection. Funny, it seems even more important then than now.)

What has your mate satisfied concerning your wants and needs in the past and the present?

(e.g., He was entertaining and he tried to take care of me.)

What does your mate do now that would satisfy you in your future?

(e.g., I'm not sure. Maybe, well certainly he loves the children.)

What has your mate given to you in the past that you didn't even know to want or ask for?

(e.g., He challenged me—made me believe in myself more. I guess when he left me alone a lot I also had to learn more about myself, about how to take care of myself.)

I want you to do a thorough evaluation of how being with your mate has made you more than you would have been otherwise. Regardless of whether all your experiences felt good or comfortable, how have you been compelled to be more of who you want to be (or appreciate being) because of the experiences you've had together? How will you be more of who you want to be in your future as a result of your past together, regardless of whether you stay together now?

You have journeyed briefly into the future. Now I would like you to generate several different possible future scenarios in the following way. Using examples of your mate's *existing* qualities and behavior—not his or her past or future possibilities— evaluate whether he or she can give you what you want. Generate one possible scenario in the future, checking for what you are getting for yourself from him or her. Compare this to a future scenario based on your mate's *possible* future qualities and behavior. Are you getting more from a future that is based on your mate's existing qualities and behavior? Or are you getting more from the qualities and behaviors you *project* as possible of your mate in the future?

Describe some of the behavior your mate does that you object to strongly. Going through them one at a time, I'd like you to determine what would have to be going on inside of you so that you would generate the same behavior. So, if what he or she does that you really hate is walking out of the room while you are arguing, I want you to imagine doing just that—walking out in the middle of an argument. What's going on that you would be compelled to do that? Is it how angry, frustrated, or threatened you feel? What are the possibilities of what lies behind that objectionable behavior which makes it understandable? (Not necessarily likeable or even acceptable, but at least understandable when you look behind the scenes.) Reviewing each of several situations where your mate has expressed such behavior, attend to the possibilities which compel him or her to be expressive in that way and imagine how it would have been different if you had responded and behaved differently. Try a few different forms of behavior for yourself in each of those past situations and recognize how it could have been different if *you* had been different. How would it have been different if you had responded to how your mate was *feeling* instead of to what he or she was *doing*?

Looking at those examples of objectionable behavior from still another perspective, determine how each is a manifestation of an attribute that in some other situation you enjoy or benefit from. For instance, with one couple, she was always late and he was incensed by this. At least he was until he recognized that her being late was a by-product of how fully she attended to the needs of whomever she was with. Then he could recall how often she had postponed, cancelled, or been late for appointments with others when he had needed her full attention. So, explore how these instances of your mate's objectionable behavior could be by-products of some appreciated and valued attribute.

As you consider your own qualities that you most value, and the ways in which you manifest those qualities through your behavior, go back to some awful past interaction involving your mate. Pay attention to yourself and to what your mate's feelings were behind his or her behavior and identify how you, too, were not being all of who you want to be or could be. See yourself there in that situation. Choose one of your highly valued attributes that would be useful in this context and see yourself generate different forms of behavior that are reflective of those attributes. See how the entire interaction is transformed by your living out your own attributes.

Now, having accumulated several examples of new, more useful behavior to influence your interactions, take them into one of those possible futures and play them out. How differently do events transpire? How much more of what you want do you get?

Knowing that you could have made the past different, and that you can make the present and future different, do you want to? Are you willing to make the necessary changes to make those interactions come out differently? Is it worth it to you?

If yes, see yourself behaving in those new ways and influencing the course of events of your relationship. As you do, feel how it feels knowing you have made a crucial difference in bringing your relationship from bad to better, perhaps even to good. Then, see your mate, recognizing his or her positive attributes that are worth appreciating, and *feel* that appreciation. When is the next opportunity for you to test your different forms of behavior to discover how much you can influence the direction of your life/relationship?

If no, ask yourself what you have to lose—what of your wants and needs will go unsatisfied if you are without that person in your life. What will you miss out on that you are getting now? How will you fulfill those needs without that person?

If the relationship evaluator is not done with both members of a couple, direct the one with whom it is done to gather the pertinent information from their mate concerning their mate's wants and needs, and the means of their fulfillment in the past, present, and future (the first three steps of the evaluation).

To recap the process, the seven steps for using the relationship evaluator are:

1. Identify what your client wants from a primary relationship now, what it is they wanted in their past (this point provides a means by which they can find that their mate perhaps was everything they wanted, but what they wanted has changed, through no fault of their mate's), and what they will want in the future.

2. Identify any differences and reinforce how wants and needs change naturally as a person progresses through the stages of life. If there are no differences, check to make sure their wants/needs

are responsive to life's stages. (If "doing everything together" is what is wanted/needed, it will be difficult to fulfill while the children are young.)

3. Have them identify how their mate has satisfied their wants/needs in the past and how he or she could possibly do so in the future. Direct them to discover what they have gotten above and beyond what they wanted, how their mate has contributed to their development as a person, and how this will extend into the future and benefit them.

4. Using only the mate's existing behavior, generate possible futures to test for how the client's future wants/needs can (or cannot) be fulfilled.

5. Identify the mate's objectionable behaviors. Ask the client to access the internal states that would cause them to generate the same behavior. Once they have accessed internal states that make their mate's behavior more acceptable or understandable, direct them to generate different external behavior in response to the objectionable behavior and reframe the mate's objectionable behavior to be a by-product of some valued trait.

6. Identify what the client hasn't done that would have been useful in response to the mate's past objectionable behavior. Identify attributes that the client identifies with and generate possible behavioral responses to the mate that are representative of those attributes. Have the client detect how the entire interaction is altered for the better.

7. Referring back to step 4, have the client re-adjust the future in accordance with the new behaviors generated in step 6. Lead the client to identifying how he or she will need to be different by seeing his or her self generate the more desirable behavior. Have them determine whether or not they are willing to make those changes. Have them test for whether it will be worth it by accessing positive aspects of their mate, then identifying what existing fulfillment of wants/needs would be lost by being without their mate.

The relationship evaluator resolves problems in two ways with couples when one or both have gone over threshold. The process of thoroughly evaluating their criteria concerning primary relationships can bring the couple to the conclusion that they are not appropriate for one another—that is, there is no possibility of satisfying each other's wants and needs any longer because they want or are only willing to give different kinds of experiences (adventures and spontaneity vs. security and tradition, for example). The process can also serve to re-engage their flexibility of behavior and sort for the internal states of the other.

In the first case, both members of the relationship end up with objective understandings that are the basis for appreciating what they have received of value from the other. These understandings are also the basis for assuredness in their decision to separate, as well as the basis for confidence in moving into the future.

In the second case, each person takes responsibility for making their life together all that it can be—by actively behaviorally manifesting their own best attributes, while equally actively recognizing and responding to the other's valued qualities. Thus, a mutual knowledge of and concern for fulfilling each other's wants/needs becomes a meaningful commitment to themselves and the future.

These interventions have been designed to be ecological for all concerned. They make substantial contributions to bringing people to those resourceful states from which important decisions are best made. I believe it is essential for people to make choices that move them closer to what they *do* want in life instead of choices that send them running away, only to fall into a similar hole in the future.

Chapter 18: Future-pacing

Although future-pacing is an integral aspect of all the techniques I have presented in the previous chapters, it merits special emphasis because of its practical as well as theoretical importance. Future-pacing is the process of insuring that the changes accomplished during therapy become generalized and available in the appropriate outside contexts. Too often, changes that occur in therapy remain anchored to the therapist or to the therapist's office, rather than being available to the client in the specific situations where the client most needs the new behavior and responses.

The primary method of future-pacing new forms of behavior is anchoring the new behavior or response to a sensory stimulus that naturally occurs in the applicable context. Step five of six-step reframing future-paces new behaviors by asking a part to take responsibility for generating those new behaviors in the appropriate context. In the reframing example with Tom, I asked him how he would know when he needed the new choices. For him, the signal was feeling pushed, so I anchored the new behavioral choices to that feeling. In changing history, future-pacing is accomplished by asking the client in what future circumstance will they again need that resource that you have worked with them to access. When the future circumstance is identified, the client then generates an internal projection of that circumstance in which that needed resource is available and expressed. In this way, the resource becomes attached to the context in which it is needed. The therapeutic metaphor future-paces by including leading or future behavior as a part of its construct. The future-pacing of those changes accomplished with visual-kinesthetic dissociation is best done by presenting the client with the actual stimulus which previously triggered the phobic response. So, if it was fear of heights, take them to a high place and learn if the desired change has been accomplished.

Future-pacing can be done very directly. One way is to ask the client, "What is the very first thing you will see, hear, or feel that will indicate you need this resource?" When the specific experience is identified, have the client generate it internally and then anchor the appropriate resource to it. Then when the stimulus occurs in external experience, it can naturally and unconsciously trigger the appropriate feelings/behavior. For instance, anchoring feelings of passion (the resource) to the feeling of smooth cool sheets, or the sound of his name softly whispered, or the sight of a yellow rose, is future-pacing the resource of passionate feelings to specific externally occurring experiences. This process can be done with couples by anchoring the new, more useful responses to phenomena that already occur naturally: how he scratches his head, the sight of their front door, the sound of the television being turned off. Any of these can serve as triggers for initiating some newly acquired behavioral choice on the part of clients. Role playing can also often serve to future-pace changes. But most preferable of all is to present the client with the actual situation in which the new choices need to be expressed. While usually impossible when dealing with sexual dysfunction, this is still the best way of testing your work and insuring the full integration of new behavior.

What is most important about future-pacing is that you don't just assume that the client's conscious mind will automatically take the accomplishments of a session into their everyday lives. Although the conscious mind may try very hard, it usually recalls the new behavior only after it has already failed (by exhibiting the former behavior). Unconscious processes, however, work automatically. It is your task to implant the new choices at the unconscious level, making sure that the triggers for these new, more useful behavioral choices will work and that they are certain of occurring at the appropriate time.

Future-pacing is *not* frosting on the therapy cake. Without adequate future-pacing, the accomplishments of a session are often lost. Future-pacing is the final step in any effective therapeutic intervention.

In Conclusion

The concepts and information contained in this presentation provide new and useful ways of understanding verbal and nonverbal communication. They are, therefore, valuable to the seasoned clinical practitioner, the developing therapist, as well as anyone interested in becoming more effective in their personal and professional relationships. Throughout this book I have presented my own methods and style of doing therapy. The structure upon which I base my own methods and style consists of three steps: one, gathering information and establishing rapport; two, evolving the client from their present state to their desired state; and three, future-pacing.

The initial step of gathering information includes determining the client's primary representational system, lead system, and the naturally-occurring anchors that trigger the sequence of internal and external processes that constitute the client's present state and desired state. This information is gathered in the form of verbal descriptions as well as by observing the client's behavior in the therapeutic context. You use your well-trained ears and eyes to gather this information from the sensory experience that each client presents. The meta-model serves as a linguistic tool for gathering the most complete verbal description possible of the present state and the desired state.

Throughout the information gathering process, you are working to establish a well-formed outcome. By meeting the five well-formedness conditions, you are assured of reliable feedback for yourself and your client. You are also assured that you will be organizing your client's resources and your own activities toward achieving changes that are worthwhile and ecological.

Once you have gathered all the information necessary to understand how the present state is structured, you choose a therapeutic intervention that will result in the client's experiencing the desired state. You then evolve the client to the desired state by employing that chosen technique or integration of techniques. The methods offered here—anchoring, changing history, visual-kinesthetic dissociation, reframing, overlapping, metaphor, looking through the eyes of someone who loves you, and the threshold neutralizer and relationship evaluator—are but a sampling of possibilities.

When the desired state has been accomplished, your task is to consolidate and integrate the changes so they can become generalized into the client's habitual behavior. This future-pacing insures the perpetuation of the desired-state experience. The process of generalization occurs by making sure that the new behavior or responses are attached to a sensory stimulus that is sure to exist in the appropriate context.

There are two components that you *must* be responsible for to effectively use this framework and set of methods. As stated earlier, these two components are flexibility of behavior and sensory experience. Flexibility of behavior refers to having choices in communication style as well as choices in methods of intervention. This presentation has offered numerous choices in techniques and methods of intervention, but *how* they are done is as important as doing them. As a professional communicator, it is essential for you to have an infinite variety of behavior available to you at all times. We should consider resistance on the part of a client to be a comment on our own behavior, not the client's. It is our job to be able to adequately pace the client's model of the world and then to elicit responses that bypass resistance. This requires flexibility on our part to be able to match the client's behavior and to use aspects of his own behavior and ours to elicit useful responses.

The importance of a therapist's ability to verbalize in a manner that is understandable to the client, regardless of cultural or educational background, is accepted. However, even this is lost if the therapist lacks the sensory experience to know by his client's responses whether or not he is indeed being understood. It cannot be emphasized too strongly that you *must* be able to vary all the aspects of your communication as well as use your sensory experience to know whether the manner and style being employed is appropriate for eliciting the desired response from your client.

When assisting clients in making changes, it is often necessary to elicit from them a wide range of responses. Acquiring your client's trust and confidence is, therefore, of primary importance. Once acquired, it may be necessary to induce anything from overt anger to abject hopelessness, or from deep sympathy to wild joy, in order to accomplish the therapeutic goal. Because of this, it is essential that you be able to vary your behavior widely, using sensory feedback in order to make the behavioral adjustments necessary to achieve success. Keeping in mind the effect that your verbal and nonverbal communications has on others, you will want to construct communications in relationship to the responses desired. When sensory experience shows that you are not getting the desired response, vary aspects of your communications, subtly or dramatically, until sensory experience indicates success.

Those therapists recognized as being genius in stature certainly display wide variability in their behaviors. Especially useful examples of the range of Milton Erickson's behavior can be found in Haley's *Uncommon Therapy* and *Advanced Techniques of Hypnosis and Therapy.* Lesser known, but no less effective, is Frank Farrelly, whose unique style is presented in his book *Provocative Therapy.* The therapeutic miracles that occur in the workshops conducted by my colleagues Michael Lebeau and David Gordon certainly evidence their infinite flexibility of behavior and sensory experience.

Possibly some might think of such tactics as manipulation. Well, if manipulation is using all available conscious and unconscious skills to assist people in making changes that they desire to make, then manipulation it is. I have often found it necessary to jeopardize the positive feelings a client may have for me in order to generate an experience that will be beneficial to his or her process of change. But even though I may seem manipulative, coarse, or even cruel at times, my highest priority is always my client's well-being. Their well-being is not necessarily enhanced by supportive or indulgent behavior on my part. It's more important for my client to change in the desired way than it is for me to win a popularity contest. They are in therapy not for my benefit, but for their own. With no limitations on behavior other than physical violence, seduction, or fraud, I am free to explore the infinite number of avenues that lead to productive change.

As with any new material, learning the patterns presented here may at first seem a monumental undertaking. In a short period of experience and you will be able to use them in a systematic way on a largely unconscious level. Since they are content-free, you can use them in any context and with anyone. Feel free to season them with your own personal style and finesse.

The task is now before you: Glean from this text that which can be valuable to you and integrate it into your behavior. Use it to enrich both your own and your clients' future experiences. Remembering always that *there are no mistakes in communication, there are only outcomes.* You *do* have the choices needed to make happy endings come true.

Each time you connect a person with needed resources that came from within him or herself, your experience will be enriched. Remember that the key to success is to discover what it is that keeps people tied to their limitations and then to undo the knots—perhaps one at a time very slowly, perhaps very quickly. And most important, continue to recognize that the future grows out of the here and now. People who are not free and eager for change will have nothing to do with inventing better futures for anyone.

Appendix I

Appendix I: The Meta-Model

Throughout the text of this book I have referred you to this appendix for a presentation of the meta-model. The meta-model is an explicit set of linguistic information gathering tools designed to reconnect a person's language to the experience that is represented by their language.

Fundamental to the useful application of this material is the concept that language is not experience, but rather a *representation* of experience, like a map is a representation of a territory. While I'm sure that you are familiar with the notion that the map is not the territory, I wonder if you have fully realized that, as human beings, we will forever experience only the map and not the territory. Actually, as persons who assist people in changing, this is to our advantage. We alter maps: that is, we change people's subjective experience of the world, not the world itself.

We make our maps out of the interaction between internal and external experience. Because we humans represent (or build) maps of our experience with language, a set of tools like those provided by the meta-model is invaluable. Essentially, the meta-model serves as an interface between language and experience.

All of the following material was developed by Richard Bandler and John Grinder, and a more detailed presentation can be found in *The Structure of Magic*. What follows is a summation of their material, reorganized to facilitate its usefulness to you.

Three Universal Modeling Processes

Because we do not operate directly on the world we live in, we create models or maps of the world which we use to guide our behavior. As an effective therapist, it is crucial to understand your client's model or map of the world. Human behavior, no matter how bizarre or resistant it may seem, makes sense when it is seen in the context of the choices generated by a person's map or model. These models we create guide us and allow us to make sense out of our experience. They are not to be evaluated in terms of good, bad, healthy, sick, or crazy, but rather in terms of their ability to be useful—useful in making it possible to cope successfully and respond creatively to the world around us. It is not that our clients are making the wrong choices, it is just that they do not have enough choices available when needed. Each of us makes the very best choice available to us from our model of the world. However, there is a surplus of impoverished models lacking in useful choices, as evidenced by the abundance of interpersonal and intrapersonal conflict. "It is not the world that lacks choices but the individual's model of the world," say Grinder and Bandler.

We create our models through three universal human modeling processes: generalization, deletion, and distortion. These processes allow us to survive, grow, learn, understand, and experience the richness the world has to offer. But if we mistake our *subjective reality* for reality, these same processes limit us and squelch our ability to be flexible in our responses.

Generalization is the process by which components or pieces of a person's model of the world become detached from their original experience and come to represent the entire category of which the experience is an example. We learn to function in the world by generalizing. A child learns to open a door by turning a knob. He then generalizes this experience by recognizing the many varieties of phenomena that fall within the set of parameters he has as "doors," and then he attempts to open all of them by turning the knobs. As a man enters a darkened room he reaches for the light switch; he does not have to learn a new strategy for acquiring light in a room every time he enters one. However, the same process can work as a limitation. If a man fails once to perform sexually in a way that he deems adequate, and then generalizes his experience to deciding that he is no good at sex, he would deny himself much indeed. Or if a woman decides that all men are insensitive based on limited and selective experiences, she loses a great deal.

Each of us makes many generalizations that are useful and appropriate in some situations and not in others. For example, a child might learn from his family's responses that crying and whining will get him what he wants, yet the same behavior will likely get him abuse from his peers. If he generalizes only the former and not the latter, he may not be able to generate more appropriate and useful behavior in the company of his peers. If a young man generalizes only those behaviors that win the respect of his fellow males, he may experience great difficulty in obtaining respect and interest from women. Whether or not a generalization is useful must be evaluated with regard to a particular context.

A second method which we can use to cope effectively or to limit ourselves is deletion. Deletion is the process by which we selectively pay attention to certain aspects of our experience and exclude others. This allows us to focus our awareness and attend to one portion of our experience over others. Thus, someone can read a book with people around him talking, or with the TV on, or with records playing. This process makes coping possible and allows us to not be overwhelmed by external stimuli. Again though, the same process can be limiting if we delete portions of our experience that are necessary for a full and rich model of the world. The adolescent who believes she is being unjustly treated and picked on, without perceiving her own participation in bringing the situation into existence, has not developed a useful model of the world. A therapist who deletes from his or her experience evidence of their boredom in a session is limiting their own experience as well as that of their clients.

The third modeling process is distortion. Distortion is the process which allows us to make shifts in how we experience sensory data. Without this process we could not plan for the future or make dreams into reality. We misrepresent reality in fiction, art, and even science. A microscope, a novel, and a painting are all examples of our ability to distort and make misrepresentations of reality. We can limit ourselves with distortion in many ways. Think, for example, of the person who distorts all criticism with the response "I'm unlovable." As a result of such distortion, any value in the criticism is lost—together with the opportunities for change and growth. Or consider the frequent distortion of turning a process into a thing. When "relationship" is disassociated from the process of relating, those involved suffer a loss. It becomes something *out there* to be talked about, out of control, and no longer dynamic.

Because these three universal modeling processes are expressed in language patterns, we can use the set of linguistic tools known as the meta-model to challenge them when they limit rather than expand a person's behavioral choices.

The meta-model is designed to teach the listener how to hear and respond to the *form* of the speaker's communication. The content may vary infinitely, but the form of the information given allows the listener the opportunity to respond in such a way as to obtain the fullest meaning from the communication. With the meta-model it is possible to quickly discern the richness and the limits of the information given as well as the human modeling processes used by the speaker. Listening and responding in terms of the meta-model distinctions creates the most understanding and learning from any specific communication.

The meta-model distinctions fall into three natural groupings:

□ Gathering Information

□ Limits of the Speaker's Model

□ Semantic Ill-formedness

Gathering information refers to gaining, through appropriate questions and responses, an accurate and full description of the content being presented. Again, this process assists in reconnecting the speaker's language with his or her experience. There are four sub-distinctions in this category:

□ Deletion

□ Lack of Referential Index

□ Unspecified Verbs

□ Nominalizations

Deletion Recognizing when a deletion has occurred and assisting in recovering the deleted information aids in restoring a fuller representation of the experience. To recover the missing material, the meta-modeler asks: ABOUT WHOM? or ABOUT WHAT?

"I don't understand."
(*response*) "You don't understand what?"
(*or*) "What don't you understand?"

"I'm afraid"
(*response*) "What or whom are you afraid of?"

"I don't like him."
(*response*) "What about him don't you like?"

"He's the best."
(*response*) "He's the best what?"

"He's the best listener."
(*response*) "He's the best listener amongst whom?"
(*or*) "Between whom?"

In the case of deletion, asking the question, "How, specifically?" will elicit information concerning the representational system being used by the client.

"I don't understand."
(*response*) "How, specifically, do you know you don't understand?"
"It's just not clear to me." (*i.e., visual rep.*)

Lack of Referential Index Lack of referential index is a type of generalization that limits a person's model of the world by leaving out the detail and richness necessary to have a variety of options for coping. With this process a person takes an experience and generalizes it in such a way that it's totally out of perspective or out of proportion. To challenge a lack of referential index, ask: WHO SPECIFICALLY? or WHAT SPECIFICALLY?

"No one wants me."
(*response*) "Who, *specifically,* doesn't want you?"

"They are obstinate."
(*response*) "Who, *specifically,* is obstinate?"

"This is hard."
(*response*) "What, *specifically,* about this is hard for you?"

Unspecified Verbs Unspecified verbs leave us in the dark about the experience being described. All verbs are relatively unspecified. However, "kiss" is much more specific than "touch." If someone says he's been hurt, it could have been from a harsh look given by someone important to them, or they might have been hit by a car. Asking for verb specification reconnects the person more fully to his or her experience. To challenge unspecified verbs, ask: HOW SPECIFICALLY?

"He rejected me."
(*response*) "How, *specifically,* did he reject you?"

"They ignored me."
(*response*) "How, *specifically,* did they ignore you?"

"The children force me to punish them."
(*response*) "How, *specifically,* do the children force you to punish them?"

Nominalizations Nominalizations are those words that have been transformed from process words (verbs) into nouns. An ongoing process thereby becomes a thing or an event. When this happens, we lose choices and there is a need to be reconnected with the ongoing dynamic processes of life. Reversing nominalizations assists a person in being able to see that what they had considered an event—over and beyond their control—is in fact a continuing process which can be changed. Nominalizations can be distinguished from regular nouns in several ways. For those who enjoy visualizing, make a picture of a wheelbarrow in your mind's eye. Now put a chair, then a cat, then your mother in the wheelbarrow. Now try putting failure, virtue, projections, and confusion into that wheelbarrow. As you can see, nominalizations are not persons, places or things that can be put into a wheelbarrow. Another way to test for nominalizations is to check whether the event word fits into the syntactic frame, an ongoing _____. If it does, it is a nominalization.

an ongoing *problem*   nominalization

an ongoing *elephant*

an ongoing *chair*

an ongoing *relationship*   nominalization

To transform a nominalization back into a process word, use it as a verb in the response:

"I don't get any recognition."
(*response*) "How would you like to be recognized?"

"Pay attention."
(*response*) "What do you want me to attend to?"

"I regret my decision."
(*response*) "Does anything stop you from re-deciding?"

"I want help."
(*response*) "How do you want to be helped?"

The next grouping of distinctions is referred to as *limits of the speaker's model*. These distinctions identify limits and, by challenging them appropriately, you can assist a person in enriching their model of the world by expanding it. The two distinctions in this category are:

☐ Universal Quantifiers

☐ Modal Operators (primarily, modal operators of necessity)

Universal Quantifiers Universal quantifiers refer to the set of words typified by "all," "every," "always," "never," "every," "nobody." Emphasizing the generalization described by the speaker's universal quantifiers by exaggerating it—both by voice quality and by inserting additional universal quantifiers—serves to challenge them. Challenging the speaker's universal quantifiers assists them in finding the exception to their generalization and thus assists them in having more choices. Another way to challenge directly is to ask whether the speaker has had an experience that contradicts his or her own generalization.

"I never do anything right."
(*response*) "You *absolutely never ever* do *anything* right?"
(*or*) "Have you ever done *anything* right?"

"You're always lying to me."
(*response*) "I'm *always* lying to you?"

"It's impossible to get what I want."
(*response*) "Have you *ever* gotten something you wanted?"

Modal Operators of Necessity Modal operators of necessity refer to those words that indicate a lack of choice: "have to," "must," "can't," "It's necessary." Challenging these modal operators takes a person beyond the limits they have heretofore accepted. There are two excellent responses that serve to challenge these limits: WHAT STOPS YOU? and WHAT WOULD HAPPEN IF YOU DID? The response "What stops you?" serves to take the person into the past to find the experience from which this generalization was formed. "What would happen if you did?" demands that the client go into the future and imagine possible consequences. These responses assist someone in achieving a richer and fuller model of the world.

"I can't do it."
(*response*) "What stops you?"

"You have to finish by Tuesday."
(*response*) "What would happen if I didn't?"

"I have to take care of other people."
(*response*) "What will happen if you don't?"

"I can't tell him the truth."
(*response*) "What will happen if you do?"
(*or*) "What stops you from telling him the truth?"

The third grouping of distinctions is concerned with semantic ill-formedness. The value of recognizing sentences which are semantically ill-formed is that it allows you to assist the person in identifying the portions of their model which are distorted in some way, impoverishing the experiences which are available to them. By changing those portions of their model that are semantically ill-formed, a person achieves greater choice and freedom. It is these ill-formed portions which frequently stop the person from acting in ways they would otherwise choose to act. The three classes of semantic ill-formedness are:

☐ Cause and Effect

☐ Mind Reading

☐ Lost Performative

Cause and Effect Cause and effect involves the belief that some action on the part of one person can cause another person to act in a particular way or to experience some emotion or inner state. Due to this belief, the person responding experiences having no choice concerning how to respond. When this belief is challenged, it allows the person to explore and question whether the causal connection is indeed true. They can then begin to wonder about what other choices of responses can be generated. The challenge is, HOW DOES X CAUSE Y?

"Your writing on the wall bothers me."
(*response*) "How does my writing on the wall bother you?"
(*or*) ". . . make you feel bothered?"

"You frustrate me."
(*response*) "How do I frustrate you? How is it possible for me to frustrate you?"
(*or*) ". . . make you feel annoyed?"

"I'm sad because you're late."
(*response*) "How does my being late make you feel sad?"

Mind Reading Mind reading refers to the belief on the part of the speaker that one person can know what another person is thinking or feeling without a direct communication from the second person. In other words, this is a way to recognize when someone is acting on delusions rather than information. Obviously, mind reading can do much to inhibit the usefulness of a person's model of the world. The listener responds to mind reading by asking, HOW, SPECIFICALLY, DO YOU KNOW X? This provides a way for the speaker to become aware of, and even to question, those assumptions they may have previously taken for granted.

"Everybody thinks I'm taking too much time."
(*response*) "How, specifically, do you know that everybody is thinking that?"

"I'm sure you can see how I feel."
(*response*) "How, specifically, can you be sure I see how you feel?"

"I know what's best for him."
(*response*) "How, specifically, do you know what is best for him?"

"He never considers the consequences."
(*response*) "How, specifically, do you know he never considers the consequences?"

Lost Performative   Lost performative refers to those statements that are in the form of a generalization about the world itself, rather than a statement recognized as belonging to the speaker's model of the world. Usually these are judgments. The speaker is using the lost performative when he takes rules that are appropriate to him and his model of the world and puts them on others. Phrased in the vernacular, this is called "laying your trip on somebody else." The purpose in challenging this is to assist the speaker to have his own rules and opinions (comfortably) while allowing the rest of the world to have its own. Frequently, with lost performative, there is no indication that the speaker is even aware of other options or possibilities. To challenge lost performative, ask: FOR WHOM?

"It's wrong to be on welfare."
(*response*) "It's wrong for whom to be on welfare?"

"This is the right way to do it."
(*response*) "This is the right way for whom?"

"That's a sick thing to do."
(*response*) "Sick for whom?"

As stated at the beginning, the meta-model is a set of tools for building better communication. The meta-model asks *what, how,* and *who* in response to the specific form of the speaker's language. Your skills as a meta-modeler depend on your willingness and ability to implement the questions and the responses provided by the meta-model.

As you practice the meta-model, pay exquisite attention to your internal processes. Since it is a formalization of intuitive behavior, the meta-model responses will occur at those times when you would have had to refer to an internally generated experience in order to understand a client's communication. For example, when a client says, "My father hurt me," in order to understand fully what is meant by this statement, you must ask "How?" The client may have been beaten, yelled at, scowled at, or simply ignored. If you decide that you understand what is meant by the word "hurt" by simply calling on your own experience, then you are in fact meeting the client at your model of the world, not his.

The meta-model is a set of tools that allows you to stay in *external sensory experience*, getting information from the client. This keeps you from *going inside*, to internally generate experience for understanding. While you are learning the meta-model, the appropriate responses can be inserted at those points when you formerly would have had to refer to your own internal experience to understand (or attempt to understand) your client's meaning. The meta-model requires that your client make his communication more clearly understandable, not that you fill in the missing pieces from your own subjective reality for him. As an example, suppose a client says to you, "I'm afraid of crowds." If you go inside and decide "Oh yeah, afraid of crowds, yes, I know about that," then you have missed the opportunity to further connect the client with his own experience. But the responses provided by the meta-model—"How do you know you are afraid of crowds?" or "What about crowds frightens you?" or "What stops you from being comfortable in crowds?"—serve to keep you with the client's experience, thus generating answers and new possibilities for growth from his own resources. Those resources might be ones you may not have yet developed.

Finding those points at which you do go inside to internal experience to understand a given communication, and inserting the meta-model questions there instead, will greatly enhance your effectiveness as a therapist as well as facilitate integration of the meta-model into your automatic unconscious behavior. One way to do this is by having a friend generate sentences that contain some (one) meta-model violation. With each one, determine how your intuitions express themselves.

For example, when hearing the statement "My feelings were hurt," if you make a picture, how did you know how her feelings were hurt, and by whom or what? If you remember (whether visually, kinesthetically, or auditorially) a time when your own feelings were hurt, then you are "understanding" from your experience, not hers. As you become exquisitely aware of your own internal processes, you will learn those cues that signal you when you are going inside to make sense instead of staying in the present. Once you have identified what your own signal is, you can utilize it by inserting the meta-model responses instead of your own internalization. So, each time you are signaled that something is missing or doesn't make sense, you will know that a meta-model response would be useful and appropriate.

The meta-model is based on human intuitions. Therefore, by becoming explicitly aware of those intuitions, learning the meta-model can be a quick and easy process. Those intuitions can be expressed in any representational system. If I say, for example, "The giraffe was chased," you have an intuition that something was left out. Perhaps your picture is incomplete or, if you represent kinesthetically, you don't know how fast the giraffe should be running. Neither of these representations is complete until you know the answer to "Chased by what?" Regardless of how your intuitions express themselves, it is at this point that the meta-model question is inserted in order to extract the fullest possible meaning from the communication.

To utilize these intuitions in teaching and learning the meta-model distinctions, begin by (1) generating sentences to the learner that contain one pattern of meta-model violation; (2) ask the learner what his experience is; and (3) once you have determined how the *learner's* intuitions express themselves concerning this pattern, have them ask the appropriate meta-model question—making it an integral portion of the expression of those same intuitions. So, if he has an incomplete picture, he asks for the rest of it. If he feels puzzled, insert the question that will put the pieces in place. If it doesn't sound right or if it's out of tune, insert the question that will make harmony of the discord. By varying the content of the statements containing meta-model violations, the repetition necessary to integrate the meta-model question with the intuition can remain stimulating. The intuitions will vary within a person for the various patterns. There may be a feeling for universal quantifiers, a picture for nominalizations, and a sound for cause and effect. Each person will have a unique set, but each person will also fall into consistent patterns. Once the patterns have been learned, these exercises can help to further integrate them into everyday behavior.

Be sure to learn (or teach) the meta-model in the three categories outlined in this appendix: Gathering Information, Limits, and Semantic Ill-formedness. In this way, you (or the student) will have appropriately organized the meta-model for easy and full integration into conscious and unconscious processes.

233

Appendix II

Appendix II: A Complete Therapy Session

In the following transcript of a complete therapy session, I fully employ the techniques of anchoring and reframing. Hopefully, this presentation will provide you with a better understanding of how these techniques can be effectively used in the context of a therapeutic session.

Sheila: Hello (*hesitates in doorway, seems slightly disoriented*).

LCB: Hello, you must be Sheila. I'm happy to meet you. (*LCB greets Sheila with extended hand, which she shakes. LCB then indicates a chair for Sheila to sit in, to which Sheila responds first by eye-glance, then by seating herself. Once seated, LCB pulls up chair across from Sheila and within easy touching distance*)

LCB: Just allow yourself to get comfortable, and we'll begin to learn from one another how I can assist you in making some changes which you desire.

Sheila: Well, uhhh . . . I told you on the phone that my therapist referred me here. She said you do something different, something called neuro-linguistic programming. (*Sheila's tonality is high, nasal, flat; she looks up and left much of the time; her hands grip the arms of the chair*) I think she gave up on me (*voice tone change, lower, softer; eyes up left, then down and right*).

LCB: (*Reaching over, takes Sheila by the hand gently*) Now, I don't even know yet what specifically you're here for, but I do know there is a strong possibility that you've misinterpreted your therapist's intention. A moment ago as you were talking of being referred here you were looking up and left. Was the picture you made of your therapist?

Sheila: Huh?

LCB: Look there again and tell me if you see her (*indicates direction to look while still holding one of Sheila's hands*).

Sheila: (*Looks up and left again*) Yes, but how did you know?

LCB: I'll explain in a moment, but first I heard you say that you think she gave up on you, and I'm wondering if perhaps that wasn't the case at all. Perhaps it was actually quite difficult for her to refer you here, to suggest to you that someone else with a different set of tools could assist you when she could not. It seems to me that her referring you here might be an expression of care and concern from her that says she wants you to achieve those desired changes even without her. But, of course, you know her much better than I. So, go ahead, take a look at her again and *see* if this possibility *feels* any better.

Sheila: (*Looks up and left, then down and right; sighs*) You know, I think really you're right. She got frustrated with me, but now that I think about it, if she didn't care she wouldn't have bothered to send me here.

LCB: (*Gently squeezes Sheila's hand*) This can be a new learning for you. I'll bet here have been other times when you assumed a negative message from what could have been and probably was a positive one. Is that true? (*LCB looks up and right, which is a mirror for Sheila's looking up and left*)

Sheila: (*Looks up, left; nods*) Why, yes.

LCB: (*Squeezes hand gently*) And you can begin now to be in touch with what the positive messages in those situations could have been. (*Looks down and left, again mirror for Sheila looking down and right.*) ANCHORING AND LEADING WITH ACCESSING CUES.

Sheila: Yes. Yes, I think I can. (*Looks down and right, smiles*)

LCB: Good. Sometime this evening I want you to remember (*looks up and right*) at least three such times and then think of what the other messages (*looks down and left*), the possible positive ones, could have been, keeping this experience (*squeezes hand gently*) firmly in mind. Okay? (*Smiles*)

Sheila: (*Smiles*) Okay. I'll do that.

LCB: (*Releases hand, sits back slightly*) Now, tell me what is it that has brought you to therapy.

Sheila: (*Responds immediately by slumping, exhaling strongly, eyes downcast*)

LCB: Whoa, whoa. (*Reaches over, touches Sheila on thigh to get her attention back.*) Hey, come back; no need to go there (*LCB demonstrates Sheila's posture, then smiles and leans forward*). I've got it. Instead of telling me what brought you, tell me how you'll know when you don't need to come anymore.

Sheila: Well, ummm, I don't know (*eyes up, left; down, right*). It's just that, well, (*eyes down left; fidgets*) I'm frigid (*this is said louder and somewhat explosively and rapidly, with upturned palms*) . . . and I've been in pre-orgasmic groups and read all the books and tried therapy, and still nothing . . . nothing . . . and now you.

LCB: (*Allows a pause, then very directly*) How do you know you are frigid?

Sheila: (*Eyes up, left*) Huh? What kind of question is that?

LCB: Now, I know that you have ways of determining what state of being you are in and what you are not. You have a way of knowing whether you are comfortable (*pauses, Sheila's eyes are down and right*) or happy (*pause*) or curious, and so on. We human beings actually understand language by associating it with our experience. While still very young, you learned to connect some combination of pictures, feelings, sounds, smells with a word. Take the word "curious." How do you know when you are being curious?

Sheila: Well (*eyes up left, then down left, over to right*) I don't know; it's just a feeling (*Sheila touches midline*).

LCB: (*Touches Sheila's right knee*) The feeling of being curious is what you're aware of, but there was something else that helped trigger that feeling. You looked up and left, then down and over (*LCB demonstrates*). Remembering my question, look up there again, then down, and tell me what you're aware of.

Sheila: Oh! (*surprised*) I see the attic door in my house when I was a little girl (*laughs*). My mother was always telling me to stay out of it. That's where she kept our Christmas presents.

LCB: And you were very curious about those presents,

239

weren't you? (*Touches Sheila's right knee*)

Sheila: You bet.

LCB: Can you hear your mother's voice telling you to stay out of there?

Sheila: (*Eyes down, left; smiles*) Yes.

LCB: So you have ways (goes through analogue cues) to know when you are curious (*touches Sheila's right knee; Sheila nods*). Now, how do you know you are frigid?

Sheila: Well . . . (*eyes up left, then down left*) because I don't have orgasms.

LCB: What did you see up there?

Sheila: Oh, uhhh (*eyes up left*), I just see the group of women in the women's group I was in. That's how all this began. I knew sex wasn't real important to me, but it didn't seem to matter much until that group. Since then, I just can't seem to get it off my mind. It's like I'm a failure as a woman unless I can have orgasms. I worked on that a lot in therapy and I know better, but I still want to have orgasms.

LCB: If I understand you correctly then, you know you're frigid because you don't have orgasms, and since you don't have orgasms you know you're frigid?

Sheila: Yeah, that's right.

LCB: All right. How do you know you don't have orgasms?

Sheila: (*Eyes up left, then down right, then up right*) Because I've never had anything like what the women in my group have described or like what they say in the books.

LCB: (*Eyes up left to mirror up right of Sheila*) Tell me what you think an orgasm would be like.

Sheila: They—the women and some of the books—said there were plateaus and peaks and explosions of feelings (*while Sheila talks, she continues to refer to her constructed images—eyes up and right—and to make the pictures with her hands*). They said it was different for each person, but I've never had anything like that happen.

LCB: I see. In thinking back to our discussion about how we understand words—like how you know when you are curious—the experience that you connect with the word "orgasm" is made up of pictures; pictures you have constructed from descriptions given you by other women and from books. My guess is that since you don't experience these pictures as a result of having sex, you've decided that you're not having orgasms.

Sheila: Are you saying I have?

LCB: No. What I am saying is that from what you've told me the word "orgasm" is being understood in only one system: visual. That's a bit like having the experience of swimming described only in smells.

Sheila: I don't understand (*eyes down right*).

LCB: You have been given descriptions in words, which you have translated into pictures. An orgasm is an entire experience, the most highly valued portion of which is usually feelings.

Sheila: But that's what I was talking about—feelings.

LCB: Can you feel a peak or a plateau? And probably your body would be unwilling to feel an explosion. Let me explain. I can describe an orgasm as a rush of warm, exquisitely pleasurable sensations that emanate in waves from the genitals to all other parts of the body, bringing relaxed, calm satisfaction in their wake. Now, if you have not had a kinesthetic experience with which to relate what I have said, you may instead translate it to a picture—say, to the sight of a stone being thrown into a quiet dark pond, and ripples moving outward in concentric circles to the edges of the pond until it is still again. That would be an excellent pictorial understanding of my description, but not what you could expect or hope to feel when you are orgasmic.

Sheila: So I know even less about the whole thing than I thought I did?

LCB: Oh, I'm sure you know much more about this than you are conscious of knowing (*touches Sheila on right knee*). And that part of you that is curious about having orgasms is probably as impatient as you were to find out about those Christmas presents in the attic. Is that true?

Sheila: (*Eyes up left*) Yeah, I'm curious and impatient, and I don't like being left out. It's like other people are getting the goodies and I'm left out.

LCB: Excellent. You have a part that is curious and explores the world for new experience and wants to make sure you get to have those pleasurable experiences that it sees other people having. Ask that part if it can see anything to stop you from having orgasms.

Sheila: What? Ask what?

LCB: Ask inside if your curious part can see anything to stop you from having orgasms. Then, since it expresses itself mostly in pictures, look up and left for the answer.

Sheila: (*Eyes down left, then up left; head shakes no*) Nothing is there.

LCB: Good.

Sheila: Wait a minute! What's a part?

LCB: A part is a way of talking about aspects of you that express themselves in abilities to do or be something. Your ability to be curious and to be impatient to have a desired experience can be called your curious part. Parts are originally developed from learnings derived from experience. We develop a cautious part from experiences like touching a hot stove, falling downstairs or off a bike. Such experiences produce pain, and so a cautious part—often visual in nature, looking out for danger—develops in order to protect us. All our parts are there for our benefit and are resources once we learn how to utilize them. That's what reframing is all about. It is a process by which you learn to contact your parts by being aware of your own internal processes: internal dialogue, visualizations, feelings, etc. Since this is how they express themselves to you, you can learn what purpose they serve and how to utilize them to achieve desired changes, as well as to lead a satisfying and pleasing life. Often, while parts are going about their business, they come into conflict with one another. Have you ever had a conflict between, say, your adventurous part and your cautious part?

Sheila: Oh, yeah. Usually I end up not doing anything and then feeling like I really missed out later.

LCB: With reframing you would contact the cautious part and find out what reassurances or precautions it needed you to make in order to let you have an adventurous experience without its interference. After all, it serves a vital function of protecting you from danger. You can express your appreciation of it doing its task by satisfying its needs, and then you can go ahead and satisfy the adventurous part of you. With that in mind, we can begin to explore the possibility of there being some part, which is unknown to you at this time, that prevents you from having orgasms.

Sheila: Well, if there is, I just want to get rid of it.

LCB: It would merely wait and come back, perhaps in a different form. Parts are born out of learnings from experiences. They are born to serve a purpose, and when an experience happens that seems to apply to that learning, they express themselves. Remember, they are serving a purpose; each has a function and is doing the best it knows how to do. What you can do is change a part, educate it to do its job in a way more suited to your present desires and needs. But enough of this. I want you to make a general declaration inside to all your parts that you are now undertaking a new process of change, and that you will do your best to consider all of them, and that you wish their cooperation on this venture. Okay?

Sheila: Okay. (*Bows head, closes eyes for a few moments; laughs*)

LCB: What happened? Did you get a reply?

Sheila: Well, I did like you said and I heard a round of applause.

LCB: Excellent. Now announce to your parts that as a demonstration of this new process of change you are going to reorganize yourself in such a way as to be able, at appropriate times, to achieve orgasm. Go ahead—tell them.

Sheila: (*Closes eyes, tilts head up left, then humphs and moves head down and right; smiles and opens eyes, looking pleased with herself*)

LCB: (*As Sheila looks down and right, LCB touches her right knee*) It appears a lot went on in there.

Sheila: Yeah, I told them what you said and first I got this voice that said "I'll believe it when I see it." And I got this sick feeling right here (*indicates stomach/ chest area*) and another voice said "You'll believe it when it's felt, not seen."

LCB: Marvelous. We know there's some parts in there already learning and willing to keep you headed in the right direction (*down and right*).

Sheila: Huh?

LCB: Now, I want you to begin to go through for yourself all the experiences you typically have when involved in intercourse. There is a series, a sequence of experiences, that leads to and follows an orgasm. Somewhere, your sequence is interrupted or leads to some experience other than an orgasm. We need to learn more about what happens to you. So ask your parts, particularly your curious one, to go inside and, taking all the time you need, remember very vividly with exquisite detail a time when you were really aroused— you were eagerly anticipating the physical experience before you—and, beginning there, (*reaches over, squeezes Sheila's left knee as a distinct expression occurs*) recall deeply how one feeling came to follow another.

Sheila: (*Sits back, breathes deeply, facial muscles relax, eyes close; as she goes through this internal process, there is REM, color comes into her face, breathing rate increases for a while, hand and foot moves rythmically, lips swell slightly, then at one point breathing stops; Sheila frowns slightly, body becomes rigid; all of this is subtle*) All right, I did it. Now what?

LCB: What are you aware of most about what you just did?

Sheila: (*Eyes down right*) That I have the same disgusted and disappointed feeling I have after I've really had sex.

LCB: I want to explain something about that awareness you are experiencing right now. What you're aware of consciously is that particular feeling. You may not be aware of your back against the chair or the hum of the air conditioning or the smell of smoke from cigarettes smoked here earlier today. At least you probably weren't aware of them until I mentioned them and brought them into consciousness. What we can consciously be aware of is limited. Otherwise, we'd be overwhelmed. We select portions of experience to be conscious of. I know that sexually you respond to body smells, breathing rhythms, temperature changes, sounds—all kinds of stimuli that you are not likely to be conscious of. Also, while you are responding to all the stimuli provided by the external world, particularly your partner—

Sheila: My husband.

LCB: —your husband, you are also responding to the portions of experience you are generating internally: internal sounds, dialogue, imagery, feelings, etc. So, I'm going to ask you to do the same thing over again, but this time a little differently. You can have your curious part (*LCB squeezes Sheila on right knee as expression comes up*) and your aroused part (*squeezes left knee; expression comes up*) go with you, and they will pay special attention to finding what stops you from achieving orgasm. Also, until this learning has taken place, you can continue to review the events of your sexual experience, becoming aware of all those aspects you missed previously. The smells, sounds, special touches, sights—all of them—perhaps attending to one, then another, then adding them to one another.

Sheila: Sounds wonderful!

LCB: I agree. So, while you're doing that, your parts can do some searching. Ask them if they are willing to participate.

Sheila: (*Closes eyes, looks up; nods head*) Yes.

LCB: Good. Tell them they can allow one hand or the other, or even both, to rise when they have made the appropriate discovery.

Sheila: (*Closes eyes*) Okay. (*Sheila goes through similar sequence of body changes as before, then goes through them a second time; just before frown is fully expressed, the right hand begins to rise*)

LCB: (*Reaches over, touches right hand*) I understand. And when you have completed the task to your satisfaction, I want you to come all the way back here.

Sheila: (*Keeps eyes closed a while longer, then opens them, blinking*)

LCB: Before you tell me what you've learned, take a couple of good breaths and give those parts a message of appreciation for what they've done.

Sheila: (*Smiles, breathes deeply*) Well, what I found out was that there are two things that stop me from having orgasms. One I knew was there, but I didn't know it kept me from having orgasms.

LCB: Okay. Tell me about them in the natural sequence in which they occur.

Sheila: (*Sheila's analogue assumes an expression previously seen in the middle of the series already exhibited; as she speaks, the sequence of expression completes itself*) Well, just when I'm really getting into it, really beginning to enjoy it, I mean I can really feel the mounting sensations (*pauses; eyes down and left*), this voice comes in and says, "Naughty, naughty. That's nasty and you're a bad girl."

LCB: Whose voice is that?

Sheila: (*Eyes down and left*) Why, it's my mother's voice—she's spoiling it for me.

LCB: Whoa, slow down. You said there were two. Continue telling me. What happens after your mother's voice?

Sheila: Well, I never really heard her before, but after her comes my voice saying, "You did it again. You'll never make it now. No matter what, you can't do it."

LCB: Okay. There are two parts that express themselves in internal dialogue. Ask inside if anything else gets in the way of your having orgasms besides these two parts.

Sheila: (*Closes eyes*) No, that's it.

LCB: Now, this mother part you have . . . it tells you that what you're doing is naughty and nasty, is that right?

Sheila: Yes.

LCB: Can you hear her telling you that now?

Sheila: Yes.

LCB: Good. Ask that part, call it a mother part if you like, what it's trying to do for you.

Sheila: (*Closes eyes*) It says—you know, it's funny, it really is my mother's voice (*shrugs*)—it says it's teaching me that sex is wrong and nasty.

LCB: Ask it if it is trying to protect you from something it thinks is wrong and nasty.

Sheila: (*Closes eyes*) Yes, yes it is. But that's crazy. I don't think sex is bad or dirty. I know better than that.

LCB: Yes, you do, but we're talking about a part that developed its learnings apparently from your mother. Let's check that out. Can you remember your mother telling you anything about sex?

Sheila: Oh yeah, she caught me and the boy next door playing doctor and she threw a fit.

LCB: Did she say anything about it being nasty and dirty?

Sheila: Yes.

LCB: As far as you know, does your mother think sex is nasty and dirty.

Sheila: She sure does.

LCB: So, you have made many more learnings in this area than she had the opportunity to make. True?

Sheila: Yeah, I guess so.

LCB: Sometimes what mothers tell their young daughters about sex is very different than what they say as their daughters become women. That is, they share teachings concerning sex that are appropriate as far as they are concerned for the stage of development their daughter is in.

Sheila: Not my mother. Sex got dirtier the older I got as far as she was concerned.

LCB: That's too bad. Now, I know that your mother was trying to protect you from experiences that for her were nasty and dirty. A part of you accepted her teachings, perhaps believing that your mother always had your best interests at heart; and usually you probably did well as a child to heed her advice. So a part— your mother part—comes in with her warning each time you are sexually excited.

Sheila: Sure seems that way.

LCB: This part's growth was stunted concerning sex. Understandably so if it received learnings from your mother and your mother's knowledge of sexual fulfillment is also limited.

Sheila: I want my mother out of my sex life.

LCB: Fine. My guess is, though, that as long as that part is concerned for your well-being—which you do appreciate don't you?

Sheila: Yeah.

LCB: As long as it thinks sex is bad for you, it will continue to interfere in unpleasant ways about your reaching a state of sexual fulfillment. Ask inside if this is true.

Sheila: (*Closes eyes*) Yes. So what now?

LCB: Ask this part what it needs in order to stay out of this portion of your life, comfortably.

Sheila: (*Closes eyes*) It says, to know I'll be okay.

LCB: Good. Ask it if it was reassured that sexual fulfillment was good for you, and even necessary for you to achieve the development of your full potential as a person as well as a woman, would it stay out of this area of your life?

Sheila: My mother would never believe it.

LCB: But this is a part of you—not your mother. It's a part that is based on *learnings* from your mother, but it is still a part of you and has access to all those learnings you have made since you were a little girl. So ask her.

Sheila: Okay (*Closes eyes*). It says yes, but how?

LCB: Do you have children?

Sheila: No, but I hope to.

LCB: Now, even though this part has your mother's voice, it was created when you were young; and it has not grown up with you. Even though you don't have children now, if you did—if you had a daughter whom you wanted to teach about the wonders of womanhood and sexuality, a daughter whom you wanted to get even more out of her sexual experiences than you have—there would be much to say to her. True?

Sheila: Yes, I'd sure do it differently than my mother.

LCB: Excellent. And now in your mind's eye, take that part of you by the hand. Walk through life's highway with her and teach her in a gentle and reassuring way about what it means to be a woman. Surprise and delight her with all you know, giving her what she needs to be an adequate mother part for you— including finding a place in your life where she will be useful.

Sheila: Okay.

LCB: Good. Just close your eyes, take all the time you need, and you can enjoy this process of teaching your mother part about being a woman, can you not? That's right. And when you've completed this journey to your complete satisfaction, you can come back, but no sooner than all parts are satisfied that the important learnings of human sexuality have been accomplished.

Sheila: (*Settles back, spends about 12 minutes sitting quietly, eyes closed, breathing regularly, sometimes deeply; blinks, opens eyes, sits up*) Okay. (*smiles, looks pleased, relaxed*)

LCB: Well, you look pleased.

Sheila: Oh, I am.

LCB: And in what area of your life have you found a place for your mother?

Sheila: In the kitchen. She can really cook and she is going to help me in the kitchen. We're going to do some great things.

LCB: And is she content to stay out of the bedroom?

Sheila: Oh, yes. Yes. You know, I didn't know I knew all those things I taught her.

LCB: I believe you. Sometimes teaching can be the best way to learn.

Sheila: Huh.

LCB: Now, as I recall, there was another voice that interfered with the natural order of things. Right?

Sheila: Oh, yeah. I forgot about that. Wow! I feel so good about what you just did.

LCB: Hey, you did it, not me. Remember that. (*Copies Sheila's analogue behavior from before*) That other voice . . . it said, "Uh-oh, you blew it, you'll never make it now." Right?

Sheila: Yeah, I can hear it now. It's my voice.

LCB: Ask that part if it wants you to have an orgasm.

Sheila: (*Closes eyes*) Yes, it says yes.

LCB: Good. Ask it if it feels this will be easier now that mother is gone.

Sheila: (*Closes eyes*) Yeah (*some hesitation*).

LCB: But it's not really sure how.

Sheila: Huh-uh (*shakes head no*).

LCB: Ask it to listen carefully while I suggest a special strategy for it to use to enhance your sexual experience. If it agrees that this is a good strategy and that it will use it, it can tell you by giving you a warm, good, satisfied feeling through here (*indicating lower abdominal and pelvic area*). Okay?

Sheila: Yes.

LCB: I'm glad you agree, but ask inside just to make sure it agrees.

Sheila: (*Closes eyes*) Yeah. (*Nods*) I already feel kind of excited.

LCB: Somehow this part is paying exquisite attention to

your sexual experience and tells you when it doesn't think you are going to achieve an orgasm. Presently, it serves to distract you from the very stimulus that will increase your pleasure. I suggest to this part that it use its skills to enhance your experience and even guide you to an orgasm.

Sheila: How?

LCB: By using that internal dialogue to describe to you all the aspects of your experience. To pace you. To describe where your body is touching his, to describe sensuously to you the smells, breathing patterns, rhythms of movement; always using positive terms, guiding you, making sure you stay immersed in the experience you're involved in. Constantly enhancing your experience. Finding what pleases you more and taking you there. In essence, utilizing that part as a primary resource, making sure it is closely associated with your ability to be aroused.

Sheila: It's happening. I almost don't believe it, but it's telling me yes just like you said.

LCB: Great. Now, just to make sure, go back, all the way back, and allow it to escort you through an imaginary sexual experience using the strategies I have suggested.

Sheila: (*Closes eyes*)

LCB: Let it take you all the way through.

Sheila: (*Appropriate analogue for described task*) God, that's great! I'm ready!

LCB: For?

Sheila: For my new sex life. My husband is going to really be surprised.

LCB: Be sure to give him some credit for your new experiences. After all, he is going to play an important part.

Sheila: Of course (*smiling*).

LCB: Ask inside if there is anything left undone in this matter.

Sheila: (*Closes eyes*) No, everything is great. I feel terrific!

LCB: Thinking back for a moment, remember what it was like to discover parts of yourself so you can find them when you need to. You often need to make contact with them in order to increase your choices with them.

Sheila: Yeah, I think I can do that.

LCB: Now I want to share with you some ways that have made your parts available to me to communicate with. We call them anchors. You may have noticed that I have touched you frequently.

Sheila: Yeah, I thought it a little strange at first, but it was nice.

LCB: Thank you, I like making contact. But, besides that, they were also ways for me to call parts of you out. Pay attention to your experience while I demonstrate. (*Fires off anchors one at a time*)

Sheila: That is incredible. I really felt myself change.

LCB: Now you do it for yourself and learn how they can work for you.

Sheila: It does, but not as much as when you do it.

LCB: It will. You just have to learn what you're going for. Whenever you wish to contact your curious part that is impatient for you to have the richest, fullest life possible, just squeeze your right knee gently and remember the picture of that attic door. That curious feeling will let you know that part is available to you. Go ahead, try it now.

Sheila: You're right.

LCB: Of course. Also, if you wish, you can let your husband in on a secret. If he would like to arouse you in a subtle and pleasant way, he can merely give a gentle squeeze to your left knee. Like this (*squeezes left knee*).

Sheila: (*Color comes to face, smiles*) What have you done to me?

LCB: That particular touch has become associated for you with the experience of being aroused—of anticipating more physical contact. We call them anchors. They become tied to particular experiences. Also, now that you know about it, you can respond even more, allowing your conscious awareness to join your unconscious response. Do you have any questions?

Sheila: Probably, but not right now.

LCB: Well, take a few moments and review the process we have gone through so you can do it on your own. Remember how you made contact with your parts, how you learned from them and about them in a way that would allow you to achieve those desired changes.

Sheila: (*Closes eyes, is quiet for several minutes*) Okay.

LCB: Good. I'd like you to come back in two weeks and we'll review the changes that have taken place and you can pick some other change you would like to make. Then you can use this process, with me available for trouble-shooting, in order to make sure you can effect change and gain new choices on your own. Okay?

Sheila: Sure, and thanks. Thanks a lot.

Notes

Part I

1 Richard Bandler and John Grinder, *The Structure of Magic,* p. 24.

2 William H. Masters and Virginia E. Johnson, *Human Sexual Inadequacy,* p. 369.

3 Edward T. Hall, *The Silent Language,* pp. 87–89.

4 William H. Masters and Virginia E. Johnson, *The Pleasure Bond,* p. 32.

5 Ibid, p. 72.

6 Since building in endurance must often be done throughout the therapy process, it is usually integrated into each specific therapeutic intervention rather than being a separate intervention. I will, however, devote a section to the concept of future-pacing to emphasize its importance in producing lasting change.

Part II

1 Edward T. Hall, *The Dance of Life,* pp. 56–57.

2 Ibid., pp. 161–162.

3 Ibid., pp. 143–144.

4 George A. Miller, "The Magical Number Seven, Plus or Minus Two: Some Limits on Our Capacity for Processing Information," *The Psychological Review,* Vol. 63, No. 2 (March, 1956), pp. 81–97.

5 Representational Systems: Each of us, as a human being, has available a number of different ways of representing our experience of the world. Following are some examples of the . . . systems each of us can use to represent our experiences.

We have five recognized senses for making contact with the world—we *see*, we *hear*, we *feel*, we *taste*, and we *smell*. In addition to these sensory systems, we have a language system which we use to represent our experience. We may store our experience directly in the representational system most closely associated with that sensory channel. We may choose to close our eyes and create a visual image of a red square shifting to green and then to blue, or a spiral wheel of silver and black slowly revolving counter-clockwise, or the image of some person we know well. Or, we may choose to close our eyes (or not) and to create a kinesthetic representation (a body sensation, a feeling), placing our hands against a wall and pushing as hard as we can, feeling the tightening of the muscles in our arms and shoulders, becoming aware of the texture of the floor beneath our feet. Or, we may choose to become aware of the prickling sensation of the heat of the flames of a fire burning, or of sensing the pressure of several light blankets covering our sighing bodies as we sink softly into our beds. Or, we may choose to close our eyes (or not) and create an auditory (sound) representation—the patter of tinkling raindrops, the crack of distant thunder and its following roll through the once-silent hills, the squeal of singing tires on a quiet country road, or the blast of a taxi horn through the deafening roars of a noisy city. Or, we may close our eyes (or not) and create a gustatory (taste) representation of the sour flavor of a lemon, or the sweetness of honey, or the saltiness of a stale potato chip. Or, we may choose to close our eyes (or not) and create an olfactory (smell) representation of a fragrant rose, or rancid milk, or the pungent aroma of cheap perfume.

Some of you may have noticed that while reading through the descriptions of the above paragraph, you actually experienced seeing a particular color or movement; feeling hardness, warmth, or roughness; hearing a specific sound; experiencing certain tastes or smells. You may have experienced all or only some of these sensations. Some of them were more detailed and immediate for you than others. For some of the descriptions, you may have had no experience at all. These differences in your experiences are exactly what we are describing. Those of you who had a sharp, clear *picture* of some experience have a rich, highly developed, visual representational system. Those of you who were able to develop a strong *feeling* of weight, temperature, or texture have a refined, highly developed kinesthetic representational system. And so on with the other possible ways associated with our five senses that we, as humans, have of representing our experiences.—John Grinder and Richard Bandler, *The Structure of Magic II*, pp. 6–7.

6 John Grinder, Judith DeLozier, and Richard Bandler, *Patterns of the Hypnotic Techniques of Milton H. Erickson, M.D.*, Volume II, pp. 34–35.

7 William H. Masters and Virginia E. Johnson, *Human Sexual Inadequacy*, pp. 65–66.

8 Robert Dilts, John Grinder, Richard Bandler, Leslie Cameron-Bandler, Judith DeLozier, *Neuro-Linquistic Programming: Volume I*, (Cupertino, California; Meta Publications, 1980).

9 The Pairing Principle: What we have noticed time and time again is that the distribution of representational systems and Satir categories in family systems and in polarities is the same . . . the most frequent and effective incongruity-into-polarity sorting was a sorting which resulted in two polarities: one, a visual/Satir category 2, and the other a kinesthetic/Satir category 1. Parallelly, in the context of couples and family systems work, the most frequent distribution of representational systems and Satir categories is one in which one of the parenting family members is a visual/Satir category 2 and the other, a kinesthetic/Satir category 1.—Grinder and Bandler, *The Structure of Magic II*, p. 133.

10 Ibid., p. 56.

11 Richard Bander and John Grinder, *The Structure of Magic*, pp. 69–73.

12 Refer to *Magic II* for other choices for responding to incongruity. I did not mention *meta-commenting*. I do not recommend this as a response. It typically elicits discomfort and, sometimes, defensiveness when you confront someone with the unconscious portions of their communications. If you question this, I suggest that you instruct a friend to meta comment upon your behavior for a period of time. It gets old and pompous quickly.

13 Theodore Lidz, *The Origin and Treatment of Schizophrenic Disorders* (New York: Basic Books, Inc., 1973).

14 Richard Bandler and John Grinder, *The Structure of Magic*, pp. 95–96.

15 Milton H. Erickson, "Self Exploration in Trance Following a Surprise Handshake Induction" *Innovative Hyponotherapy*, The Collected Papers of Milton H. Erickson, Volume IV, Ernest L. Rossi, Ed. (New York: Scranton Publishers, Inc.) pp. 437–438.

16 See Frank Farrelly and Jeff Brandsma, *Provocative Therapy*.

17 Brander and Grinder, *The Structure of Magic*, pp. 13–14.

18 William H. Masters and Virginia E. Johnson, *Human Sexual Inadequacy*, p. 126, p. 144.

19 Ibid., p. 142, pp. 256–257.

20 Social scientists know that the process of maintaining and improving rapport is dependent upon body language: All the nonverbal signals which human beings send to one another communicate an individual's responses whether he or she realizes it or not. Certain constellations of body postures, gestures and expressions have also been recognized as having cultural meaning (and even cross-cultural meaning in some cases). Examples of this include the nonverbal communication that is understood by others as happiness, sadness, surprise, anger, aggression, etc. If you are interested in learning more about cultural behavioral complex equivalences (my term for them), I suggest you begin by reading the works of Edward T. Hall and Desmond Morris.

Selected Bibliography

Ard, B., and Ard, C. *Handbook of Marriage Counseling*. Palo Alto, CA: Science and Behavior Books, 1973.

Bandler, R., and Grinder, J. *The Structure of Magic*. Palo Alto, CA: Science and Behavior Books, Inc. 1975.

————. *Patterns of the Hypnotic Techniques of Milton H. Erickson, M.D.*, *Volume I*. Cupertino, CA: Meta Publications, 1975.

Bandler, R., Grinder, J., Satir, V. *Changing with Families*. Palo Alto, CA: Science and Behavior Books, Inc. 1976.

Belliveau, F., and Richter, L. *Understanding Human Sexual Inadequacy*. New York: Little, Brown and Co., 1970.

Berne, E. *Sex in Human Loving*. New York: Simon & Schuster, 1970.

Cameron-Bandler, L., Gordon, D., Lebeau, M. *Know How: Guided Programs for Inventing Your Own Best Future*. San Rafael, CA: FuturePace, Inc., 1985.

Ellis, A. *Sex Without Guilt*. New York: Lyle Stewart, 1958.

————. *The Art and Science of Love*. New York: Lyle Stewart, 1960.

————. *The Sensuous Person*. New York: The New American Library, 1974.

Farrelly, F., Brandsma, J. *Provocative Therapy*. Cupertino, CA: Meta Publications, 1974.

Fried, E. *On Love and Sexuality*. New York: Grune & Stratton, 1960.

Gordon, D. *Therapeutic Metaphors*. Cupertino, CA: Meta Publications, 1978.

Haley, J. *Advanced Techniques of Hypnosis and Therapy: Selected Papers of Milton H. Erickson, M.D.* New York: Grune and Stratton, 1967.

————. *Uncommon Therapy*. New York: Grune and Stratton, 1968.

Hall, Edward T. *The Silent Language*. Garden City, New York: Doubleday and Co., Inc., 1959.

————. *Beyond Culture*. Garden City, New York: Anchor Books, 1977.

————. *The Dance of Life*. Garden City, New York: Anchor Press/ Doubleday, 1983.

Jaynes, J. *The Origin of Consciousness in the Breakdown of the Bicameral Mind*. New York: Houghton Mifflin, 1976.

Laing, R.D. *The Politics of the Family*. New York: Random House (Vintage Press), 1969.

Marshall, D., and Suggs, R. *Human Sexual Behavior*. The Institute for Sex Research, 1972.

Masters, W., and Johnson, V. *Human Sexual Response*. New York: Little Brown and Co., 1966.

————. *Human Sexual Inadequacy*. New York: Little, Brown and Co., 1970.

————. *The Pleasure Bond*. New York: Little, Brown and Co., 1975.

Newell, A., and Simon, H. A. *Human Problem Solving.* Englewood Cliffs, NJ: Prentice-Hall, 1972.

Perls, F. *The Gestalt Approach and Eye Witness to Therapy.* Palo Alto, CA: Science and Behavior Books, Inc. 1973.

Pribram, K. *Languages of the Brain.* Englewood Cliffs, NJ: Prentice-Hall, 1971.

Slater, P. *Footholds.* Canada: Clark Irwin Co., 1968.

Watzlawick, Weakland, and Fisch *Change.* New York: W. W. Norton Co., 1974.

Dear Reader,

An individual's ability to establish and maintain a fulfilling and loving relationship is influenced by the strength and richness of his or her self-concept. A person's self-concept, in fact, influences to a great extent how successful that person will be in achieving and enjoying any of life's potential pleasures.

I have developed a simple procedure which works quickly and effectively to secure a strong and positive self-concept. It is a well-tested format that you can apply to yourself—for your own benefit—in addition to using it to help others.

If you would like a written copy of this self-concept procedure, I would be delighted to send it to you. It is a way for me to thank you for your interest in this book.

Send me your name and address and I will mail it to you at no charge:

Leslie Cameron-Bandler
% FuturePace, Inc.
P.O. Box 1173
San Rafael, CA 94915